Prisoners of Hope

PRISONERS
OF HOPE

*The Story of Our Captivity
and Freedom in Afghanistan*

DAYNA CURRY *and* HEATHER MERCER

with
Stacy Mattingly

DOUBLEDAY

New York   London   Toronto   Sydney   Auckland

WATERBROOK PRESS

Colorado Springs

WATERBROOK
PRESS

PUBLISHED BY DOUBLEDAY
a division of Random House, Inc.
1540 Broadway, New York, New York 10036
DOUBLEDAY and the portrayal of an anchor with a dolphin are
trademarks of Doubleday, a division of Random House, Inc.

WATERBROOK and its deer design logo are registered trademarks
of WaterBrook Press, a division of Random House, Inc.

This book is copublished with WaterBrook Press,
2375 Telstar Drive, Suite 160, Colorado Springs, Colorado 80920,
a division of Random House, Inc.

Book design by Erin L. Matherne and Tina Thompson

Library of Congress Cataloging-in-Publication Data

Curry, Dayna.
 Prisoners of hope : the story of our captivity and freedom in Afghanistan / Dayna
Curry and Heather Mercer with Stacy Mattingly.
  p. cm.
 1. Curry, Dayna. 2. Mercer, Heather. 3. Christian biography—Afghanistan. 4. Political
prisoners—Afghanistan—Biography. I. Mercer, Heather. II. Mattingly, Stacy. III. Title.

BR1725.C846 A3 2002
266'.0092'273—dc21   2002025984

ISBN 0-385-50783-6 (Doubleday)
ISBN 1-57856-645-2 (WaterBrook)
ISBN 1-57856-659-2 (WaterBrook International TP)

PRINTED IN THE UNITED STATES OF AMERICA

July 2002
First International Trade Paperback Edition
1 2 3 4 5 6 7 8 9 10

To those who gave heart and soul through prayer and practical service to bring us home alive. Words cannot express our thanks. May you be blessed for your courage, love, and sacrifice.

To the Afghan people whom we so dearly love. May you see the day of true liberation for your country and this generation.

To our Lord and Savior Jesus Christ. Your everlasting love has healed our hearts and set us free. May we honor and love you with all that we are for all of our days.

CONTENTS

Prisoners of Hope

PROLOGUE

Dayna: I was already behind schedule when I pulled the Aamirs' door shut and stepped into the courtyard. The air was hot and dry, and the late-afternoon sun played over the dirt yard. The gate to the alley, which the family usually left open, was bolted. Soofia's mother, who was washing clothes in a plastic tub, unlocked the gate and let me onto the mud alley. She was the only family member out-of-doors. I had left everyone else in the room with Heather watching that film, which was playing in the DVD drive of my laptop.

I looked both ways before stepping from the alley onto the dirt road to make sure no Taliban guards were out. We always took this precaution when leaving Afghan homes, as the country's ruling Taliban forbade foreigners to visit with Afghans. The street was quiet. My taxi driver, Abdul, was waiting for me at the bottom of the hill. I quickly slipped into the back seat and we started down the unpaved road toward the Taliban checkpoint marking the entrance to Sherpur, the name for this Kabul neighborhood of mud houses.

The time was 4:30. I was due to meet Lillian and the others downtown before having to be back in our neighborhood, Wazir Akhbar Khan, by 6:00 for a meeting with my Shelter Now International (SNI) coworkers. At Lillian's, I was to meet an Afghan woman whom we were considering introducing to our Afghan friend Rashid. I would have only a short time to visit and was thinking about the meeting as Abdul started down the bumpy road out of the Aamirs' neighborhood.

We hadn't gone ten feet when a young man dressed in civilian clothes and a colorful skullcap approached the passenger side of the car. He ordered Abdul to stop the taxi, but Abdul continued on. The young man repeated himself several times in an angry tone: "Stop! Stop!"

Finally, Abdul relented, and the stranger got into the front seat. I remembered having been warned that if an Afghan man ever got into my taxi I was supposed to get out and find another taxi. You were never to ride in a car with an Afghan man, and especially not a strange one.

"*Chera?*" I asked Abdul in Dari, or Afghan Farsi. Why? Abdul was one of our regular taxi drivers and had been taking Heather and me around Kabul for months. He knew better than to let this man into the car.

Before Abdul had time to answer, the stranger turned to me and said, "Where's the other woman?" He spoke first in Pashtu, the language of the Taliban. Then he asked again in Dari so I could understand.

"I don't know you," I replied, unsure what was going on. "It's not right for you to ask about another girl. Who are you?"

The man ignored me.

"I'm going to a meeting," I said politely, though making it clear I was upset. "I don't know where you're going. I don't know if we're going in the same direction. Maybe I should get another taxi."

"Be quiet," the man snapped. "You don't need another taxi." He turned around and looked at me. His piercing blue eyes stunned me with their hatred. I had experienced the same feeling a month earlier when an Arab man standing on a corner in downtown Kabul spit in my direction as I walked by and then pelted me with a clod of dirt.

The man in the front seat took a walkie-talkie from his pocket and spoke into it, and within seconds a white Toyota Corolla hatchback pulled out in front of us carrying half a dozen men wearing large white turbans. These, I realized with a growing sense of unease, were the religious police from the Taliban's Ministry for the Promotion of Virtue and Prevention of Vice—the men who whipped women begging alone on the street and beat men off their bicycles for failing to be at the mosque during prayer.

Now, with greater urgency, I told the man in the front seat as we drove on: "I have a meeting. I have to be there. Who are you? Where do you work?"

He didn't answer.

"Who are you?" I repeated. "Who are you with? Where do you work?"

The man seemed greatly annoyed with my talking. *"Ryaasat, ryaasat,"* he said sharply. Government, government.

I changed my approach: "Please take me to my boss. He lives just over here in Wazir. I am a girl alone. This is not right."

"You can see your boss later," he said.

Abdul kept a cool expression, but I saw fear in his eyes. He looked at me apologetically in the rearview mirror.

We came to the end of the neighborhood road and slowed down to take a right onto the main street. Many taxis waited at the intersection. I thought I would try to get out of Abdul's taxi and into another one. I opened the car door while we were still moving.

The man in the front seat saw what I was thinking and radioed to the Toyota of Taliban in front of us. We stopped abruptly. Before I could make a move, one of the white-turbaned men got out of his vehicle and came around to the back seat of our car. He got in beside me and laid a whip across his lap.

"This is wrong for you to be in this car with me," I again complained. "I am a single woman."

"*We* are not infidels," the man in the front seat remarked gruffly, turning around.

"I'm not an infidel either," I exclaimed. "I love God." He looked at me with disgust.

In another few minutes, we arrived at a building in the center of Kabul. Behind the building's high wall I could see rows of black Toyota pickup trucks, the Taliban's vehicle of choice. As Abdul brought the taxi to a stop, I saw Taliban armed with guns and whips circling the area.

The man in the front seat took my bag and rifled through it. "It is not here," I heard a man say. "It must be with the other one. Someone will have to go back." He then got out of our car, walked over to the accompanying truck, and exhanged his skullcap for a turban. Some men moved me to another vehicle, and Abdul drove away in his taxi.

This government building was in a somewhat busy area next to a city park. Civilians walking by looked into the car at me. I hoped another foreigner or someone I recognized would pass by and notice me. I tried to recall every Bible verse about fear that I knew. I quietly sang songs to God. Remembering the whip on the man's lap, I said, "O Lord, please get Heather out of there."

Heather: After I hugged and kissed the Aamir women, Aly walked me out into the courtyard. His little body swayed under the weight of Dayna's computer bag as he tried to stand up straight. None of the other children accompanied us. They usually mobbed me all the way out to my taxi, pleading with me to take them along while their mothers waved goodbye from the doorway. On this day, however, Aly and I went alone.

From the courtyard gate, I could not see who was out on the street, so I asked Aly to look for any Taliban guards who might be loitering by the neighborhood grocery stands at the bottom of the road. He would not go into the street by himself. *Perhaps he does not understand me,* I thought. My Farsi skills, elementary as they were, did not always serve me well. Since I was already late for my six o'clock staff meeting, I gave up trying to explain again and went ahead. *There won't be anyone on the road,* I told myself.

The day was exceptionally warm, and the neighborhood seemed subdued. It was Friday, the Muslim day of prayer, and few people were on the street. I was tired from a long day of activity but anxious to see my friends at the meeting in Wazir. Aly followed me halfway to my taxi and passed me the computer. Then we said goodbye. I walked the rest of the way down to where Abdul was waiting and got into the back seat.

"How long have you been here?" I asked Abdul regretfully. I had planned to be out by 5:30 so I could get to the meeting on time, but it was already a few minutes after six. I wanted to pay Abdul for the extra time, but he did not answer my question. He glanced at me in the rearview mirror; our eyes connected. His face, taut and pale, wore an odd expression. *How strange he won't answer me,* I thought. I decided I would ask him about the money again when we arrived at the meeting, only a few blocks away.

Abdul and I wended our way out of the Sherpur neighborhood, bumping along the unpaved road at twenty miles an hour. Suddenly we stopped and a man in civilian clothes climbed into the front seat.

"Who is this?" I asked Abdul. "What's going on?" No answer. The other man glanced back at me; he turned to Abdul, and they began talking. Why was Abdul allowing a strange man to ride with me? Perhaps the stranger was Abdul's relative, maybe his brother. After all, Abdul had stopped the car to let him in. I waited attentively to see what would happen next.

We had traveled only several more feet when Abdul slowed again and another man, also in civilian dress, got into the car, this time in the back seat with me. The man was tall with a narrow face and a large, protruding nose. In his hand was a walkie-talkie. Immediately, I knew the men had come for me.

"Who are these men?" I asked Abdul. "This is not permitted. I'm late for a meeting. I will find another taxi to take me."

Everything was happening so fast. Were these men kidnapping me? Only days earlier, an Afghan man had pinned me to a wall in our neighborhood as Dayna and I were walking to a prayer meeting. Did these men, too, intend to harm me? Would they try to rape me?

The car came to a stop, and I nonchalantly opened the door. The big-nosed man next to me grabbed my arm as I stepped out. I thought I might be able to run down a familiar side street and cut back over to Wazir Akhbar Khan, the neighborhood where we lived. Then I looked around.

Pulling out in front of us was a Corolla station wagon full of Taliban; I could see their oversized turbans through the vehicle's tinted windows. Abdul had stopped right next to the Taliban check post, and nearly a dozen men surrounded me. Some were armed with Kalashnikovs. I scanned the area. A few men from the neighborhood lingered in the street, but none offered to help. I did not see anyone from the Aamir household, no familiar faces. My choices were limited: I could run and risk getting shot or return to the car. The taxi door was still open, so I got back inside.

As we started driving, I changed my strategy and attempted to negotiate. "I am late for a meeting," I offered. "You can drive me there. My boss speaks Pashtu and knows many Taliban officials. We can meet with him to discuss this matter." The men paid me no attention.

Could they be apprehending me for visiting an Afghan home? I wondered. Did they know I had shown the film about the life of Jesus? How could they know? I was carrying the CD in Dayna's computer bag. What would happen if the Taliban found the film? I was thankful Dayna had gotten away. At least *she* was safe.

We turned onto a main road and I stared out the window at the faces of passersby. If I could just spot a familiar face, I could roll down my window and shout for help. But I saw no one I knew—no neighbors, no street kids. I sat still, trying to appear calm.

Our caravan approached the turnoff for my meeting in Wazir. "We can turn here," I proposed. "My boss is this way."

"No," the man in the front seat retorted. "Your boss is at the office where we're taking you." So this had been planned out. Well, at least we were making progress—I had finally gotten a direct answer from someone. I became slightly more confident that the men would not try to harm me. Thankfully, Georg would be at the office to help me work this out.

After ten minutes, we pulled up to what appeared to be a government building, though it had no identifying signs. The street teemed with activity—shepherds herded their flocks through a throng of traffic; drivers honked their horns; pedestrians darted across the rows of vehicles. I could hear the ring of a nearby blacksmith's instruments. In the Shar-e-Nao park next to the building, a crowd of young men and boys played soccer.

Abdul positioned our taxi behind a white sedan. I could see someone sitting in the sedan's back seat. Was it Georg? I looked closely, and my heart sank. Dayna was sitting in the car—alone. I imagined the Taliban had captured her when she left the Aamirs' house nearly two hours before. The big-nosed man ushered me over to the sedan and instructed me to get in. He took the heavy computer bag off my shoulder, and with it, the film. As I approached the car, I spoke to Dayna through the window. "It's okay," I said, summoning up my strength. "God is with us."

part one

KABUL TOWN

one

THE ROAD TO KABUL

Most people only get to read about it.
—E-MAIL HOME, MARCH 29, 2001

Heather: Much has been written about the road from Peshawar, Pakistan, to Kabul—Afghanistan's capital city. Before I arrived in Peshawar for the first time, I dreamed of driving on the Kabul road through the famed Khyber Pass, the strategic mountain gateway where Alexander the Great positioned an army of troops and elephants and managed to become the only foreign military leader to defeat the region's fierce Pashtun tribal warriors.

I had heard stories of this thirty-three-mile passage through the snow-covered mountains of the Hindu Kush. As one writer noted, "The story of the Khyber Pass is composed of such colour and romance, such tragedy and glory that fact really looks stranger than fiction in this case."

Silent witness to numerous invasions and remarkable events, the pass is rugged, arid, and foreboding. Mountains loom over tiny, scattered villages. Spontaneous dust storms sweep over the land. The prospect of traversing such awesome, unpredictable terrain exhilarated me, and when I finally did it I was not disappointed. My first journey over the pass in the summer of 1998 proved to be all that I had hoped and more.

In a land where every man carries a gun, we began our travels from Peshawar with an Afghan driver and an armed Pakistani guard, whom we hired for our protection to accompany us to the Afghan border. Known as the Northwest Frontier Province, this no-man's-land that precedes the border with Afghanistan is governed by Pashtun tribal law, and its culture is as mythic as its terrain.

The Pashtuns, nearly half of all Afghans, are a passionate people, doggedly loyal to family and tribe. Gatherings of tribal elders, called *jirgas,* settle Pashtun disputes, and it has been said that most disputes among Pashtuns revolve around *zar, zan,* and *zamin*—gold, women, and land. To be a Pashtun is to be a Muslim, usually a Sunni Muslim. Dishonoring a Pashtun is as good as killing him, but if you are the guest or friend of one of these warriors, you can be sure that only over your host's dead body will harm come to you. If you become a Pashtun's friend you become a part of his family. In the words of a famous Afghan proverb, "The first day you meet, you are friends. The next day you meet, you are brothers."

The road through the Khyber Pass, land of the Pashtuns, is always changing—rocks fall from cliffs, bombs at one time fell from the sky. Our Afghan driver took the sharp mountain turns at an unnervingly fast speed considering the steep drops of several hundred feet—in places nearly a thousand feet—to our left and right. At times the driver would fling our vehicle around blind single-lane curves as if he were fully confident no oncoming truck piled high with bags of rice, no boulder or bomb crater, would be awaiting him on the other side.

The constant side-to-side motion of the vehicle was enough to keep all of us perpetually on the verge of nausea.

On one occasion our driver's antics almost proved catastrophic. We were racing down the road, dodging potholes and bumping over rocks, when we came to a bridge. Our water bottles, frozen solid when we departed, were now fully thawed. Sweat dribbled down my forehead. As we started across the bridge, we found ourselves approaching a ten-foot crater at the center of the overpass, the work of a recent explosion. Seeing we had one option if we hoped to get to Kabul, our fearless driver pressed ahead uninhibited by the sight. From my vantage, the view was anything but comforting. Looking out the windows on either side of the van, I noticed we were only a hairs-breadth away from the twenty-five-foot drop to a rock-hard riverbed. A flock of spotted goats grazed on the few strands of grass below.

Our automotive dance with destiny on the Kabul road unfolded against an acoustic backdrop of blaring Hindi music, which our driver would cut off abruptly once we started running into Taliban check-points on the Afghan side of the border. All nonreligious music was banned in Afghanistan under the Taliban, as attested to by the Taliban checkpoint poles wrapped with layer upon layer of tape—the innards of countless audio- and videocassettes (also banned)—as a caution to wayward travelers.

As we approached each checkpoint, our driver would yank the Hindi cassette out of the tape player and hide it; on occasion he simply lowered the volume and waved at the Taliban guard as we passed by. Like many Afghans, our driver played a constant game of chance with his Taliban overseers. Better to live freely some of the time and risk getting caught, he figured, than to live in fear and misery all of the time trying to keep the increasingly stringent law of the land.

All along the roadside on the way to Kabul, we noticed oblong mounds of rocks and dirt. Marked by headstones and footstones, the mounds were graves or shrines where loved ones would come to pray for the dead. The bodies of the deceased were positioned above the ground, not underneath, with their faces toward Mecca, the Muslim holy city. Long branches adorned with colorful pieces of torn fabric staked many of the mounds. With every flap, these pennants are thought to release a prayer toward heaven.

Somewhere outside Jalalabad, the halfway point on our journey, we encountered a massive cloud of dust whirling down the highway and swallowing everything in its path. Within moments we lost sight of the monstrous mountain range in the distance. I thought perhaps we could outrun the cloud, but it fast overtook us. Our driver braked to a dead stop, and everything outside of our windows disappeared. We rolled up the windows, but dust poured into the van, caking our scalps, coating our luggage. Dust stuck to our sweaty faces, and grains of sand and dirt even got wedged in between our teeth. But the storm passed almost as quickly as it came: Within five minutes we were on our way; and I learned never to wear nice clothing on the road to Kabul.

Several hours into our trip, we kindly asked our driver to make a pit stop. Finding appropriate bathroom facilities on the Kabul road required some ingenuity. The occasional teahouses did not provide bathrooms, meaning we had to venture behind large rocks or down the mountainside near the river. The presence of thousands of land mines made creating a suitable toilet a dangerous business, and we had to be careful not to stray too far from the road. Mines of another kind, piles of dried-up feces left by earlier travelers, were strewn across the landscape. As women, we did what we could to ensure privacy by shrouding one another with our head scarves.

We kept our money out as we traveled, because we never knew when we would drive by a child or elderly man crouched in the road shoveling gravel and dirt into potholes. People of all ages engaged in this activity, and the shovelers were covered in dust stirred up by passing vehicles. Often, the shovelers worked miles from the nearest village in scorching heat and without water. We would observe them jump up and begin to work when they saw our vehicle approaching. As we passed, we would throw Afghani bills out the windows. Usually, the road menders made only about thirty cents a day; but their services actually benefited travelers. On occasion we noticed some of their more sophisticated handiwork: newly mended barricades between the road and the river.

Camel caravans were a familiar sight as we made our way toward Kabul. The shepherds leading the caravans were Kuchi people, nomadic Pashtuns, dressed in bright, colorful clothing that stood out against the drab browns and grays of the Afghan landscape. The shepherds carried long switches tied with strips of fabric, and the lethargic camels carried loads of overstuffed burlap bags. A strikingly beautiful people with dark hair, olive skin, and light-colored eyes, the Kuchi nomads travel in groups in search of fields where they can pasture their under-fed flocks. Years of war, drought, and famine have taken their toll on the Kuchis.

Our eyes were allowed a reprieve from dust and desert about two hours outside of Kabul at Sirobi, a town situated in a valley on a gorgeous, crystal-clear lake surrounded by trees and lush vegetation. From the mountain passes approaching the town, the view was breathtaking. I wondered, *Is this still Afghanistan?*

The land became dry again and mountainous as we approached the Kabul Gorge. Here the road ran high above the Kabul River, which has nearly dried up in recent years owing to the drought. Our driver resumed his wild, mountain-road maneuvering until we got to the other side of the gorge. At last, Kabul—a broad, dusty stretch of earthen, flat-topped houses—fanned out across the valley below.

My own personal road to Kabul often has seemed just as exhila-rating, just as spectacular, and at times just as treacherous and heart-breaking as the actual road. I have often told people, "It took me years to get to Kabul." It did—four years, in fact. There were days after my arrest and imprisonment by the Taliban in August 2001 when I wept specifically because I had waited so long to get to Kabul, only to be jailed four and a half months later with a potential death sentence hanging over my head and a global catastrophe erupting outside our prison walls.

For as long as I can remember, I have been drawn to adventure and risk. I grew up in upper-middle-class America, and my early-childhood years were rich with opportunity. I was free from the fear of needing or wanting anything. My parents loved me, provided for me, instilled in me a concrete sense of right and wrong, and created chances for me to grow and explore. I looked at the world and dreamed of its possibilities, and I desired to experience as much of life as I could. From the age of eight, I was determined to grow up and become an astronaut.

By the time I was twelve I had lived in three foreign countries and visited eleven others. My friends were kids from all over the globe—Egypt, Kenya, India, Holland, and Italy. I learned to value people who were not like me, and I discovered that the world extended beyond my own concerns and ambitions. I also learned that most people did not live with the same luxuries to which I was accustomed. Most people lived more simply, with only the basics—if they were fortunate enough to have those. Somewhere in my heart a compassion for the less fortunate was being developed.

As a high school student living in northern Virginia, I was driven and purposeful. Even at that young age, I wanted to be successful and make a difference in society. I defined myself largely by my physical appearance, my performance in school, and my circle of friends. To others I seemed to have my life together, but I struggled tremendously with insecurity, fear of failure, and fear of rejection. I wondered where I fit. What was my place in the world?

During this critically formative season, my family also struggled. My parents separated and my life drastically changed. My behavior changed—my decisions became knee-jerk reactions to the chaos around me. My mom and one of my sisters moved to a different state. I rebelled against my parents, breaking all of their rules.

Still, somehow I knew the choices I made at that time could affect my future and my destiny. Deep inside I wanted to do the right things. In high school I chose to stay out of the party scene and got involved with extracurricular activities—student government, the school newspaper, cross-country, and track and field. I threw myself into my activities. I worked hard, believing that if I could be successful, then somehow I would be able to find a way out of the emotional challenges I faced. But hard as I tried, the striving didn't gain me the kind of success I had in mind.

Even though I worked harder than just about anyone I knew, I ultimately couldn't measure up to the standard I had set for myself. Others around me seemed more talented and capable, and I became frustrated when their talent beat out my hard work. One year I ran the mile relay in the district championship for track and field. We ended up winning the district title that year, which opened the door for our team to go on to the regional tournament. But my coach decided not to run me again. Instead he put in another sprinter who was faster than me. I was devastated. It didn't seem to matter that I had trained so hard and won the event at the district tournament. The other girl beat me out of a spot because of her talent. I felt like a failure. Would I ever measure up? Was hard work enough, or would I always be second best?

One of my closest friends in high school was a Christian, and she lived out her authentic faith in our friendship. She was a friend in good times and bad. She always seemed upbeat about life and at peace with herself, and I knew there had to be a reason for it. I had friends on the track team, too, who followed Jesus, and their faith seemed to give them the motivation and the strength to live honorable lives. Observing these friends, I became curious. When my close girlfriend invited me to church with her, I was open to going.

One afternoon in biology class, my friend invited a handful of us to a concert at her church. It was November 13, 1992. Hundreds of youth packed the sanctuary that evening, and after the concert, a young man—perhaps in his mid-thirties—shared a story about a man I had heard of before but never thought much about. A man who was revolutionary for his day and time. A man with a message. The speaker explained that this man loved me, and that the love was not contingent on anything I could do. I could not earn the love. It was free; it was unconditional. The speaker told stories of this young revolutionary healing people's bodies and hearts. The man the speaker described even had a plan for my life. That caught my attention. "This man's name," he said, "is Jesus."

Why have I never heard this message before? I wondered. I had gone to church. I celebrated Christmas and Easter. I knew that Jesus died on a cross and came back to life three days later. But this was different. This was relevant.

After the speaker finished, he offered to pray with any of us who desired the love that Jesus offered. I thought to myself, *If this Jesus guy is really who he says he is, and if his love is truly real, then of course I want it.* I had strained to be satisfied with love from other people in my life but had come up feeling empty. I wanted something lasting and life-changing, something real. This message of love resonated in my soul. That evening as the speaker prayed aloud, I prayed along with him. I asked Jesus to give me his love and heal my broken heart. I told Jesus I would follow him if he would show me where to go.

Almost immediately I felt different. I didn't understand why. Once the event was over, I went up to the front of the church to talk with the speaker. "Sir," I said, "I prayed that prayer and . . ." Unexpectedly, I began to bawl. I could not control myself. I was horrified, humiliated. All of my peers were watching me lose it. With a sympathetic smile, the man hugged me. He explained that I had received a new life and that Jesus was healing my heart. I returned home embarrassed by my behavior and uncertain of what my decision really meant.

Gradually, I witnessed adjustments in my life. My attitudes were different. My desires and goals were changing. I became more interested in people around me, and I began to see in others the same pain I had carried for so long. I assumed that if Jesus was big enough to mend my heart, then he could do the same for my friends. Though people did not always understand or agree with my newly discovered faith, I did not mind. Jesus became my center. He became my vision and my purpose.

When it came time to apply to college, I looked at universities that created an environment where faith was fostered. As a young adult, I also wanted to venture to a new place and start over. In 1995,

I landed at Baylor University in Waco, Texas, a school with a Baptist affiliation. I had never even been to Texas, but then again, I always enjoyed the less-traveled route.

I grew up at Baylor. For the first time I was independent and responsible for making my own decisions. A world of possibilities opened up for me. I worked all the way through college, part-time at the cafeteria and campus library. I became involved with campus ministry to college students and led Bible studies for freshman girls. Eventually, I co-led small fellowship groups that met in students' homes. I spent time one-on-one with several young women and encouraged them to pursue a deep friendship with Christ and show the love of God to others.

It took me some time to find the right church in Waco, though not for any lack of choices. In this Bible Belt city, there are houses of worship on seemingly every block. I tried several churches but found myself particularly drawn to a group of passionate students who attended one of the local Baptist churches, a congregation that later helped establish the nondenominational church I currently attend, Antioch Community Church. The people at the church fervently loved Jesus, and I wanted to love Jesus with my whole heart, too.

Through my church's teaching, I started to learn more about people from other cultures and nations. Poverty, disease, and famine plagued several of the countries we studied. As I read the Bible, I noticed that many scriptures addressed serving the poor. One particular passage caught my attention: "'. . . He defended the cause of the poor and needy. . . . Is this not what it means to know me?' declares the LORD" (Jeremiah 22:26, NIV). I came to realize that my love for God would be directly expressed through my service to the poor. Love had to be demonstrated—how could it be authentic otherwise? Further, I had been blessed with so much in life, I had a responsibility to give of myself to those with less. I considered this scripture: "'And from everyone who has been given much shall much be required'" (Luke 12:48, NAS).

Throughout my years at Baylor, I looked for ways to build friendships with the poor. I did not want to patronize people; I wanted to know them. I hung out with the homeless on Waco street corners and under the interstate bridge. At one point, I tried to rent an apartment in the inner-city projects to be closer to people in need so I could identify with their struggles.

Eventually—and it did not take long—I began dreaming of serving the poor overseas and expressing the love of Jesus to those who had never heard about him. My heart burned to go abroad. I came to a point where all I could imagine was going to the ends of the earth to serve the poorest of the poor. Sometimes people suggested other noble things I could do with my life, but those prospects always seemed second best to my dream. The thought of not going abroad, or the thought of doing anything else with my life, broke my heart.

My vision became so expansive that I decided I would quit school after my sophomore year to get training and move overseas. "What am I doing with these books when there are so many broken people in the world who never have experienced or heard about God's love?"

I came around to see the practical wisdom in completing my degree, which was in German and physical education; but my heart still ached to go. When the church announced it was opening up a short, exploratory trip to Afghanistan in the summer of 1998 for anyone who wanted to consider doing humanitarian aid work there long-term, I immediately signed up.

As my vision about sharing God's love with the poor overseas became clearer, I had begun to pray this way: "Lord, send me to the hardest place. Send me where others do not want to go—or are afraid to go." I had never been satisfied with the status quo. I never desired to lead what might be considered a normal life. I dreamed about pursuing the unusual and extraordinary; I desired to live on the edge of impossibilities. Helen Keller once said, "Life is either a daring adventure or nothing."

Further, when I considered the people whose suffering I could help alleviate and the sense of satisfaction I would gain by living for a purpose larger than myself, the sacrifice of my personal comfort and security seemed well worth the risk.

Still, I was not confident I had much to offer a devastated nation like Afghanistan. I had no experience to qualify me—only average talents and abilities. In prayer I felt God ask me if I could do three things: *Can you love your neighbor? Can you serve the poor? Can you weep as I weep for poor and broken people?* I came to see that God did not need someone with extraordinary gifts and achievements. He just needed someone who could love, share her life, and feel for others as he did. God was looking for compassion, not commendations. He was looking for faithfulness, not fame. God assured me that if I would be committed to loving and serving with a soft heart, then even if my life seemed small in the eyes of the world, before God it would be great.

Naturally, my parents were not keen on my taking even a short-term trip to Afghanistan. My protective father did not want his daughter to put herself in harm's way and suggested I try some other country. Ironically, where my dad was concerned, the apple did not fall too far from the tree. My sense of adventure and desire to dream came from him. He left his family at a young age to travel and see the world. He served God and country as a U.S. Marine in Vietnam. My destiny was taking me somewhere slightly different, but just as my father did what he had to do, so I had to pursue what I knew I was made to do. In the end, my dad was supportive and gave me his blessing.

Although the 1998 summer trip to Afghanistan was meant to be a kind of toe-in-the-water excursion, our small group from Waco stepped onto the Kabul stage during one of the most dramatic moments experienced by the capital's foreign community during the Taliban's rule. Taliban forces had captured Kabul in 1996. Birthed out of the Pashtun tribal areas in southern Afghanistan during the early 1990s, the Taliban—"religious students"—implemented strict Islamic law and brought some order to a chaotic, deeply fractured nation. But Afghanistan was hardly stable.

Our arrival in Kabul coincided with a Taliban-imposed deadline for all foreign aid workers to relocate their offices and residences to the city's bombed-out polytechnic institute, a compound with no electricity or running water. The foreigners in town had decided to wait out the ultimatum. No one ever knew whether the Taliban would follow through on its decrees. Even when the Taliban did follow through, there was usually room for negotiation through relationship channels. But not on this occasion.

On our first full day in the city, the actual day of the Taliban deadline, my friends and I were taken on a tour of various medical facilities. Partway through the tour, our guide went inside to notify the staff of our visit, and when he came back out, we knew something was wrong. He told us that only minutes earlier the Taliban had entered the clinic, which was run by an aid organization, and kidnapped one of the clinic's Afghan employees. We were instructed to go back to a friend's house and stay there until we received further direction.

Over the next twelve hours the Taliban became increasingly unpredictable, and our expatriate hosts worked frantically to send us back to Pakistan, along with all other nonessential relief workers. By the next day my teammates and I were back on the Kabul road headed toward Peshawar. I learned we made it across the border just before Taliban border guards began confiscating the property of foreigners fleeing the country.

No one was sure what the Taliban's crackdown would mean for the future of the aid community, and relief workers were left to sort through significant questions. What would become of their projects, their families, and the people they came to serve? Oddly, nothing about the ordeal scared me. Somehow in all of the chaos I had become deeply attached to Afghanistan.

After our evacuation, our team remained in Pakistan for two weeks touring the Afghan refugee camps in Peshawar. One afternoon we visited a medical clinic. My heart broke over the conditions. The facilities were without air-conditioning and equipped with only a few fans to fight the 115-degree heat. The clinic floors were stained with blood, and the linens were filthy. I wondered what became of most of the patients treated in this clinic. The medical staff did the best they could, but their resources were so limited.

When I walked down the hospital corridor toward the children's unit, I could smell sickness and death. Most of the children suffered from severe malnutrition. One young girl immediately caught my attention. Every bone in her emaciated body protruded against her skin. Her cheek and temple bones jutted out so dramatically, she literally looked like a skeleton. Iodine used to clean mouth sores caused by a vitamin deficiency had dyed her lips purple. Her right hand was wrapped in gauze to keep a temporary IV in place. She lay on a blanket stained by her own chronic dysentery.

I did not know how to respond. I watched as the little girl's mother attempted to cool her by waving a straw fan. *How could this have happened?* I wondered. How could this child's illness have been allowed to get this bad? Before I left the room, I placed my hand on the girl and prayed for her healing. I had read often in the Bible about the miracles of healing Jesus performed. I knew this girl needed one or she would die. As I left the room to carry on with the clinic tour, I burst into tears. Nothing else in life made sense at that point except living and working among the Afghan people.

When the time came to fly home, I sat on the plane weeping and asked God if he would let me return to the people I had grown to love. I sensed in my heart that my work in Afghanistan had only begun. I would return someday—perhaps someday very soon.

By the following summer, the Taliban had allowed the aid community to return to the country, and I went back to Afghanistan to stay with a married couple from our church. The trip was less exciting than the previous one, but no less satisfying. I confronted the mundane aspects of life: the practical needs of the Afghans, the high altitude, and the slow pace of daily activity. When I left, I was more resolved than ever to come back and serve the Afghan people.

In August 1999, I graduated from Baylor and enrolled in a ministry training school, my final stage of preparation before moving to Afghanistan long-term. I made a three-year commitment and planned for a start date of March 2001. The training school, which emphasized character development and biblical principles, met for ten months and ended with an overseas trip, which I spent in Turkey. It was now the summer of 2000. I returned to Waco intending to begin raising financial support for Afghanistan. But four days after my arrival, my middle sister, Hannah, died of an accidental prescription-drug overdose.

Our family was devastated by Hannah's death. My parents lost a baby girl years ago, and the death of another child seemed too much to bear. My heart was broken. For years I dreamed that Hannah, who suffered chronically from physical and emotional pain, would make it out of her dark world with an incredible story to encourage other suffering people. But it was not to be, and I did not understand. How could her young life have come to such an abrupt end? She had so much potential, so much life still to live.

At times the sense of loss pressed on my heart almost like a physical weight. But Jesus was my comfort. During times of prayer, I sensed intuitively God reaffirming his love and kindness toward my family and me. In the end, I believed that somehow good would come out of my sister's tragic death and that our family would grow stronger as a result. The grieving was not easy, but I came out more certain than ever that God was faithful. I could still trust him.

Never during that time did my heart's desire to go to Afghanistan wane. I knew I still had to go. I longed to go. My mother, however, vehemently disagreed. She had never been totally on board with the idea of my going to Afghanistan for a three-year stint, but Hannah's death understandably roused her to fight my decision with renewed zeal.

The vigor of my mother's opposition hit an even higher level two months before I was scheduled to leave. In January 2001, Mullah Mohammad Omar, supreme ruler of the Taliban, issued a decree imposing the death penalty on any Afghan Muslim who changed his or her religion. Some reports suggested that the death penalty could be meted out to foreigners who shared their faith with Afghans. In my mother's mind, the decree confirmed her worst fear—that Afghanistan would prove a death trap both for Afghans with whom I might share about Jesus and, potentially, for me.

"Heather," she confessed, "I am afraid you will get on that plane in March and I will never see you again."

She proceeded to write to government officials and religious leaders, hoping to find a means of stopping me from going. I understood. She had just lost one daughter and was going to do everything in her power to keep from losing another, even if that meant lying down in front of my airplane. Eventually, though, she learned there was nothing she could do. She came to the airport to see me off in the end. My father by now had relented, too—I was an adult, he said. The parting was peaceful, but I knew I was breaking their hearts.

I already had counted the cost of living in Afghanistan. I already had reconciled myself to a life of uncertainty when it came to my own safety. Obviously, I did not wish to put any Afghan in harm's way; and in the months to come, I would grapple with that issue a good deal. Yet while I willingly cut my ties in America to embark on a potentially dangerous years-long odyssey, my parents were forced to deal with the consequences of my decision. They paid the price, but they were not allowed the luxury of counting the cost. They could only watch me go.

two

BEHIND THE VEIL

Dayna: The streets of Kabul are chaotic and diverse, a world unto themselves. The main downtown roads, though paved, are pocked with potholes. Drivers weave from side to side, dodging both the holes and an onslaught of pedestrians and bicycles. Men pull two-wheeled carts piled high with sacks of flour, and merchants push four-wheeled carts of produce and other wares. Shepherds maneuver sheep and goats through the crowds; on rare occasions cows, horses, and even camels contribute to the press. The streets resound with shouting and the sound of engines, and the air is filled with the scent of exhaust and animals. In Taliban days, black Toyota 4-x-4s owned by the government would speed and skid through the crush of traffic as if to assert authority.

When I first moved to Kabul in August 1999, what struck me most about this lively scene were the activities and wanderings of countless blue ghosts—women covered in *burqas*, shiny garments that fit over the head and cover the body with mesh screens for the eyes. Watching the Afghan women go about their business, I longed to touch their lives in some way—to help them, but also just to know them in friendship. Out in the open, their lives seemed hidden and remote.

Under the Taliban, burqas were required garb for women. Some women would take risks on occasion and flip back their burqas when walking on out-of-the-way neighborhood streets. Young girls, some elderly women, and Kuchi women—whom the Taliban tended to leave alone—wore big *chawdurs*, or head scarves, covering their hair, arms, and backsides. We foreign women wore *chawdurs,* too. But for the most part, you rarely encountered a female face on the streets of Kabul. Most Afghan women still wear burqas—some for cultural or religious reasons, others out of fear ex-Taliban will attack them on the streets.

Once you become accustomed to seeing veiled women about town, the mystery of the sight fades, and you begin to notice the difficult and mundane aspects of Afghan women's daily existence. Every day women come down from their mud houses in the hills surrounding the city and wash clothes in putrid water on the side of the Kabul River, which runs through town. The women make several trips up and down the hills to fill jugs of water for household use at wells and water pumps. Many women wake early to knead bread dough and carry it to the bakeries in time to have bread for that day's eating.

Even the simple things are hard. For covered women, traversing the streets of Kabul is a hazardous undertaking. Women in burqas have difficulty seeing the ground, and many trip on the uneven streets. Burqas also limit women's peripheral vision, and at times careless drivers sideswipe women pedestrians.

Often you will see women teetering precariously on the backs of bicycles, perhaps holding children in their arms. Women ride side-ways with their legs dangling to one side while their husbands or male relatives pedal. Women can be seen both queuing up on the street for taxis and riding in taxis. Under the Taliban, women could ride on buses, but they had to sit in curtained-off areas in back. The back windows also were curtained, and the women depended on the drivers to call out the stops.

Burqa-clad women daily crowd the Kabul bazaars. Occasionally you might encounter Kuchi women with their faces uncovered selling glass and plastic bracelets along the roadsides in the bazaar areas. Otherwise, men work all of the shops and stands. You can hear women haggling in loud voices with salesmen at stalls for fabric or meat or household goods. The women shout to be noticed. You can easily ignore them, because you cannot see their faces.

When I lived in Kabul, women usually walked through the bazaars in small groups accompanied by children. It was unlawful under the Taliban for women to venture out unescorted by at least one close male relative, but many women broke the rule. Rarely would you see a woman all alone without even her children. Such women were usu-ally beggars, and their solitary state made them subject to beatings by Taliban police.

When women acquaintances approached me on the streets, I would try to recognize them by their voices. It was strange not to be able to see their faces. I would notice other women talking together in the bazaar and wonder how they recognized one another under their burqas. To some extent you can identify a woman's burqa once you get to know her, but doing so in a crowd of covered women is a feat.

It is less difficult to distinguish the poor women from the rich—or from the women who at one time had wealth. Women of means wear shiny, bright blue burqas. Some wear very high heels and stock-ings, even fishnet stockings. Afghan women like to dress up and will wear high heels through the winter. Since burqas are shorter in front than in back, you can catch glimpses of women's garments just below the knee. Wealthier women wear high-quality dresses and *tombans*—

pants that go underneath their dresses. Wide-legged tombans are the rage, and you may see luxurious lace sewn onto the pant and dress hemlines. Occasionally, sequins or sparkly velour fabric may flash underneath a woman's burqa.

Poor women wear tattered tombans and dresses underneath their burqas, which usually are stained, patched, and faded. The women wear plastic slipperlike sandals called *chaplacks*; often the sandals are torn and barely wearable. Some poor women wear black rubber Holland-style shoes in winter. Many women cannot afford socks.

After years of war, an extraordinary percentage of Afghan women are widowed, and they must do what they can to earn money for their children. Many women sit in the bazaar areas all day with their children, begging for assistance. Walking in the bazaar with a foreign male friend one day, I noticed a whole row of Afghan ladies begging. I went inside the corner bakery, bought more than a dozen pieces of fresh, hot bread, and began to hand the bread out to the women. An Afghan man approached my friend and me and rebuked us: "If you are going to give, then you should give to all of them." I told him I was sorry. I thought helping a few of the women would be better than helping none, but he did not agree.

Many times in the bazaar, or on Chicken Street—a famous street frequented by foreigners and lined with souvenir and antique carpet shops—women holding babies would approach me and ask for money to feed their children. I worked at a woman-and-child health clinic my first year and a half in Kabul and would encourage these women to breast-feed. Often I would tell the women about the health clinic, which would be able to offer them medical assistance.

In the summer, women would come to the health clinic and take off their burqas, nearly hyperventilating from the heat. Being underneath a burqa during the Kabul summer can be like standing in a furnace, and the women's faces would drip with sweat. Some of the women who came to the clinic were displaced people from the northern Shamali Valley—where the Taliban, at war with the Northern Alliance, had burned villages. These women were living in the bombed-out Russian embassy building and had little or no access to water. Their hands were nearly black with dirt. I did not know how they kept going.

Throughout Kabul, you will see women sitting along the sides of the main roads waiting for passersby to give them money. Other women loiter near the homes of foreigners, aggressively begging for handouts, sometimes following foreigners on errands through the bazaar.

I talked most often with Afghan women at my home. Women would come to the gate at lunchtime to ask for assistance. We would stand together at the gate or we would have tea inside. The women would flip back their burqas and tell me heartbreaking stories about the loss of loved ones, debts taken on to feed numerous children, chronic illness, hunger, abuse by husbands, and mistreatment by the Taliban. I would see utter desperation in the women's eyes. They tried to keep their heads up, but the pain would always emerge if our conversations went deep enough. I think I was able to help a little just by listening. I loved the Afghan women and wished with all of my heart for them to know better days.

I desired to extend friendship to veiled women long before I ever went to Afghanistan—perhaps because I had known isolation myself. There were years in my own life when I badly needed someone to break through and reach me. As a teenager growing up in Nashville, Tennessee, I had few goals outside of partying and meeting boys. I made good grades, but only because I knew I would be in trouble otherwise—my parents both worked in academia. I tried shoplifting on a few occasions. I experimented with drugs. I drank a lot. I got physically involved with a boyfriend. There was a kind of dark haze over my life that I recognized was hurting me, yet I couldn't seem to get free of it.

My early years were not as bleak. In fact, for most of my childhood my parents considered me an angel. They sent me to a small Christian elementary school, where I was ambitious to do well. I made top grades, and I was the valedictorian of my sixth-grade class. I participated in Girl Scouts, basketball, and cheerleading. I acted in several school plays and a musical, and I told my parents I wanted to be a singer when I grew up. During the summers I played on a softball team and was on a swim team.

I attended summer church camp and especially enjoyed singing songs to God during campfire worship services. One song I liked had the lyric "Father, I adore you, I lay my life before you." I remember praying to God on an almost nightly basis as a child and asking Jesus to come into my heart.

At the same time, though, harmful influences filtered into my life. Some of the kids I knew would play games that included moderate molestation. I began kissing boys early. One kid's parents kept pornography around the house. I began to develop a rather perverted mind, and I watched R-rated movies at friends' houses.

After sixth grade, my parents enrolled me in another private school; and, to my shock, they divorced. My mother moved into another house, and at first I frequently shuttled back and forth between my parents' homes. I felt terribly insecure, and my ambition flagged. After I failed to make the basketball team in eighth grade, I forsook all extracurricular activities. For some reason, I gave up trying to please my parents. Instead I spent a lot of time at the shopping mall and the roller-skating rink, and I looked for acceptance from boys.

I switched schools again in ninth grade, this time to a public school where I didn't know anyone except a stepcousin. My only desire at that point was to make some friends and find a boyfriend. I began to drink freshman year, and I went to parties. I did make friends. Some were into shoplifting, so I tried it a few times; but I was too scared, and felt too guilty, to keep it up. I started working at a restaurant and soon was able to pay for the things I wanted.

Eventually, I became the only one of my friends who remained a virgin. I had a boyfriend of several months and thought I loved him. According to my own moral code, it seemed right that I should be intimate with the first guy I loved. One night my boyfriend persuaded me. I badly regretted it, and I told myself I did not want to do that again until marriage.

Junior year I met an older boy at a party, and we started dating. He experimented with drugs, and I followed his lead. One night after we had been dating several months my boyfriend took advantage of me. Tears streamed down my face, and I remember thinking: *I tried to stay pure, but what's the use? I'm dirty now, and nothing can change that. I might as well go along with it.* Afterward, we became sexually involved.

During the same period, I began attending a new church with my mother. I enjoyed the modern music and worship style. People at the church seemed happy. They would dance and sing out to God from the heart, and I enjoyed it. I would bring my boyfriend with me and wanted him to like the church. I was beginning to believe we were not living right.

One time the preacher talked about "riding the fence," having one foot in the church and one foot in the world. I knew he was talking about my life, but I had no clue how to get out of it. I had no friends living the kind of life the preacher was talking about—a clean life. I felt totally defiled, as if I already had blown every chance for purity. How was I supposed to change?

At some point, I began to worry that I might become pregnant if I wasn't careful. I wanted to break off the physical relationship with my boyfriend—I had a sense I was being warned. But I could not seem to follow through. It wasn't long before my concerns caught up with me: I got pregnant on my seventeenth birthday.

Fear took over. I was afraid of shaming my family. I was afraid my father would disown me. I was afraid my mother would send me to a convent or that I would have to go before the preacher. Someone at school mentioned that I might get expelled if anyone found out I was pregnant. I did not know if that was true, but the prospect contributed to my fear. I began to think abortion was the only way out. One girl asked me in the bathroom at school if I had considered adoption. I don't believe I ever thought it through. I just reacted by saying, "There is no way." And I never heard the suggestion again. Some of the women at the restaurant where I worked had gotten abortions and knew where to take me. The abortion law in Tennessee did not require parental consent.

I remember being so confused in the waiting room. My now ex-boyfriend—we broke up before I knew I was pregnant—sat beside me weeping. I, on the other hand, was hard as a rock. If he wanted me to keep the baby, why was he here? I would have kept it if only he had agreed. I felt angry and betrayed. I remember praying to God, "Lord, let this baby go to heaven and send me to hell." I was so mixed up.

After the abortion, I felt like a stone. I felt dead inside for several months. I made a pact with myself that I would never be intimate with a guy again until marriage; but two weeks later, I went to a party with my cousin, got completely drunk, and ended up having a one-night stand with a stranger. I was utterly ashamed of myself. I thought, *I'm out of control. I need help.*

Eventually, my father found out about the abortion and my one-night stand from my aunt. He invited me to dinner and confronted me. It was my worst fear come true. I was so humiliated, devastated, and broken. But my father just looked at me with tears in his eyes and told me he loved me. Later I told my mother about the abortion. She cried, too. She did not understand why I had not shared the news of my pregnancy with her. She said she would've helped me through it, but I had not thought of that.

Back at church I began to experience awareness that God was drawing me to him. When I sang from my heart I would feel joyous and peaceful inside. I was still living fast on the weekends, however, and I knew I needed power to get out of the cycle. I needed something. I would go to a Chinese restaurant with my fake ID, order mai tais, smoke cigarettes, and tell my friends, "I know God is real. I know there is something more."

When it came time to apply to colleges, my mother chose Baylor University for me. Among other criteria, she was looking for a school with a good business program and a Christian emphasis. I was not interested in the application process. I only knew I wanted to get as far away from Tennessee as possible. I wanted a new life. That was it. My mom would not let me go farther than a day's drive, so Baylor—located in Waco, Texas—fit the bill. Baylor did not allow smoking in school facilities, either—another plus from my mother's perspective.

Once I got to Baylor I encountered a group of students from a Baptist church that later helped establish my current church—Antioch Community Church. The students were so alive and loving and passionate for God. I never knew people like that existed. When I visited the church, I experienced freedom in singing and worshiping God like I had never known. But I still carried a heavy weight of guilt for the abortion. I remember meeting someone who had been adopted and thinking, *Wow, if this person's mom had opted for an abortion he wouldn't be here—this sweet, wonderful person wouldn't be here.* I so wished I, too, had thought about adoption, or that I had gone to my parents. I knew I could have made it nine months.

At the end of an evening get-together on campus, a pastor said to those of us gathered, "There may be some of you who feel like wounded puppies. It's as if you are under a table and do not want to come out because you're afraid. If you would like to raise your hand, we would love to pray for you." My heart was pounding in my chest. I raised my hand along with a few other people. The pastor instructed the students to gather around and pray for those with their hands raised. Three students started praying for me. I just cried and cried. It was as if waves of heat were washing over me. I knew God was touching me. "It's a terrible sin," I told the students. But for the first time I felt I was forgiven.

Later that year, I thought God wanted me to talk openly with my new friends about the abortion. I was afraid they would reject me, but I believed I needed to share. I told some friends about my experience at a small group-prayer meeting for freshman students. Afterward, each of the girls kissed my cheek as a sign of acceptance. I felt incredible freedom and joy. I could not quit smiling. In those days, whenever I started to feel shame or guilt, I meditated on this scripture: "Those who look to [the Lord] are radiant, their faces are never covered with shame" (Psalm 34:5).

Meanwhile, I faced some temptation to go to parties. One night I went to a party, but I managed to get out of there without drinking alcohol. When I got back to my room, I made a declaration to myself: "Okay. I'm just going to give this Jesus thing a try. I'm going to give myself to you, Lord, a hundred percent and see what happens, see if you really meet my needs." I started reading the Bible regularly for the first time and was awed by what I read—stories about healings and other miracles and the lives of Jesus' apostles. *Oh my gosh,* I thought, *no one told me all of this was in here.* I read the Bible and other books about God all the time. Some days I would pick up a take-home lunch from the cafeteria and spend time talking with God. I went to the church every time it opened. My heart overflowed with love for God. I was beginning to see my way out of the terrible place I had inhabited. I thought, *This relationship with God is what I was created for.*

On an outreach trip to Mexico spring break of my freshman year, a pastor and others prayed for me during a special prayer time. I immediately felt a sense of God's presence and love and began to cry. While the pastor prayed, he said, "Dayna, one who has been forgiven much loves much."

The pastor's words helped me understand why I had such incredibly passionate and tender love in my heart for God. I loved God more than I ever imagined was possible. I could have ended up addicted to drugs or alcohol. I could have contracted a sexually transmitted disease. But God helped me get off the wrong track, and I was so grateful.

Later, during one college summer break, I wanted to make some things right. I went back to the stores where I had shoplifted and paid back some money. I gave $100 to one store. The manager seemed a bit shocked, but he took the money. The other store had closed down. I also called the ex-boyfriend with whom I had gotten pregnant and told him I forgave him. I explained that God had changed my life. Nothing in my life was hidden any longer. I felt free and clean.

As an outgrowth of the profound change I had experienced, I got involved in the lives of young girls as a mentor through the Waco Center for Youth. Many had been sexually abused, abandoned, or convicted of crimes. I befriended them. I took them to church with me. My heart broke for girls who were down and out, pregnant, addicted to drugs and alcohol, or in any kind of serious trouble. I wanted to give them the kind of support I could have used myself not so long ago.

This same motivation took me to Guatemala and Siberia with church groups during summer breaks. I even told a gathering of Siberians about my abortion experience and the power of God's forgiveness. My desire was to serve people who had never had the opportunity to hear about God's love for them through Jesus. Knowing God as a loving father, experiencing his forgiveness—these things had completely changed my life. I wanted others to experience that same kind of love.

I graduated from Baylor in 1993 with a degree in social work and decided to do a year of discipleship training with my church. At the end of my training, I learned that the church needed people to go to Uzbekistan to help teach new Christians. I was not sure what to do with my life at that point—to serve overseas, to apply to graduate school, or to pursue a career. I prayed that my pastor and church leaders would give me the right direction about my future plans. Before a scheduled meeting, I picked up my guitar and began to play a song I had not sung in years: "Here am I, send me to the nations, as an ambassador for you, as an ambassador for you, my Father."

At the meeting, my pastor and church leaders suggested I pray about going to Uzbekistan. When they mentioned it, I felt great excitement. Thanks to my mother, I was not saddled with debt from my education. I was free to go. I reflected on the verse of scripture written into the song I had played on my guitar: "Then I heard the voice of the Lord saying, 'Whom shall I send? And who will go for us?' And I said, 'Here am I. Send me!'" (Isaiah 6:8). After much prayerful consideration, I believed God simply was looking for someone who was willing to go wherever there might be a need. I wanted to be such a person, so I committed to go to Tashkent for two years.

In Tashkent I learned Russian and some Uzbek, worked at an English library, and taught Christians mostly from Russian backgrounds.

For much of the time I was the only longtime worker from Waco in Tashkent. The church sent people to the city in shifts to support me, and soon after I arrived a married couple came and carried the pastoral weight of our group. But at various points I served as the unwitting leader of some thirty new Christians.

Our meetings were discreet. The government of Uzbekistan, once part of the former Soviet Union, approves certain brands of Islam along with Russian Orthodox Christianity and other Christian denominations; but the law places heavy restrictions on religious activity. In our group—which later became two groups—we studied the Bible, sang worship songs, and prayed together. We supported one another in friendship. I taught a few people how to play the guitar.

In Tashkent I first saw women fully covered in Islamic dress. I would see the women walking in groups on the city's main square, and I would want to talk to them. They wore black coverings called *chadors.* I could see the women's eyes through slits in the fabric. I remember thinking, *How do you approach such a woman? How do you offer her love and comfort? How can you reach her?*

In the second year of my stay in Tashkent, a young married couple from our church came through on their way to Afghanistan. Chris and Katherine Mason met with our group and talked about the desperate needs of the Afghan people. Once the Masons left, our group began to pray regularly for Afghanistan. The Masons also told me that they hoped I would join them in Afghanistan one day.

In 1996, I returned to Waco for nearly three years and took a job as a social worker in an alternative school for troubled youth. I wanted to experience workaday life in America. I enjoyed my job with the kids at school, but I soon began to long to go abroad again. I missed the slower pace of life in Central Asian culture. I missed being a part of overseas prayer and worship meetings. My exposure to the life stories of Mother Teresa of Calcutta and Jackie Pullinger—a British woman who traveled alone to Hong Kong while in her twenties to serve the poor and drug-addicted—stirred the longing in my heart to demonstrate God's love to the poor in other nations.

My pastor began to encourage me to get my feet wet again. I had hoped to get married and go back overseas with a husband, but I could not put my life on hold waiting for a husband to materialize. The needs of the people in Afghanistan were as great as ever, and our church wanted to send people to join the Masons long-term as aid workers in Kabul. I took an exploratory trip there in the summer of 1998 with a small team that included Heather.

When our group was evacuated from Kabul after the Taliban clashed with the foreign community, we spent the rest of our time touring the Afghan refugee camps in Peshawar. One day I had the opportunity to give my blood in a refugee hospital to help save a little Uzbek girl's life. I was deeply moved that the needs of these people were so acute that my small act could have such an effect. I thought, *OK, I can do this. I can come and work here.*

I read in the book of Isaiah: "[I]f you spend yourselves in behalf of the hungry and satisfy the needs of the oppressed, then your light will rise in the darkness. . . . The Lord will guide you always; he will satisfy your needs in a sun-scorched land and will strengthen your frame" (Isaiah 58:10,11). Afghanistan qualified as a sun-scorched land. The Afghan people were most certainly hungry and oppressed. If I would just give myself to the Afghans wholeheartedly—if I would give my life over to the poor and needy—then God would satisfy me.

A few months after that 1998 summer trip, I heard someone describe overseas Christian service like this: "Whether you feel called and go, or simply volunteer and go, the end result will be the same. Your fulfillment and reward will be the same." In other words, I did not need some big dramatic sense of calling or vision to go to Afghanistan. I could just go. It actually seemed crazy not to go, since so few people were willing to serve in such a desolate place. I was not afraid to go, and I was not bothered by the idea of living humbly. I said, "God, if you provide me with the finances, I will go." Within a few months—thanks to the support of friends and family—I had enough money, and I committed myself to working in Kabul for a year.

My decision frightened my father. He was concerned for my

safety, with the war between Taliban and Northern Alliance forces raging in the northeast corner of the country. Also, though he later saw how fulfilled I was by my work, my dad was initially disappointed in my choosing to go to Afghanistan. In the big picture, he hoped I would go to graduate school, earn a good salary, and start saving for the future. I felt bad about letting him down, but I did not want to live what many consider a typical American life. I desired to serve people and show them God's love in places where others did not want to go. By living and working in America, I learned that God loved me whether I stayed or went; but I also realized that serving overseas was a tremendous privilege and an incredible adventure.

My mother—an adventurer herself and one of my motivators— agreed. As a young woman, she had considered joining the Peace Corps to teach French in Africa. By the time I committed to going to Afghanistan, my mom was used to my own overseas wanderings and even had visited me while I lived in Tashkent. She offered to do my taxes and send out a regular newsletter for me while I was in Afghanistan; and she said she would see me in Kabul. In fact, she made it to Pakistan in 2000 but could not get an Afghan visa. When she finally did get into the country, it was to visit her daughter the prisoner.

As I prepared to move to Kabul in August 1999, I envisioned a simple life of helping the poor. I also planned to pray for Afghanistan—I strongly believed prayer would make a difference for the Afghan people. The country was under tight religious restriction, so I knew I would not be able to share my faith openly. I wasn't sure how I would fare without being able to talk about Jesus, but I thought if I could look just one desperate widow in the eyes and tell her God loved her, then the time would be worth it. I was delighted to find later that God would provide many opportunities to speak about him.

three

HARD QUESTIONS

Heather & Dayna: Before we committed to working in Afghanistan long-term, we each asked ourselves hard questions. We also answered hard questions posed by our families and friends. Extraordinary are the parents who do not balk at the idea of their child moving to a third-world, war-ravaged, drought-stricken country—and, in this case, a country serving as a hub for international terrorist activity. That we had decided to go as Christian aid workers to a country where a harsh, unpredictable regime severely curtailed religious freedom gave most of our loved ones pause at best, and otherwise prompted serious alarm.

We were asked: "Aren't you being foolish? Why would you jeopardize your own safety?"

Of course, countless individuals choose to put themselves in harm's way every day because they believe in what they are doing. Police officers, firefighters, journalists, U.S. Special Forces, United Nations peacekeepers— these people sacrifice their own security to pursue their passions, convictions, and dreams. We were no different. Our dream was to go to hard-to-reach places and demonstrate God's love by serving the poorest of the poor.

Just as some people are motivated in their vocations by political ideology or patriotism, we were motivated to serve the poor by our love for Jesus. He loved us enough to rescue us from our destructive behaviors, selfishness, bitterness, and isolation. He was a faithful friend who protected and provided for us. We wanted to do the things that he considered important.

In reading the Bible, we learned that feeding the hungry and clothing the naked were of paramount concern to Jesus. When you do these things, he told his disciples, you do them to me. If Jesus lived among the poor and dying, the widowed and orphaned, then we, too, wanted to live among such people. We knew we did not have to go to Afghanistan to serve the poor—Waco, Texas, is home to plenty of people without adequate means to live. We wanted to go to Afghanistan because we knew few others were willing to do so.

"But aren't you really going to Afghanistan to try to convert people to Christianity?" we were asked. "Isn't the work with the poor just a way into people's lives so you can preach to them?"

We certainly hoped we would have opportunities to share about Jesus with those who were interested. Jesus turned our lives upside down in a way that brought us enormous joy and hope. Of course we wanted to share this with others. If something touches your life in a powerful way, you do not keep silent about it. To use a simple analogy, if you have been sick for a long time and finally locate a doctor who can prescribe a cure, then you want to share the name of that doctor with others. For us, Jesus did something that defied even what we could imagine in our own minds—he healed our emotions; he gave us the ability to love and forgive; he mended our relationships; he showed us he had purpose for our lives. That is good news. Naturally, we wanted others to hear it if they desired.

But the word "convert" does not accurately reflect our intentions; it implies something vaguely manipulative, even dishonest. What we wanted to do was serve the Afghan people because we felt God had put a special love for them in our hearts. If the Afghans asked us, "Why are you doing this? Why did you leave your good life in America and come to this place?" we wanted them to know: "Because God utterly changed our lives and healed our broken hearts with his love. He loves you that much and has a purpose for your life, too."

Ultimately, many Afghans asked us questions about Jesus. The Afghans were very curious about our beliefs, and the topic of religion came up in conversation on a daily basis. Even while we were in prison, Taliban officials frequently asked us questions about our faith. We honestly talked more about Jesus in Afghanistan than we ever did in America. Was this because we were out trying to force our religious beliefs on others who did not want anything to do with us? No, it was because the Afghans would not stop asking us questions about our God.

Further, in a war-torn country where people barely survive from meal to meal, hearts are worn on the sleeve—talk of God comes naturally. A taxi driver might say, "Oh, the country is being destroyed. There is no hope."

We might respond, "We are praying for your country—that God will restore and rebuild it."

He might agree: "We hope God will do that, too, but it does not look like it."

People showed up in desperate straits at our door every day asking for help. Even our Taliban neighbors came to us and asked whether we could do anything for their disabled son. Our conversations with Afghan women would include mention of spiritual things, largely because the women were so depressed about their circumstances. When talking to a widow despairing over her sick, malnourished children, we naturally would tend to comfort her—as we would comfort anyone here in America—with the things that had given us hope.

"God loves you and he wants to help you," we might say. "When we're sad we tell him about our problems, and he gives us peace. Can we pray for you and ask God to give you peace?" The Afghan women welcomed our prayers. We would ask permission to pray in the name of Jesus, and permission was always granted. Always. We would give them food and medicine, too, but these alone were not enough to address the wounds of the heart.

Some people have asked us: "By targeting the people with the greatest needs, aren't you trying to influence them to become Christians? At the very least, aren't you creating the impression that becoming a Christian would be advantageous from a material standpoint?"

We did not mislead anyone through giving. When people approached us saying they wanted to become followers of Jesus, we would explain specifically that their decision would not gain them anything special from us such as extra money or visas to America. By following Jesus, they would get Jesus—his constant companionship, his promise to love them and never leave them—not groceries or appliances or cash. All we could promise would be our friendship, and that we gave to anyone who sought it.

We understood that the Taliban prohibited non-Muslims from sharing their faith with Afghans. Of course, this law violated international norms. The Taliban, which had a miserable human rights record, guaranteed its citizens no religious freedom and very limited freedom of speech. At that time, only three countries—Saudi Arabia, Pakistan, and the United Arab Emirates—even recognized the Taliban as a legitimate government. Though we were not planning to go to Afghanistan and thump our Bibles on the streets of Kabul, we hoped to be able to share deeply about Jesus in a natural way with our friends, just as we do here in America. Friends share their hearts with one another. We wanted to exercise that freedom.

We did understand that by answering a friend's probing question about Jesus we might indeed be breaking the Taliban's law, though even then the lines were unclear. In their own language, the Taliban forbade foreigners to "invite Afghans to other religions." We simply were making ourselves available to those Afghans who wanted to know about our faith. Nevertheless, we recognized that if the Taliban perceived us as having broken their law or crossed their line, we would have to be prepared to accept the consequences. In the end, we were willing to take punishment because we really believed God had called us to Afghanistan.

Further, our faith compelled us to talk openly about Jesus where opportunity arose. In the Bible, Jesus directed his followers to go and share his truth with people all over the world. We recognize that not everyone agrees with our view that the Bible is true, or with our interpretation of the Bible; but like anyone else, we have to live out our convictions. We wanted others at least to have the chance to hear about Jesus if they were interested. What they chose to do with the message we shared would be between them and God. We could not force people to embrace a religious faith even if we tried. No individual can reach that deeply into the heart of another. The inclination of a person's heart is God's business, not ours.

Why couldn't we just accept that the Afghans were Muslims and keep our faith in Jesus to ourselves? some people asked us. We respect Muslims—their devotion to prayer and desire to be fully submitted to God are remarkable. In addition, Christians could learn a great deal from the Afghans' unflagging commitment to hospitality. At the same time, we believe the Afghans—like all people—should at least have the opportunity to hear about the teachings of Christ if they choose. Do the Afghans not have a right to study other religions if they wish and make decisions about matters of faith for themselves?

The most difficult of all the questions we faced concerned those Afghans who might decide to become followers of Jesus based on a connection with us. The Taliban ruled that for Afghan Muslims, changing religions was a crime punishable by death. The same law holds in some other Muslim countries. Some people close to us wanted to know how we in good conscience could go to Afghanistan and share anything about Jesus with Afghans, knowing that in the end those same Afghans might wind up with death sentences.

In dealing with this reality, we decided that we would share about faith in Jesus on a deep level only if Afghans approached us on their own initiative and were persistent in their inquiries. The Afghans, too, knew the risks. If they demonstrated determination to learn more about Jesus, we could not in good conscience deny them. We tried to be extraordinarily careful and we allowed the Afghans to set the boundaries for our interactions. If an Afghan approached us wanting to become a follower of Jesus, we would explain the very real dangers tied to that decision and encourage the individual to consider the matter with great care. "You could lose everything," we would say. "You could be beaten. You could die."

Ultimately, some Afghans were willing to take a chance. In fact, even as the Taliban seemed to be tightening its control over religious minorities in the months leading up to our arrest, Afghans seemed more curious about Jesus than ever. Looking back on events, perhaps we should have been more cautious answering the Afghans' questions during such a tense, restrictive season in Taliban history. But at the time, it was very difficult for us to turn away people who wanted to know more about Jesus.

four

KABUL LIFE

Heather & Dayna: In March 2001, we arrived in Peshawar and hired a newspaper van to take us to Kabul. A Pashtun-language expert—a Westerner—rode with us, ensuring us greater safety but less room for our luggage. I, Heather, carried more bags than Dayna because I was moving to Kabul for a three-year term; Dayna had only been back in the States for a two-month break. We decided to leave some of the luggage behind and retrieve it later when we could get free spaces on an International Committee of the Red Cross (ICRC) flight back to Peshawar.

We would need to return shortly to Peshawar anyway to purchase items we would not be able to find in Kabul for our new house. Those of us from Waco were in the process of moving across town to be closer to our coworkers with Shelter Now International (SNI). Formerly, our group from Waco lived in an area of Kabul called Karte Se on what we referred to as the "non-electricity side" of town. Now we were going to live on the city's "electricity side."

Our friend Chris Mason found the two of us a house in Wazir Akhbar Khan, a neighborhood of choice for Taliban, Arabs, and other foreigners. Most of the houses on the street were large, freshly painted, two-story concrete homes. Ours was the smallest, most decrepit house on the street. The previous tenants, Sudanese mercenaries, used the house for an artillery storehouse and the backyard for a bunker. The wall enclosing our yard was riddled with bullet holes, all of the trees in the backyard had been cut down for firewood, and the inside of the house had to be completely remodeled. Going into the project, workers estimated they could complete the overhaul for under $1,000; all told we spent more than $3,000.

Even after the workers finished, the house looked less than pristine from the street. For starters, in front of the house the workers left a mound of grayish dirt by the sidewalk, and passersby used the mound as a trash heap. Stray dogs slept in the mound at night and hid in a nearby sewage ditch, making excursions after dark somewhat treacherous. The house itself was whitewashed, though badly in need of fresh paint. We liked it that way. We had come to Afghanistan to serve the poor and did not want to appear as wealthy foreigners living in a posh, high-end residence. The contrast between our lives and the lives of most Afghans already was stark enough.

From the street you could see our house's flat-roofed second story above our concrete wall. A wall surrounds most every Afghan home. Our wall had a walk-in gate for visitors and a larger gate through which a vehicle could pass. To the right of both gates you could see a tiny square window in the wall; the window belonged to the watchman's bathroom. A watchman, or *chowkidar,* protects the house and answers the gate. Most foreigners and Afghans with means hire day and night *chowkidars.* Night *chowkidars* sleep in a watchman's room across the courtyard from the house and abutting the wall. Our watchman's room was located at the wall's front right-hand corner. We kept a *toshak*, or futonlike cushion, in the room, along with a little stove and teapot, and a cabinet for cookware.

The front door to the house was glass, and a curtain could be pulled across the door at night. Next to the door hung our coatrack, though we kept no coats there, only our *chawdurs*. Straight through the entranceway was our living room, or *saloon*, where we arranged *toshaks* and large pillows on the floor to form Afghan-style couches. Other furniture included a low, square coffee table; a cabinet for our television; and a low corner table. Framed prints we had picked up in Pakistan hung on the walls. Most of the pictures were portraits of Kuchi people.

Under the Taliban, Afghans were not allowed to own pictures representing people or living things. Such pictures were outlawed because according to the Taliban's interpretation of Islam, representations of living things distracted one from the worship of Allah and tempted one to idolatry. Most Afghans couldn't afford wall hangings of any sort, and we often wished we had left our walls bare even of decorative fabrics and hats so that the women who visited us wouldn't feel bad about the austere condition of their own homes.

Adjoining our saloon was a dining room with table and chairs loaned to us by one of our coworkers. If Afghans were eating with us, we would spread a large plastic sheet, or *destarkhaan*, across the saloon floor and eat sitting on our *toshaks* in traditional Afghan style. In our kitchen we were fortunate to have a half-sized refrigerator, which we picked up in Peshawar; most Afghans do not have access to refrigeration and have to go to the bazaar to buy food every day. We also had a Russian-designed gas stove and ample cabinet and shelf space thanks to the handiwork of an Afghan carpenter. We kept a solar-powered oven in the backyard, and our day *chowkidar,* Khalid—a slight, cheerful man with salt-and-pepper hair—did most of our cooking.

In the afternoons, it was best to keep your windows closed. Dust storms would arise out of nowhere, and if you were caught unawares with open windows, everything would be coated with dust within minutes. Dust storms notwithstanding, Khalid swept our floors every other day just to keep up with the grit.

In our bathrooms we had Western toilets in place of the typical Afghan squatty potties, ceramic toilets set into the floor with places for your feet. We installed a flush squatty potty in our *chowkidar*'s bathroom, though. Afghans did not know quite what to do with Western toilets, and neither did we feel comfortable using squatty potties: You had to develop certain leg muscles to be able to maintain your position. On occasion, after women and their children had visited our house, we would notice children's footprints on the toilet seat in our downstairs bathroom.

We were cautious when we invited Afghans inside for reasons of security, though it was difficult to gauge when the Taliban might enforce the no-visiting rule between foreigners and Afghans. One of our foreign friends, for example, had relationships with many Taliban officials whose homes he visited. The wife of the Taliban commander who lived next door to us visited our home and had tea with us a handful of times. The commander himself even showed up at our gate one day with a hospitality gift of freshly baked bread in return for a cake and M&M's we had sent, hoping to develop a friendship with our neighbors.

When we first moved to Wazir, crowds of street children and poor women in burqas would gather outside of our gate at all times of day to ask for food, medicine, money, and work. Such crowds gathered at foreigners' gates all over town. One day our Taliban neighbor informed our *chowkidar,* Khalid, that he did not approve of crowds loitering in front of our house. We knew that if one widow were standing outside the gate talking with us, then it would be only moments before a dozen people joined her, so we began asking the women to step inside the gate. Often we invited the women into our house for tea.

Perhaps inviting the women in was somewhat risky, but short of telling the women they could not come to see us, we did not know what else to do. After all, these women were the reason we had come to Afghanistan. A Talib had viciously beaten a crowd of women standing at the gate in front of Chris and Katherine Mason's house when our friends lived in Karte Se, and we did not want the same scenario playing out at our gate in Wazir. We decided we would continue letting the women inside until our Taliban neighbor told us to stop. He never did.

We arranged for women and children to come to our gate at lunchtime during the week—Sunday through Thursday in Muslim countries—and we made appointments for visitors to come on Fridays and Saturdays. We usually gave the women some food and tried to create jobs for them. We hired one woman to wash our sheets and towels and another to wash our clothes. Other women we hired to embroider items like tablecloths, coasters, bookmarks, wall hangings, Christmas ornaments, and purses. We commissioned some women to make clothes for us and for other poor Afghans we knew. We paid one woman to make our curtains with fabric we purchased in a Pakistan bazaar. Another woman made the *toshaks* and pillows for our *saloon*.

If a widow came to our gate and she did not have a bread or widow card from an aid agency to get food each month, we would take down her name, address, age, number of children, and other information. Then we could write up an official document and take it to an aid agency ourselves so the widow could qualify for assistance. If a woman had a recent prescription from a doctor, we occasionally would give out money so she could get the prescription filled. Since some beggars carried around ancient prescriptions asking for money, we would always look at the date and then indicate in writing on the prescription that we had given money to purchase the medicine. More often, we personally took the prescription to get filled or asked Khalid to go in our place.

We almost always offered to pray for women who were sick. We would explain that when Jesus was on earth he healed everyone who asked. "He's alive and still heals people when we pray in his name," we would say. And the women would urge us to pray.

As we helped them, the women often said, "God will give you merit." We loved saying, "We're not giving to earn merit. We're giving because God loves you and so do we."

Our weekday mornings in Wazir started to the sound of dozens of children chanting portions of the Qur'an in Arabic at the Taliban commander's house on the other side of our wall. The commander ran a *madrassa,* or Islamic school, for girls and boys. Girls generally were permittted to attend religious school up to age eleven; otherwise they were denied access to education. The Afghans, however, were determined about educating their girls, and we knew of several underground girls' schools. A taxi driver we met raised money for girls' education. We even hired a teacher to set up a coed school for the sons and daughters of some women we knew. On occasion we heard reports of Taliban police sweeping through areas of the city looking for girls carrying books. The police might track down a school that way and make an example of it—imprisoning, fining, or beating the women in charge. Other girls' schools would quiet down in the wake of such a raid, but soon they would be flourishing again.

On weekday mornings, we left the house a few minutes before eight o'clock and walked around the corner to our regular SNI prayer meeting, usually held at the home of one of our coworkers. The minute we stepped onto the street, we were besieged by the mob of street kids who worked the residential blocks of Wazir. Many of these children walked great distances over the course of a day. From time to time, we would spot one of the ragtag children from Wazir wandering somewhere miles across town engaging in his perpetual, often one-sided dialogue with passersby. *"Bakhshish?"* he would ask. Alms? Thousands of children, some young enough to be wearing diapers, made the same petition all over Kabul on any given day.

Our first encounter on the way to our meeting was with a pack of shoeshine boys who daily vied for our business: "Can I shine your shoes today?" they would all ask at once.

Dayna: Because there were so many boys, I gave guaranteed work twice a week to one—a boy named Omar. I let others spontaneously do my shoes, but I gave Omar the most work. He was the most polite and least pushy of the bunch. His dad recently had died, and I knew his family desperately needed the money. Heather invested a good bit of her energy in the shoeshine boys. She bought them shoe polish and sometimes bought new sandals for the street children. She was a hot item on the street; they called her "the compassionate one."

Heather & Dayna: On our walk, we passed a large lot that looked like a trash dump where children grazed their goats and sheep. Other kids gathered paper and twigs out of the rubbish for their mothers' cooking fires and carried their finds in burlap sacks. Often as we passed by, some of the children would approach us and say, *"Khaarijee, bakhshish?"* Foreigner, alms?

Afghans were always looking for something to burn—most of the trees in Kabul are naked of branches all the way up to the tops of their trunks. With so many trees all but stripped bare, we often wondered if the city was headed for a serious environmental problem.

The ICRC office and the compound where the organization's staff lived were on the route to our meeting. Other aid organizations also had offices on the street. The street was full of foreigners, perhaps explaining why a large number of beggars worked the area.

An older man in a wheelchair often followed us in the mornings asking for help. His wheelchair was in good condition and had a turn handle to make the wheels operate. In a society where women and men never publicly looked one another in the eye, this disabled gentleman's advances made us very uncomfortable. We urged him to approach other men rather than ask for alms from two young single women.

Women beggars in their burqas approached us in the mornings, too. One in particular always greeted us with enthusiasm and, in typical Afghan form, with a flurry of questions: "Good morning, how are you? Are you healthy? Are you fine?" Then she would say, *"Bakhshish?"* or *"Komak?"* Help? We normally did not give help on our way to and from the SNI meeting to discourage crowds from waiting outside the meeting door. But our coworker, Peter Bunch—a friendly, easygoing Australian in his fifties—almost always handed out money after the meeting, so crowds usually assembled anyway.

At other times of day, we gave bread, fruit, or juice to the beggars we encountered. A small shop and produce stand were located at the end of our street, and when women beggars approached us, we would ask them to follow us to the shop and pick out the things they needed. If a woman said, "No, I need money," we usually apologized and renewed our offer to buy her something.

Heather: After the morning SNI meeting ended at eleven o'clock, street kids would follow us back to our home. We would have scheduled appointments with Afghan women from 11 to 12:30, and at 12:30 we would hand out bread and fruit to the street kids and let the boys shine our shoes again. We made it clear to the kids we would only be available at 12:30 and not before; otherwise, they would press on the doorbell at the gate until someone answered.

Khalid would help me deal with the kids. He was a stern disciplinarian and could easily determine which among the bunch were troublemakers. The kids listened to Khalid and followed his instructions. He would sit them all down in a row on the curb opposite the door. Then Khalid and I would go down the line and give each child some help for the day.

I wanted to be able to help as many kids as I could, but in the case of the shoeshine boys, I simply did not have enough pairs of shoes to support their multiple small businesses. The market on shoe shining was overexhausted—too many entrepreneurs and not enough consumers. Usually, I hired the kids on rotation. One day I would let two or three boys polish shoes, and the next time some other boys would have a turn. Often I would dole out one shoe to each boy and split the pay.

I always made sure no one walked away empty-handed. To those who did not get paid, I gave fruit or, occasionally, a bottle of shoe polish or a pair of sandals.

Distributing plastic sandals turned out to be a far larger enterprise than I had imagined. I gave out the first pair to a kid who owned no shoes. Afterward, children came to me constantly with the top ten reasons why they, too, needed new pairs. Some kids truly did need the shoes. Others, however, just liked the idea of getting something new. Interestingly, with one exception, I never saw any of the kids wearing the shoes I had provided. Some gave the shoes away to relatives as a tactic for getting more; others sold the shoes for money. It was difficult to discern the kids' true intentions. Eventually, Dayna and I learned how to gauge which kids were sincere. But most times, we just risked being deceived in order to help them.

Dayna: Just before one o'clock Heather and I would get ready to go to our respective SNI activities. Heather usually left before me and took a taxi to the downtown neighborhood of Shar-e-Nao, where she spent the afternoon at language school. The language school was in the SNI office compound on the same street as the Afghan passport office and about a ten-minute ride from our house in Wazir.

Meanwhile, I would finish up with the Afghan women who had come to our house, and Khalid would go out to find me a taxi. The nice taxis were yellow Toyota Corolla station wagons. Less comfortable were the old Russian-model cars. None of the taxis were equipped with seat belts. A few drivers regularly took us places. One of our drivers, Abdul, would park on our street until we came out needing to go somewhere. Waiting for us likely proved more lucrative for Abdul than driving all over town in search of random passengers who might not have the means to tip him.

Driving around town, we would often pass buses or vans packed to the gills with people and carrying men or boys on the rooftops or clinging to the sides. No traffic laws seemed to exist in Afghanistan. Especially when we traveled to Karte Se on the non-electricity side of town, we would pass several bombed-out buildings with shattered windows and cars on the side of the road punctured with bullet holes. We would have to be deliberate about telling ourselves, "This is not normal."

On weekday afternoons, I had the taxi take me to the SNI street kids project building, located just past Shar-e-Nao and only a couple of minutes from the United Nations guesthouse. Many of the street kids who participated in the project walked to the building from Sher-pur, a neighborhood of mud houses on the hillside behind Wazir.

When Heather and I arrived in Kabul, SNI's projects in the capital city were smaller in scope than the work it was doing elsewhere in Afghanistan. SNI factories in Kandahar, Helmand, Jalalabad, and Khost produced concrete roof beams and roof slabs, which were provided to Afghans at a subsidized price. In Logar, a small village outside of Kabul, SNI helped rebuild hundreds of houses following an earthquake. In Ghazni province—where Heather, I, and our six fellow SNI prisoners were jailed just before our rescue by the U.S. military—SNI helped repair thousands of wells and built a medical clinic. The organization's Ghazni office was ransacked, we learned, following our arrest.

In Kabul, SNI administered a winter distribution of food, blankets, and firewood for two thousand families, and helped repair water systems and two orphanages. The organization launched the street kids project in May 2001 after one of our coworkers, a young German woman named Katrin Jelinek, could no longer handle the numbers of kids turning up at her home at lunchtime for fruit and bread. Kati, a hardworking, cheerful woman in her late twenties, designed a program to provide street kids with a hot meal and then a number of job-training classes, which the kids would be paid to attend. The Taliban allowed us to open the program only to boys, the vast majority of whom did not attend school.

Lunch was served to the boys around noon—usually beans, rice, fruit, vegetables, and maybe some meat. I couldn't make it to lunch at the project because so many women gathered at our gate in Wazir at lunchtime, and I could never get away earlier than just before one o'clock. After lunch the boys played soccer outside in the big court-yard. We filled a small, concrete, basinlike area with water so some of the boys could swim. And a few others helped us tend the garden for a modest income.

We offered the boys only two classes when we started the project: a printing class, in which we taught the boys to make stationery depicting various Kabul scenes; and, for the smaller children, a paper-flower-making class. Afghans use paper flowers for decoration in wedding ceremonies. We talked about adding carpet weaving and tailoring classes eventually. Days before Heather and I were arrested, we opened a carpentry class.

For most of the summer an Afghan man and I taught the printing class. Later we trained another Afghan to take my place, and I became more of an administrator for the whole project. I interviewed boys who wanted to participate and kept data on which boys were getting shoes, medicine, and clothing from us. At the time of our arrest, the project was feeding and training about seventy boys every day. A typical interview went like this:

"Akmal, do you have a mother and father?"

"Yes."

"Does your father work?"

"No, he is sick at home."

"Do you attend school?"

"No."

"Did you attend in the past?"

"Yes, for one year."

"Why did you stop?"

"The Taliban came."

"Which class would you like to take here?"

"Printing!"

"Right now that class is full, but we will be starting carpentry soon. Would you like to do that?"

"Yes."

"Do you need *chaplacks?*"

"Yes."

"Let me see yours." The boy would show me his tattered plastic sandals sewn together in many places.

"Okay, let's go next door and get you some new ones."

"Thank you, Miss Dayna-jan." Afghans add "-jan" to a name as a term of endearment.

Heather & Dayna: Our evenings generally were booked with meetings. On Sunday nights, we met at a foreigner's home across town for prayer; Tuesday nights we had SNI worship meetings in Wazir; on Wednesday nights, our small clan of Waco friends gathered at the Masons' for dinner; and on Friday nights, SNI held a gathering open to all foreigners in the city.

Whenever we could carve out time for social activity, we usually visited with foreign friends in one another's houses. We shared meals and sometimes watched movies. A number of the longtime Kabul residents in the foreign community owned enormous video libraries. Afghans were not permitted to watch movies, though the law didn't keep anyone from doing it. Many Afghans with money hid TVs and VCRs in their homes and continued to see films in secret. It was common knowledge that the Taliban watched movies and satellite television. The warden in one of our Taliban prisons actually wanted the satellite dish from our SNI leader Georg Taubmann's house, as Georg could have no use for it in prison.

Weekends—Fridays and Saturdays—we usually reserved for appointments with our Afghan friends and errands in the bazaars. There were numerous bazaars in Kabul—some covering dozens of blocks and city streets, others stretching out along single streets. We often traveled to Kabul's largest bazaar, called Mandaee, which sprawled alongside the barely flowing Kabul River and surrounded the famous mosque Masjidi Puli Khishtee. Stands were set up just outside of the mosque for selling prayer beads, white skullcaps, prayer rugs, and other Islamic paraphernalia. Women often sat with their babies near the mosque, its blue dome towering over the scene, and begged for handouts.

Branching out from the mosque were areas of the bazaar designated for spices and songbirds. In the spice bazaar, the air was always thick with exotic aromas. Nearby, men would stir-fry vegetables and meat in heavy black skillets, adding to the olfactory experience. Walking through the snaking pathways of Mandaee, you also would come upon a sprawling money bazaar, where people sat by the side of the road with stacks of Afghani bills waiting to make exchanges for dollars and rupees, Pakistan's currency.

Rows of shops extended as far as the eye could see. At Mandaee, you could find most anything you needed—burqas, appliances, dishes, cosmetics, linens, *destarkhaans,* teapots and serving trays, flour, sugar, and more. You might see merchants with blankets spread out on the sidewalk and piled high with shoes or other goods. Countless rows of stands were divided into sections for carpets, fruits and vegetables, shoes, makeup, used clothing, plastic buckets and basins, and other items.

The largest section at Mandaee was for cloth sellers. Often, if you bought something from the cloth sellers, they would offer you tea. Some foreign friends of ours once joked that they could spend an entire afternoon at the bazaar going from shop to shop drinking tea.

The bazaar was almost always wall-to-wall people. Covered women beggars, street kids, and men on bicycles clogged the streets and narrow passageways. In the air hung the scent of *boulanee*—fried potato pastries—commingled with the smell of sewage running through the streets. You could hear merchants shouting out lists of their offerings. "Come here!" they would call. "Look at this!" Or they would practice their English: "Hello, can I help you?"

Children walked around the bazaar trying to sell things. Once we bought several squares of toilet paper from a little boy for a few cents each. We liked to encourage the children to work instead of beg.

Heather: Shortly after we moved into our house in Wazir, we traveled to Mandaee to buy material for the *toshaks* and curtains in our *saloon*. Young boys seemed to be stationed every few feet begging. We decided to help them and stopped at a fruit stand to buy a dozen oranges. I did not want to create a mob scene handing out the fruit, so I waited until we got deeper into the bazaar. With a knot of boys in tow, we made our way through a maze of narrow mud walkways tightly lined with booths and came to a spot near the fabric sellers where I could hand out the oranges one at a time.

Almost immediately after I began passing out the fruit, the boys went berserk and started grabbing oranges out of my hands. Oranges fell to the ground. The boys shouted at one another. Some of the boys took more than one. We looked at them disapprovingly. "Your behavior is extremely poor," we said.

"I did not get one," exclaimed one of the younger boys, so angry he was close to tears. A nearby shopkeeper made a remark that provoked the boy, and the boy threw a rock in reply. Then the shopkeeper bent down and picked up a rock. We held our breath. Thankfully the man restrained himself, perhaps due to our presence. We were so relieved. Even when we were trying to help Afghans, we sometimes caused problems—the people were so desperate.

Heather & Dayna: Near the SNI office compound in Shar-e-Nao was a smaller bazaar street famous for having the best meat selection. The meat markets were gruesome places to be in the mornings. Bloody animals would be piled up outside the butcher shops. We might pass a sheep, goat, or cow lying in a pool of blood with its throat cut. Carcasses also hung on hooks and played host to swarms of flies and bees. The air would be rank with the smell of dead flesh.

Chicken Street, a frequent destination for foreigners in search of handwoven carpets and lapis jewelry, was also located in Shar-e-Nao. On nearby Flower Street were shops offering Western products like Oreos, Pepsi, Pringles, Frosted Flakes, and Campbell's soup.

We frequented one Flower Street shop called Chelsea's, where the owner, who spoke excellent English, would serve us ice-cold Capri Suns or juice boxes. A lifelong citizen of Kabul, the owner had seen the rise and fall of several Afghan governments—trails of hippies, Russian invaders, and Arab Al-Qaeda terrorists all had walked the aisles of his store.

Every time we would go to pay the owner for our purchases, he would say, "If you don't have enough money, no problem—you can pay later."

The owner kept a record of charges for foreigners who didn't have enough money, and he trusted them to come back and pay for whatever they took.

When he offered to spot us, we would reply, "Thank you, we think we have enough money this time."

Then he would say, "Where are you going? We will get a taxi for you." His brother would insist on carrying our items out to a taxi for us. Often we would try to carry the things ourselves, but to no avail. The brother would sweep up our packages and escort us to a taxi.

Dayna: At the bazaars, we foreigners attracted attention. When I lived in Karte Se on the non-electricity side of town, I had to walk through the bazaar every morning to catch a taxi. I would pass by the shops, the bread bakery, and the hanging meat. As I walked, men and some women would turn toward me and motion to their friends to look: *"Khaarijee!"* they would exclaim. Kids would call out *"Khaarijee, Salam!"* Hello, foreigner!

We didn't ever feel quite safe pushing through the crowds of people in the Kabul bazaar areas. Once when Heather and I were purchasing some meters of material at Mandaee, a crowd of about thirty men gathered around to watch us try our hand at bargaining for a better price. One of the men made a comment, and the whole crowd erupted in laughter. We had not been able to catch the man's remark, but it obviously wasn't good. We bought the cloth and got into our taxi as quickly as we could.

One day a foreign girlfriend and I ventured into a burqa shop in one of the larger bazaars. I wanted to buy a burqa and proceeded to try on several. I was having some difficulty finding a burqa long enough to suit my height and wide enough at the top to fit over my Western head. The fashion show went on for some minutes before I realized a crowd of Afghan men and curious Taliban had assembled at the door of the shop to watch! The sight of a foreigner donning a burqa was entertainment, indeed. Luckily, the shopkeeper ushered me into a small room where I could continue away from the gaze of the strange male spectators.

On another occasion, I accompanied one of my foreign guy friends to the Khair Khana bazaar, one of the largest in the city. I helped my friend select some souvenirs. He wanted a turban and some colorful skullcaps. Before we knew it, a crowd of at least thirty people—mostly men and boys, but also a few women—had gathered around us and proceeded to follow us from shop to shop while we made our purchases. As we finally got into a taxi to leave, some of the teenage boys in the mob started spitting at us and yelling out, *"Khaar-ijee!"* One boy spit into our taxi window, hitting my friend on the leg. Another boy threw an apple core into the car. The poor taxi driver tried to reprimand the boys: "You are very bad!" he kept saying. As he drove off, he apologized to us and excused the boys as undisciplined and uneducated.

Heather & Dayna: The Taliban's attitude toward foreigners and things non-Islamic seemed to become increasingly hostile over the spring and summer. A few weeks before we arrived in late March, the Taliban caused an international uproar when it destroyed two thousand-year-old Buddhist statues in the cliffs of the Hindu Kush Mountains near Bamiyan. The move shamed some of our Afghan acquaintances, who felt the Taliban had defiled their national identity.

In May, the Taliban released a flurry of edicts affecting foreigners and religious minorities: Hindu women were ordered to wear burqas; non-Muslims were told to wear tags identifying themselves; foreign women were forbidden to drive and were told to wear burqas, too. None of the edicts was enforced, to our knowledge, but they mirrored the tension we could detect in the streets.

Heather: We tried to stay clear of Taliban on the street. They were men who enjoyed their power. You would see Toyota pickups full of Taliban flying through intersections. One day I was walking down our street in Wazir with one of my SNI coworkers, when some Taliban in a white Toyota Corolla station wagon nearly ran me off the road. I jumped onto the curb and turned my head to stare at them. When I did, a Talib stood up out of the window and spit on me. He yelled something and glared at me with utter hatred. Then the vehicle sped away.

Other foreign women we knew had similar experiences. One evening a Talib in a pickup truck spit in Dayna's face as she was walking down the street with our night *chowkidar.*

Civilian men also were aggressive on occasion—they were not above spitting, as poor Dayna also discovered. But there were worse things than being spat on. One night, Dayna and I were walking to an all-night prayer meeting at the SNI guesthouse compound around the corner from our house. We intended to pray for the thousands of Afghans pouring into the refugee camp in the western city of Herat because of the drought. Many of the refugees were digging holes in the ground to get some relief from the heat, and the camp lacked enough water to meet the people's needs. The refugees were so desperate, they did not even have money to afford burial cloth for the sixty to a hundred people dying daily. SNI was in the process of opening an office at the camp to conduct a joint aid project with another organization, and the SNI Afghan employees wept when they saw the suffering of the people.

Dayna and I had organized the all-night prayer meeting for the Herat refugees, and when we set out for the meeting it was just before 10 P.M., Kabul's curfew. We knew we were pushing the limit on safety, but we had only a few short blocks to travel. As we started walking, the stray dogs that congregated near our gate started chasing us and biting at our heels. The dogs snapped at the air and also tried to bite our bags. We picked up our pace. Why were these dogs being so aggressive?

When we went to turn the corner at the grocery stand half a block away, we noticed a strange man standing in the middle of the intersection. He yelled out: "Where are you going?" We looked the other way and kept walking. Before we could realize what was happening, the man ran after us, grabbed hold of my arm, and pinned me against the wall of a residential compound. Dayna, who was standing in the street, started to scream forcefully: "Stop!" What would this man do to us? Did he have a weapon? I, too, began to scream at the top of my lungs. "Help us! Stop!" Once we both started screaming, the man let go and walked away.

Heather & Dayna: Despite mounting hostility toward foreigners on the streets, our woes under the Taliban were nothing compared to those of the Afghans. We were guests in the land and afforded most every privilege. You could see the difference the moment you crossed the border with Pakistan and entered the country: Whereas foreigners usually were waved through the Taliban checkpoints, Afghans waited in their vehicles for hours while border guards searched for tapes, videos, and other such contraband.

It was difficult to keep up with all of the laws governing Afghans' daily lives, and even more difficult to know when the laws might be enforced. Much about the Taliban's exercise of power seemed arbitrary, making the government's rule more menacing for the average Afghan.

If a man was walking in a neighborhood during prayer, a Talib might beat him severely with a stick and reprimand him for failing to pray. This happened to one of our foreign friend's *chowkidars*.

We knew a *chowkidar* at another aid organization's building who had gotten his head shaved by the Taliban for wearing his hair too long—the beard was to be long, but the hair kept short. For a while, the Taliban set up armed roadblocks in order to inspect the length of men's hair.

Women might get beaten for wearing nail polish, or for not wearing panty hose or socks with their shoes. Women could be punished for working outside the home. If a woman was traveling in a taxi unescorted by a husband or male relative, the religious police might beat the taxi driver for agreeing to drive her.

Shops had to close down for prayer time or the owners would be whipped, fined, and even put out of business. Merchants would push us out of their shops at the appointed hour out of fear the Vice and Virtue police would see they were still open. Barbers would throw people out onto the street mid-haircut at prayer time out of fear of being beaten. The customers then would wait perhaps twenty minutes for their haircuts to resume.

The Taliban were particularly brutal to Hazaras, recognizable by their Asian features. Taliban often called Hazaras dogs or donkeys and treated them with fierce disrespect. One day some Taliban pelted the son of a Hazara woman we knew with rocks, cutting his eye. People lived under a cloud of fear.

All through the spring and summer of 2001, our community prayed deeply for Afghanistan. The nation was suffering a severe drought, famine, war between the Taliban and Northern Alliance opposition, and an enduring wave of drug addiction fueled by the vast poppy-growing industry. People were dying—both physically and emotionally—or they were fleeing to already overwhelmed refugee camps in neighboring countries. Few children attended school. No women were being trained as physicians. What would happen to the next generation? We asked ourselves: Could a country be more desolate than this one?

It was early summer when we began to pray with fresh confidence that Afghanistan would experience a new day, and we sensed that a change for the nation was on the horizon. The reason for our optimism was inexplicable, and just exactly what might take place remained unclear. We did not know whether a change of government was in store, or perhaps just a power shift in the favor of moderates within the Taliban. We knew the Afghans couldn't take any more war. How could the land be devastated any further? The land was rubble, and it was soaked with the blood of generations. Restore, build up, and prosper the land—this was our prayer.

five

PEOPLE WE KNEW

Heather: Before I could begin work on any of SNI's aid projects, I was required to complete a six-month course in Dari at the language school in Shar-e-Nao. I had reached only the halfway mark when we got arrested—I literally reached the halfway mark the day before the Taliban took us—so my season as a humanitarian aid worker in Kabul never officially got off the ground. I did build relationships with Afghans, though, and most of these friendships came out of my contact with the Wazir street kids and the women who came to our gate for help.

Marghalai and Soofia, two preteen cousins, presided over the gang of thirty-plus Wazir street kids. Marghalai, the older of the two, was the ringleader. A beautiful, slim girl, Marghalai was feisty and would do whatever it took to get what she wanted. She pushed the shoeshine boys around at times and mothered the younger children. We often saw her walking down the street with a child in her arms. Soofia—a gentler, taller girl—followed Marghalai's lead.

We met Marghalai and Soofia within days of our arrival in Kabul. Our house was not yet finished, so Dayna and I stayed in separate houses in Wazir with some coworkers. Walking back to our respective houses from our morning prayer meeting one day, Marghalai struck up a conversation with Dayna. I barely knew a word of Dari at that point, so Dayna translated as the conversation progressed.

"Do you pray?" Marghalai asked Dayna.

"Yes," Dayna replied. "I pray every day."

"Are you a Muslim?"

"No, I am a follower of Jesus."

"You can become a Muslim if you just say these words," Marghalai offered, repeating the Muslim confession.

Dayna looked at her apologetically: "Oh, I do not want to become a Muslim."

"Why?" asked Marghalai. All of the street kids were listening at this point.

"Because Jesus changed my life and made me clean. And now I can go to heaven and be with him when I die."

Marghalai looked surprised. "How do you know you will go to heaven?" More Afghans walked up, so Dayna politely steered the conversation in a different direction.

Since we wanted to encourage the street kids to work for money rather than beg, we asked Marghalai and Soofia to come to our new house when we moved in later that week and help us clean it up. Our relationship with the girls took off after that. We saw them multiple times a day, and they were always at our gate when we handed out fruit at lunchtime. For weeks they would ask us almost daily, "Can we come and work again?"

Not long after we got settled into our house, Marghalai approached me with news of her mother: "My mother is very sick. She is in the hospital."

What a great opportunity to show this family we care about them, I thought. Early that evening, I went to visit Marghalai's mother with my coworker Diana, a petite Arab Australian woman of fifty. We traveled to the ICRC hospital situated on the poor side of town among several bombed-out buildings. Marghalai and her sidekick, Soofia, came with us in our taxi.

Marghalai's mother was lying in bed with bandages around her abdominal section and an IV in her arm. Her surgery had been routine, we understood. We visited awhile, making the most of our paltry language skills. Diana, who was also a nurse, had studied Pashtu in Pakistan for years but did not speak much Dari. We fumbled our way through the conversation, because we loved to relate with the Afghans. I longed to know the Afghan people and determined to get by as best I could on my meager vocabulary, learning the language as I went along.

Before Diana and I prepared to leave the hospital, we offered to pray for Marghalai's mother in the name of Jesus, and she agreed. Since I did not know enough Dari even to form a coherent prayer, I prayed in English.

As soon as I finished, something like a small-scale riot erupted—everyone around us wanted prayer. The relatives of patients entreated: "Will you please pray for my daughter?" "Will you please come pray for my sister? She's over here." "Please, can you come this way and pray for my relative?" Several people lined up, and we ended up walking around the hospital laying our hands on sick people—some seriously ill—and praying for them in English in the name of Jesus.

We walked into the burn unit that evening and met some women who had set themselves on fire with gasoline. A couple of the women were only in their late teens. One had been married off to a Talib and hated her life so much that she thought setting herself on fire was her only way out. Another young woman, only nineteen, wanted to take her life to escape the shame of poverty. For some of these women, the act was just a cry for help—a painful, dangerous cry; many women ended up dying in the hospital of complications.

When Diana and I left the hospital, a line of people followed us outside. "Please, wait," they called out. "You haven't prayed for my relative yet. Will you please come back and pray?"

"We have to go now," we apologized. "But we will pray for you as we go on our way."

Not long after that experience, I sought permission from the hospital to volunteer on Fridays. Dayna and I attended an international church service on Friday mornings, but we had the afternoons off. "I have no medical skills," I explained to the person in charge, "but I can sit with patients. I will give people baths, help the nurses, bring food—whatever needs to be done."

Since the patients' extended families did much of the nursing for their sick relatives, I asked if there were any patients without family who needed someone to look after them. I was introduced to a fourteen-year-old girl with cerebral palsy named Lida whose family had abandoned her on the street. She was severely malnourished and about the size of a seven-year-old.

Lida and I developed a sweet friendship. She couldn't manage a walker without someone's assistance, and she couldn't talk. She couldn't do anything for herself. She could only make sounds and clap her hands, which she would do each time I arrived at her bedside. Clapping meant she was happy.

I would bring Lida food and clothing and give her baths. Sometimes I would get to the hospital and find her covered in feces and flies. The flies in Kabul were biting flies, and many Afghans would break out in terrible, scarring sores, a condition called leishmaniasis. Aid agencies set up special clinics just to treat these bites.

I sang songs to Lida, prayed for her, and read her some children's stories I had translated in my language class. Sometimes I took her on short walks in the courtyard. We would sit on a cement bench by the courtyard wall, and Afghan women would gather in a horseshoe around us. I tried to communicate with the women as best I could.

One day I attempted to tell a story. I drew a picture of a frog and asked some of the women to tell me the Dari word. "What is this?" I asked. They told me, and I proceeded with my tale of the wide-mouthed frog. I must have looked ridiculous as I stumbled through the narrative, embellishing it with different animated faces and gestures. Meanwhile, all of the women sat around laughing at the foreigner making a fool of herself.

One Friday I went to Lida's bed and found she had been moved. In the bed next to her old bed I encountered a sad sight—a young Kuchi girl of perhaps eleven with a bloody stub of an arm and a bandaged foot. Her face was marked with scratches and bloody scabs. I found out later that the foot had been blown off while the girl was picking up a rock on the mountainside outside the city. She had come face-to-face with a land mine.

The little girl moaned and cried while her mother stroked her hair and tried to feed her. My heart hurt to see such a beautiful girl so disfigured by an instrument of terror. Her life would never be the same. I ended up going back to see her several days later. By that time she had been moved to the children's ward and looked better, but she still suffered a tremendous amount of pain.

After Lida's family had abandoned her, she in essence lived at the ICRC hospital. During the week, she did not receive the kind of care she needed—no one was available to help her learn how to use a spoon or even bathe her regularly. She was so frail, she couldn't move herself in the bed, and often she would remain in the same position for as long as a whole day. Eventually, Dayna and I paid someone to nurse her. But after a while, the hospital needed to release Lida to a family; she could not live in the hospital forever.

Over the summer, Dayna and I began looking for an Afghan family who would care for Lida. At a government-run orphanage, we conducted a series of interviews with potential adoptive families, but our efforts were cut short when the religious police arrested us. We had been communicating with an Italian nurse at the hospital during the interview process and desperately hoped she had taken up Lida's cause.

Our arrest derailed several projects we had set in motion over the summer. Dayna and I used our own personal money to pay Afghan women for things like embroidery and washing, but we shared a pool of benevolence money with our Waco friends for larger endeavors like helping families start businesses.

Close to the time of our arrest, we had started a business for the family of one of the Wazir street kids. Shafique, ten years old, was a gentle boy, unlike most of the street kids. He rarely asked for anything and expressed gratitude for what we gave him. He seemed to wear a permanent smile. Shafique dressed in the same green pants and tunic every day and carried a burlap sack around the streets of Wazir collecting wood and paper for his mother's cooking fire. We often let him inside our gate to collect wood chips from a large pile of debris the construction workers left in our carport area.

Shafique suffered from a persistent, oozing eye infection. On occasion he shared with me about the dire conditions in which his family was living. They barely were able to buy bread, and his mother was sick.

"Have your mom come to the house so I can meet her," I told him, "and we will try to help her."

Soon afterward Shafique came with his mother, Omira, a young lady in her thirties who was very gaunt and looked much older. We invited Omira inside and sent our *chowkidar,* Khalid, to the bazaar to buy her some food. Omira explained that she suffered from a stomach illness. We gave her some money for the doctor and asked her to bring us the prescription so that we could fill it. We prayed with her before she left.

Omira began to come to the house regularly after that. She would always cry and kiss our hands in reverence. "No, no," we would insist. "We are just normal people like you. We want to help you. Do not feel ashamed."

One day I arranged to go to Omira's house to determine what kind of help the family needed to survive long-term. I took a taxi up into the hills behind our neighborhood and came to a two-story mud house unfit for any person. There were no toilets, no electricity. The walls were filthy. Only torn-up pieces of fabric covered the floors. The windows were wide open, and the house was infested with flies. The children all wore rags.

I learned that Omira's husband at one time had run a small business selling fruits and vegetables off a *karachi*—a four-wheeled cart with a canopy that merchants pushed through the streets in the bazaar areas. We heard that for some reason either the Taliban had run over the husband's *karachi* with a vehicle or had stolen the *karachi* and locked it up somewhere. Whatever the case, we decided to use benevolence money and buy the man a new cart along with the necessary produce to start his business again. We committed to fronting him the capital for produce every week for six weeks on a decreasing scale.

Dayna and I asked Khalid to take the family to the bazaar and purchase the cart along with the first batch of produce. As foreigners living under Taliban rule, we could not accompany an Afghan family to the bazaar area. Moreover, Khalid could get better prices on goods—whenever a foreigner showed up at a shop or stall, prices doubled or tripled.

The first night the family's business was up and running, Omira, beaming with joy about her future, brought a melon as a gift to our gate. But by the time we were arrested, we had given the family only two weeks' worth of their six-week allowance.

I remember Khalid saying to me on the day I visited Omira's home, "I am very worried for you, Khatera-jan." My Afghan friends knew me only by this adopted Afghan name. "What you did was dangerous, going to that Afghan house alone. I am worried for your safety."

In fact, Dayna and I probably related with Afghans in their homes more than most people in our circle. We tried to be careful about it, but we could hardly keep up with the demand. Our educated Afghan neighbors across the street would have had us over for tea regularly if we had been able to carve out the time. Even Khalid invited us to his home. He and his wife served us a beautiful meal. I trusted Khalid and dearly loved him. He was a loyal friend. Once he said to me, "You are like my family. Your house is my house, and my house is your house."

Dayna: When I returned to Kabul with Heather in March after my two-month break, it took me a while to get back in touch with my Afghan friends. Previously I had lived in Karte Se on the other side of town—first with the Masons for a year, then with some other single women. It would take some doing to reconnect with my friends now that I was established in Wazir.

When I lived with the Masons, a small group of beggar kids congregated daily outside our gate. Anytime I stepped onto the street, the kids would run to greet me, calling out requests for food and money. Four of the children were related and had relocated to Kabul after the Taliban destroyed their family's home and crops in the Shamali Valley. Each day the parents sent these four children out to beg. We often gave the kids food, and once I took them to the bazaar to buy plastic sandals. Sometimes we invited the kids into the Masons' backyard to play on the swing set, and the kids had the time of their lives.

One dusty, ragtag little girl, Noorzia, would grab my hand and walk with me in the street for a while in whatever direction I happened to be going. She had the cutest freckles, but her complexion was severely cracked from overexposure to the sun and vitamin deficiency. Noorzia always smiled and hugged foreigners whenever she saw them. It was hard to believe that a girl who had absolutely nothing, not even shoes for her feet or clean water to drink, could be so genuinely happy. Her example encouraged us.

Another child who stood out among the Karte Se street kids was a taller boy with a gentle disposition. He usually asked us for things in a soft, hesitating voice. When I finally visited his family's home, I learned that this boy was actually a girl. The family dressed her up as a boy so she would be able to beg on the street and do more for the family.

Dealing with these kids' requests for help day after day began to drain me, so I came up with an idea. I told the four kids from the Shamali Valley that I would give them something every Saturday if they wouldn't ask me for anything during the week. They agreed. I went to the bazaar weekly and bought them kilos of rice and beans, several oranges, oil, soap, shampoo, and other things. Someone from our church in Waco sent me ten dollars a month to help.

Once I moved in with the single women on a less conspicuous street a few blocks away from the Masons' house, I would invite the kids inside on Saturdays, read them a story, and give them their food. The arrangement brought some stability to the kids' lives and did wonders for our relationships. During the week the kids would come hold my hand and walk with me on the street as before, but instead of asking for things, they would talk to me about their lives.

After I moved to Wazir with Heather, I was able to bring the kids a large supply of food once a month. They all quickly fell in love with Heather. The international church was located in Karte Se, so whenever Heather walked from the church to the hospital on Fridays, the kids would follow her. She usually bought them bread or fruit in the bazaar.

One of the many women from whom we bought eggs in Karte Se was a widow named Leena, a petite Hazara woman barely more than twenty. I met Leena, too, while living with the Masons. A soft-spoken, timid young woman, Leena was illiterate and had grown up in a small village. She seemed naive about many things in life. Her only relatives in Kabul were her two small children and her ailing mother.

The Taliban had taken Leena's husband one day while he was out working in the bazaar. She did not know whether her husband had been arrested or perhaps forced to fight for the Taliban against the Northern Alliance. She had not seen him for more than two years. Katherine Mason helped Leena get a widow card, which qualified her to receive flour, rice, chickpeas, and oil each month; but Leena needed some other sort of income for things like soap, washing powder, tea, and clothing.

To make ends meet, Leena would go to her neighbors' houses, collect eggs from their hens, and sell the eggs to foreigners for a small profit. Katherine would usually buy twenty to twenty-five eggs a week. An egg was selling for about seven cents at that time. Leena made a profit of a couple of pennies per egg, but she had to take two buses to get to Karte Se and forfeited a percentage of her earnings on the trip.

After the Taliban beat a group of Afghan women standing outside the Masons' gate one day and forbade the women to return, we arranged for Leena to bring eggs to the women's health clinic where I worked. Leena would sell me the eggs once a week, and we would sit and talk, usually in a back office. Leena cried often, particularly about her living arrangements. The older woman who let her a room in a compound of mud houses was beating Leena's children. When I prayed with Leena about it, she would cry out, "Oh, dear God, dear God."

One day I visited Leena in her compound outside of the city in a rural area with no running water and little, if any, electricity. As we sipped tea, Leena told me about a terrible incident, weeping as she talked. The husband of one of the women living in her compound had entered Leena's room in the middle of the night and lain down beside her. The man awakened Leena as he touched her. "No!" she exclaimed. "I am not that kind of a person. Leave me alone!" He left her, but she was badly shaken. Such violations of a woman's person are anathema in Afghan culture. I told Leena it was not her fault and that God loved her.

We tried to think of ways we could help Leena earn more money and eventually used our benevolence fund to buy her some hens; that way, at least she would get to keep all of the profit on her eggs. When Heather and I moved to Wazir, we asked Leena to come to our house and sell eggs. We always paid her more to cover the extra bus fare.

Heather and I also gave work to a woman named Tamana, whom I knew from the Masons' gate. Tamana had a round, youthful face and was only in her thirties, but she got around slowly due to chronic pain in her leg. We commissioned Tamana to make our *toshaks* and some clothing.

A widow, or so we thought, Tamana came often to the Masons' gate when I lived in Karte Se, seeking food and work. We helped her secure a widow card from an aid agency so she could feed her six children, and we gave her some sewing jobs. One day Tamana came to Katherine Mason anxious about her daughter, who was at home with a fever.

"Do you mind if I pray for your daughter to be healed in the name of Jesus?" Katherine asked. Tamana accepted, and by the time Tamana arrived home, her daughter's fever was gone.

"My daughter got better," she told Katherine afterward. "Who is this Jesus you prayed to?"

Later I gave Tamana a cheap radio like those for sale in the bazaar and told her that if she wished to learn more, she could listen to various radio programs about Jesus.

More than a year afterward, Tamana had two dreams. One night she dreamed that Jesus came to her, touched her leg, and healed her. Another night she went to bed very worried for her six children—how she would feed them, what kind of future they would have. In her dream, Jesus came into the room and put his hand on each child's head. He said, "Don't worry. I will be their father. I will take care of them."

After the dreams, Tamana brought all of her children to the Masons' gate and asked how they could get closer to this Jesus. I was there at the time. We let the family into the house, and Chris explained to Tamana that becoming a follower of Jesus would be very dangerous.

"Do you understand what this means?" he asked. "Do you understand the risk? You could lose everything, even your children. You could die."

Tamana was afraid. She asked whether we would be able to help her if something bad happened. We told her we couldn't give her assurances of material help, but that we would pray for her and support her in friendship.

Tamana, and eventually her oldest children, decided to take the risk.

We later showed Tamana and her children a film about the life of Jesus in order to give them some understanding about the faith they had chosen. Tamana was illiterate and her daughter couldn't read very well, so we thought the film would be helpful.

The family loved the scenes in which Jesus calmed the storm, healed the blind man, and fed thousands of people with a few loaves of bread and some fish. Tamana remarked how kindly Jesus treated women. He showed compassion to a prostitute. He was good to the poor. The whole family sobbed during the scene when Jesus was beaten and crucified.

The Taliban showed up at Tamana's home some weeks later. Tamana's neighbor had reported the family to authorities for failing to fast during the Muslim holy month of Ramadan, a common complaint used by Afghans to work out rivalries. When the police ransacked Tamana's house, they discovered a book about Jesus. The oldest son was beaten severely, and the Taliban imposed an enormous fine on the family. We were devastated.

After the beatings, Tamana came to my gate in hysterics. She pounded frantically on the gate, and when I let her in, she pulled down the neck of her dress to expose long, thin, red welts on her back. I prayed for her and tried to comfort her.

"I wish I had been beaten instead of you," I said to Tamana. And I meant it with my whole heart.

Several days later, Tamana came to visit again, and as we conversed we heard an Afghan woman in the house next door let out a piercing scream. The woman continued to scream for some time, and it soon became apparent that her husband was beating her. We stopped talking and listened. I was visibly unnerved. Tamana told me we could do nothing to stop the man, as there were no laws to protect wives from such abuse.

She looked at me and remarked gravely: "Those screams are nothing compared to the screams that came from my house when the Taliban were there." My heart ached for her.

Tamana's oldest daughter, a teenager with her mother's round face, visited me at the women's health clinic that same week. She, too, recounted the beating story and cried when describing how badly the

Taliban police had beaten her brother. Then she said something that startled me: "It's okay," she said, "because Jesus was beaten for us." In Dari she said *"lat khord,"* meaning Jesus "ate lashes" for us.

I was so moved I did not know what to say. Really, it was incredible none of the family had been killed.

After Heather and I moved to Wazir, Tamana confessed that, in fact, she was not a widow and had two more children. She sat with us in the Masons' new house in a neighborhood nearby and explained that she had been hiding something. She told us she was having nightmares about us discovering her lie. She would wake up scared that we were going to walk in and see her other two children.

We told her we loved her but that in good conscience we would have to go back to the aid agency that gave her the widow card and tell the truth about her status. "We're so sorry we have to do this," we explained. She understood, which we found remarkable given the amount of guaranteed food she would lose if her widow card was revoked.

Amazingly, when Katherine Mason and I went to the agency and explained the situation, the staff allowed Tamana to keep the card. They reasoned that the challenge of providing for eight children and a sick husband was close enough to a widow's plight to qualify Tamana.

The Masons and the rest of our Waco group were planning to set Tamana's husband up in a small shop, but Heather and I were arrested before we had gotten very far in the process. The husband had found a space to rent and made a list of the supplies he wanted to sell. We were in the process of reviewing the list at the time we were taken.

Heather & Dayna: On Saturdays we tried to coordinate our schedules and visit our Afghan friends together. Often we would flag one taxi on a given Saturday morning and monopolize the car for the day, which suited our driver. As discreetly as possible, we would travel to our friends' houses in poor neighborhoods located in different areas of town, sometimes stopping at this or that bazaar to pick up gifts for our hosts.

Walking from the taxi up to the gates of our friends' mud houses in summer was an experience that left something to be desired. Metal piping running along courtyard walls would empty human waste from the mud houses into the alleys, and we would have to be careful stepping over puddles and rivulets. Black clouds of flies hovered over the liquid waste and piles of trash left out in the streets. At times we would have to pass through the black clouds to get to a friend's gate. The stench was overpowering. In winter the alleys weren't as gruesome— the human waste would freeze over and the flies would be gone.

We remember one Saturday in early summer as being particularly eventful. As on most Saturdays, an Afghan woman came to our house at 10 A.M. and dropped off some embroidery work. We did not visit with her long on this morning and were out of the house by eleven with much activity ahead of us.

One of the young women in the burn unit at the ICRC hospital had died and we planned to pay our respects to the family. Also on our agenda was a visit to the compound where the clan of beggar kids from the Shamali Valley lived—we needed to take them their monthly supply of food items. And we needed to visit our egg lady, Leena, and her new roommate, a young widow with a desperately malnourished child.

We left in a taxi with one of our regular drivers, a nice Pashtun man, and stopped first at Chicken Street in Shar-e-Nao to pick up food for the grieving family of the burned girl. We bought some kabobs and a plate of *Kabuli palau,* an Afghan dish containing rice, carrots, raisins, and meat.

Next we traveled to the hospital to ask for directions to the family's home. We looked in on Lida while we were there. When she saw us, her eyes lit up and she clapped. Thankfully, one of the Afghan nurses at the hospital had been to the young burn victim's funeral and knew where her aunt lived. The nurse offered to ride with us in our taxi and show us to the aunt's home; the aunt, in turn, could ride with us to the home of the young girl's family.

As it turned out, we would never have found the house without assistance. Once we picked up the aunt, we proceeded through a number of narrow, rocky alleys deep into a neighborhood of mud houses. Our driver had trouble clearing the turns; in places we barely had an inch to spare on either side of the car. Finally, we arrived at a squalid mud home.

We walked through a beat-up gate and entered a dirt courtyard containing only a metal pump well. Beyond the courtyard was another courtyard where bricks were stacked. We took off our shoes at the door of the house, as is customary when you visit an Afghan home, no matter how poor.

The atmosphere inside the house seemed very somber, but the mother of the girl who had died greeted us with kisses. We gave the family the food, and they gratefully received it.

Heather: I hugged the girl's mother for an extended time. She and I had visited together in the hospital while her daughter was still alive. Now I cried with her and whispered in her ear, "I am sorry."

Heather & Dayna: We sat down with the mother and the aunt in a simple hospitality room containing a red carpet, *toshaks,* and a small cabinet for the teapot and glasses, essentials in any Afghan home. The walls were bare and the paint was peeling.

The mother asked another one of her daughters to make us tea.

"Don't go to the trouble," we urged, but it was hopeless. You cannot stop Afghans from serving their guests tea.

In a typical tea service, Afghans first would ask us if we wanted black or green tea. Usually they would serve the tea in a metal teapot—or a decorative thermos if they had some money—on an aluminum tray with a small bowl of candies. The cheapest Afghan candies were hard, pastel-colored nuggets in the shape of lima beans. Sometimes Afghans would serve chewy toffee candies wrapped in paper along with the hard candies. Candy was usually served since sugar was too expensive for most families. You were supposed to put the candy in your mouth as you drank the tea to make it sweet. If the family was very poor, you would drink tea in clear glasses without handles. This particular family served our tea in teacups with handles, but offered no sugar.

The mother wept and showed us pictures of her deceased daughter and the daughter's husband. We learned that in fact the girl's husband was not the reason she took her life. She loved her husband. The husband's parents were the problem. Every day the parents told her she was worthless—nothing but a poor girl who would never amount to anything. To this young girl, setting herself on fire seemed the only way to get out of her straits. The mother shared with us that now her other daughter—the one who made us tea—was threatening to kill herself too.

Heather: The girl, only about fifteen years old, looked like her sister who had died. She was beautiful, with olive skin, a spotless complexion, and piercing eyes. She squatted down at the end of the room, and I began to talk to her.

With tears running down my cheeks, I looked her in the eye and told her that my sister, too, had died.

"I still miss her very much," I said to the young girl. "I understand how it hurts. But Jesus helped me. He comforted me when no one else could help."

I turned to Dayna and asked, "How do you say 'special'?"

Dayna gave me the word, and I continued: "Jesus loves you. You are a special person and your life is important. God has a plan for your life. Do not take your life. God loves you."

I asked her to remember the qualities she loved about her sister and offered to be available anytime to talk. I welcomed her to visit me Friday afternoons at the hospital whenever she wanted, and she ended up coming the next week.

Heather & Dayna: As our conversation progressed, we learned that the mother suffered regular abuse at the hands of her husband. She pulled back her small *chawdur* and showed us bruises and scrapes on her forehead by her temple; her ear looked disfigured. We were saddened and felt helpless to do anything. We asked the women if they had ever listened to any of the radio programs about Jesus. They told us their radio was old and that they had no money for batteries. We encouraged them to listen to the programs if they ever had the opportunity. "You will find hope," we said.

Before we left we offered to pray. The mother and the aunt accepted, and we took turns praying for God's peace and provision in the home. We prayed that God's love and comfort would fill the women's hearts. The women kissed us as we stepped back into the foul-smelling alley to walk down to our taxi.

Our next stop was a nearby bazaar, where we picked up food items for the beggar clan from the Shamali Valley and for Leena's new roommate. When we arrived at the beggar clan's compound, we ducked through a rotten wood gate and entered a courtyard. Some women came out of one of the mud houses, kissed us, and invited us in.

"No, no," we said obligingly. "We have to go to Noorzia's house in the adjoining courtyard." Noorzia was the smiling beggar girl with freckles and cracked skin.

There were water wells and small, withering gardens in each of the mud courtyards, and the houses themselves looked pitiful. There were no doors on the entrances, no glass in the windows. The walls and floors were filthy, and only rags and pieces of plastic covered the floors.

Dayna: When we walked into Noorzia's house, Heather looked at me and said, "This is the poorest home I've visited yet."

Heather & Dayna: Noorzia's mother—an attractive, light-skinned woman in her early thirties—greeted us with a nursing baby at her breast. Other mothers in the compound were nursing new babies, too. All of the mothers and children who were home joined us for conversation.

"We can't stay long," we explained. Noorzia and the gang were out begging but came in some minutes later. All of the kids looked as if they had not bathed in days, and many had sores on their faces from fly bites.

We handed out the food supplies, and the kids asked us to sing them a song. We sang a song we called "God Made the World." The kids loved the song—it included hand motions and got them laughing and smiling.

"Who made the world?" the song went. "Who made the flowers? Who made the fish? God made the world, God made the flowers, God made the fish."

Dayna: Before we left, Noorzia's mother asked if we possibly could buy them a pump for their well. She showed me her hands—they looked callused and red—and explained that pulling the bucket up from the well was terribly difficult. Some weeks after this visit I learned that the family's well had gone completely dry, so I used benevolence money to hire a man to dig the well deeper and install a pump.

Heather & Dayna: From Noorzia's house, we traveled to the house where Leena had moved. The older woman who beat Leena's children had thrown Leena out of the other compound; Leena's new lodgings were some distance from town. We drove for thirty minutes, passing neighborhoods of mud houses, fields of crops, several small bazaars, and a few Taliban check posts. The mud house where Leena lived was tucked back off the main road.

When we entered the house, we found Leena's roommate there with her two children, Leena's ailing mother, and Leena's two children. Leena was out for the afternoon. We took down the roommate's personal information so that we could make sure her house was surveyed to qualify her for a widow card. She told us she had to beat her seven-year-old son every day to get him to go out and beg. Women with sons were not allowed to beg door-to-door.

"He does not understand that we will have nothing to eat if he does not go," the roommate said tearfully.

We gave her the food items and soap we had purchased at the bazaar. We also laid out some outfits that we had hired our friend Tamana to sew—clothing for the women and children both.

Before we left, we offered to pray. First we sang a song in English: "Holy Spirit come, we have need of Thee. For you are the one who sets the thirsty free." Then we prayed in Dari, particularly for Leena's sick mother, whose asthma was so severe you could hear her gasping for air with almost every breath.

Heather: I offered to get Leena's mother some more asthma medicine and took her prescription with me as we left.

Heather & Dayna: It was nearly dark by the time we got home. We were exhausted but deeply fulfilled. To unwind we ate popcorn and watched a movie, *Remember the Titans,* albeit a pirated DVD version from Pakistan.

six

LIFE INTERRUPTED

Heather: In the weeks before our arrest on August 3, Marghalai and Soofia, the two cousins we encountered every day on the street, pressed us to visit their home in Sherpur. "My mother wants to see you," Marghalai would insist. "When are you coming to our house? You said you would come to our house. How come you haven't come to our house?"

We already had visited the family's compound a handful of times over the spring and summer. My initial trip to the ICRC hospital to see Marghalai's mother opened a door for Dayna and me to meet the girls' extended family. In addition, the girls' grandmother, a large, dark-complexioned woman, worked at the hospital every other Friday washing linens and clothing, and I would visit with her there. On occasion the grandmother washed Lida's clothing, as Lida had no relatives to care for her.

The first time Dayna and I went to the Aamirs' compound, we wanted to look in on Marghalai's mother, who was recovering from her surgery. Since a taxi turning through the narrow mud streets in poor neighborhoods usually attracted attention, we decided to walk the ten minutes to the family's house. Khalid made us a plate of *boulanee,* fried pastry with potato filling, and we carried it to Marghalai and Soofia's neighborhood on foot.

Walking proved to be a mistake. As soon as we entered Sherpur, an entourage of close to a dozen kids surrounded us, jeering as they walked. Some were shouting, *"Khaarijee!"* We often heard people yelling out "Foreigner!" as we walked through Kabul, but these boys seemed especially cruel. Two of the boys gestured with their hands as if to shoot at us and made accompanying rifle noises. Closer to the house, one boy made a motion across his neck implying he wanted to slit our throats. "We want to kill you," he cried.

As we continued on, we noticed we would have to walk past a Taliban check post to get to the Aamirs' gate. There we were, two foreigners, obviously going to visit an Afghan home and fending off a crowd of rude, noisy kids, and a Taliban guard was watching the whole procession.

"Maybe we should just ask the Talib for permission to bring the family some food," I suggested to Dayna. At least by asking the guard for his consent, we would dispel any suspicion on his part.

Dayna agreed, and we approached the check post, a tiny shack with a white flag and a small lookout window; the post was situated near some grocery stands.

"Sir," Dayna said, "we would like permission to bring an Afghan family this plate of food. The family is poor and we want to help. Would it be okay?"

Amazingly, the Talib agreed. We walked the rest of the way up the street to the Aamirs' gate with the guard's official sanction. But we never traveled on foot to the home again.

When we arrived at the gate, we entered the courtyard and greeted and kissed the women. They invited us inside to drink tea with them. Perhaps twenty people lived in the family's compound of mud houses, and it was difficult to determine how all of the people were related. The grandmother had several sons, some of whom had either died or disappeared; and in the men's absence, she presided over their wives and children. Two of the wives were the mothers of Marghalai and Soofia.

We sipped tea and talked with the family. Typical conversation in an Afghan home would begin with small talk and then circle around to a somber discussion about the family's needs—life is hard, we do not have any food, our husbands and sons cannot find work, and our children are not going to school. We listened to the Aamir women as they told their desperate, all-too-common story.

Then Dayna and I taught the children the Dari song we called "God Made the World" and showed them how to perform the hand motions. This song became a favorite of the Aamir children, and they often sang it to themselves and with their friends.

Just before we left, the grandmother brought in a small girl with a large sore on the inside of her mouth. Her cheek was swollen and infected. We offered to pray for her in the name of Jesus, and the family gladly received our prayer.

On our next visit some weeks later, the grandmother told us that the child's cheek had healed soon after we prayed. Now she asked if we would pray for her, too.

"Would you pray for my back?" the grandmother requested.

Other family members with ailments would ask us to pray each time we visited. Soofia's mother, a striking, blue-eyed woman, usually experienced shooting pain in her back and legs due to a sciatic nerve problem. She would grab our hands, place them on the area of pain, and have us pray for her that way.

The kids always asked Dayna and me to sing the "God Made the World" song. "Sing the song with us!" the kids would plead.

Occasionally, we would read stories to the children, including some about the life of Jesus. I also told animal stories and read Shel Silverstein's *The Giving Tree,* which I had translated in my language class. After each story the kids would pipe up: "Read us another one!" They were hungry for entertainment.

One of the older Aamir boys, Aly, could read a little bit. The stories in a book Dayna brought to the house were written in English, phonetic Dari, and Dari script, and the Dari was simple enough for Aly to understand. After one of our visits, Aly asked Dayna, "Can I have this book?"

Dayna told him no, explaining that she used the book to develop her own language skills. But she promised to go into town and make him a copy.

On various visits, the Aamirs asked us questions about our faith. They were particularly interested in the practices of prayer and fasting.

"Do Christians fast?" the grandmother asked one day when Dayna kindly refused some candies being offered.

"Yes," we said.

The grandmother explained to us that Muslims fasted during the month of Ramadan, denying themselves food and drink between sunup and sundown. We shared that we had no set method for fasting, but that we did so whenever and in whatever manner we believed God desired.

"If we have a problem, we might pray and fast from food in order to seek an answer from God," we offered. "Or sometimes we fast as a way of telling God that we need and love him more than food."

One day as the family continued to ask questions about our faith, another foreign friend and I explained that we could show them a film about the life of Jesus if they were interested. That way they would better understand our responses to their questions. They said they wanted to see the film.

A few days later, my friend and I went back to the house—again without Dayna—and showed the film using a laptop computer with a CD-ROM drive. Some of the mothers and children were there to see the film, but at times we had difficulty following the story line because the younger kids were misbehaving. One of the mothers kept getting up and leaving because her baby was crying and throwing fits.

Two of the older girls wept as they watched the scenes of Jesus being beaten and crucified. They covered their faces, peeping through the cracks in their fingers every few seconds, while the mothers dabbed tears from their eyes and cheeks. During the resurrection scene, the family at first seemed confused about what was happening; but once they realized that the Jesus character had come back to life, they all smiled and rejoiced out of relief.

When the film ended, we talked with the family as they shared their thoughts and, as usual, prayed with them before leaving the house.

One day at dusk Marghalai and Soofia came to our door in Wazir and told Dayna and me that one of the mothers in the family needed to see us right away. There had been an emergency, the girls insisted.

It was getting dark, making the prospect of visiting an Afghan home somewhat dangerous; women, whether Afghan or foreign, normally did not traverse the streets of Kabul after dark. While we often traveled to evening meetings by taxi, in this case we would have to venture into an unlit Afghan neighborhood and walk down an alley to get to the house. The prospect made us uneasy. Nevertheless, the girls urged us, claiming the family desperately needed our assistance, so we decided to go.

When we arrived, we found there was no emergency at all. The Aamir family only wanted to visit with us. They missed us, they said. We were disconcerted by the lie but encouraged by the family's motivation of friendship.

On that visit we met another member of the Aamir clan—a young man who had just come home from living abroad. This young man knew that we were followers of Jesus. He explained that he had heard about Jesus while living in another Muslim country. The young man had seen the film about Jesus a number of times and recounted several of the scenes for us with enthusiasm. Before we left, the family told us they wanted to see the film again.

A week or two later, Dayna and I brought the film with us to the compound. This time we met another male relative who looked to be in his thirties; he was older than the man who had been living abroad. This older relative made small talk with us for a moment and then asked a surprisingly direct question: "What will being a Christian do for me?"

We were taken aback. No one ever had asked us about following Jesus in such a brazen manner before. We answered as best we could, telling the man that following Jesus was an issue of the heart, not something a person did to get things. If anything, we said, he would get a relationship with Jesus, eternal life, spiritual blessings. Yet though we answered the man in earnest, we noticed that his tone was strange, perhaps cold.

As it turned out, we did not show the Aamirs the film that day; not everyone who wanted to see it was at home, the family told us. Meanwhile, the children were milling around with little to do, so Dayna took out her children's storybook.

"Would you like to hear a story?" we asked.

"Yes!" the children exclaimed.

We read a couple of stories from the book—one about Jesus calming the sea during a storm. As we were reading, the older male relative we had just met came into the room and listened. After we finished, he asked Dayna if he could have her book. She told him no, but assured him she would make him a copy since she was already planning to make one for Aly.

Afterward Dayna gave the grandmother a radio from the bazaar, since the family did not have one. If they were interested in learning more about Jesus, Dayna explained, they could listen to some of the radio programs about him.

Before we left, the family told us they wanted us to come back and show the film as soon as they were finished rebuilding one of the single-room mud houses adjoining their courtyard. Then we could show the film in a nice new room, they said. Then the whole family would be available to watch.

Dayna: After meeting the older male relative at the Aamirs' house, I decided to go downtown the next day and make copies of my children's storybook for both him and Aly. Kabul had dozens of little copy stores.

Though the family members had asked me for the book, I was slightly nervous about copying a book that contained stories about the life of Jesus. Even so, since all of the stories were written in English and Dari, I did not believe the book would attract unnecessary attention. I had used the book for language learning.

Of more concern to me was coming up with a suitable place to meet Aly and give him the copies. I decided our gate would suffice, and when he asked me for the copies, I told Aly to come to Wazir.

Aly showed up at our gate with two strange boys. I had seen the boys at the street kids project, but I did not know them. I did not know their intentions—perhaps they spied for the Taliban. With street kids you never knew. Whatever the case, I chose not to give Aly the package in their company.

"I'm sorry," I said. "I can't give the package to you now."

Aly became very upset. "Why can't you give it to me? Why don't you want to give it to me now? I want it now."

"I am sorry," I said again. "I can't do that."

Then Aly did something out of character. His brother was coming toward him on a bicycle, and Aly turned around and whacked his brother across the face. It was a fierce expression of anger. Heather saw it, too, and we were both amazed. All we knew of Aly was that he was a gentle boy. We had not seen this side of him.

"Come on," Aly said, turning to his friends. "Let's go."

Early the next week, we invited three of the Aamir girls—

Marghalai, Soofia, and another relative—into our home for tea. "Will you please come to our house now?" the girls implored. They said the new house in their compound would be ready at the end of the week and told us their family was anxious for us to come.

That same week, three people from our church in Waco—two men and a young woman—arrived in Kabul for a short visit. Some SNI staff members had guests in for the week as well. Heather had just hit the halfway point in her language training and was taking the following two weeks off. I planned to drive out of Kabul with her on Sunday, August 5, to escort all of the out-of-town guests back to Peshawar.

The woman visitor from Waco stayed the week with Heather and me in Wazir. She shadowed us throughout her visit to get a feel for how we lived, and as usual, all of our days were packed with activities. Friday, our day off, proved to be no exception—we were booked straight through to ten o'clock at night. Our guest from Waco planned to join us for all of our appointments, including our scheduled visit with the Aamir family.

On Thursday night we attended a swing dance party at one of the foreigners' houses in town. The guys visiting from Waco were excellent dancers, and we had asked them to bring some music with them from the States. We all danced until we were covered in sweat and hardly able to stand—probably one of the better things a person could do the night before going to prison.

We got up the next morning and went to the international church service on the other side of town. On my way out, I ran into a friend, Lillian, who worked for another aid organization. She invited me to come by her house that afternoon to meet an Afghan woman whom we thought we could introduce to another Afghan who we knew was looking for a wife.

I was somewhat overwhelmed by the day's schedule already, but Lillian stressed the meeting's urgency, so I agreed to meet at her place in Shar-e-Nao as close to 4:30 as I could. I figured I would have to leave Heather and our Waco guest at the Aamirs' in Sherpur at around 4:20 to get to Lillian's on time.

Heather: I do not remember who preached at the international church on Friday, August 3. I do recall a message preached perhaps the Friday before—maybe some weeks before. The international church did not have a steady pastor. People signed up to share messages every week, and others signed up to lead music. Dayna often led songs with her guitar. Peter Bunch, our Australian coworker, presented the memorable message. He spoke about loving your enemies—those who persecute you and those who hate you.

Peter was among the six others arrested a couple of days after Dayna and I were taken.

Another of our friends preached a message that summer about following Jesus where he leads, even if the choice involves pain and suffering. Persecution and even death were concepts we frequently addressed in our community. We read in the Bible about the first followers of Jesus and the religious persecution they faced. We soberly considered that perhaps we, as followers of Jesus, would have the same kind of experiences. I do not believe anyone really expected to encounter serious persecution right away, but you never really believe it until it happens.

After service on August 3, I took our Waco guest with me to the ICRC hospital, where we spent some time with Lida. The nurses continued to urge me about finding Lida a place to live. "We cannot take care of her anymore," they said. "She needs a place to go."

We also visited the children's ward, looking for the little girl with the land mine injury. She was there with her mother. I could not communicate very well with the girl—being a Kuchi, she spoke Pashtu—but I asked her in Dari if she wanted me to sing her a song. Some of the women in the room tried to translate, and the girl smiled in agreement. As I sang her the "God Made the World" song, about thirty women and children gathered around the bed, laughing as I made the hand motions. The singing brightened the atmosphere in the room; joyful singing was not everyday fare in the hospital.

Our Waco guest and I ended up staying at the hospital much later than we had planned. It was always difficult to leave the hospital once

I got there; spending time with the women and children was a high-light of my week. Still, we were due at the Aamirs' house at 2:30, and it was after two o'clock now.

As the taxi neared our house in Wazir, our guest turned to me and said she felt too tired to go with us to Sherpur. She wanted to rest before our SNI meeting at six o'clock. Typically, I would have tried to encourage her to go to Sherpur anyway—I would have said something like, "Oh, what a great experience it would be to visit an Afghan family. You really don't want to miss it. You really should go. You will only be here a couple more days." But for whatever reason, I did not push it. We went into the house, and I freshened up and then left for Sherpur with Dayna.

Dayna: Everything Heather and I tried to do over the next couple of hours seemed difficult. Since Heather was running late, I wondered how we would be able to show the film at all that afternoon. The film ran for roughly two hours, and we would need some time to visit with the Aamir family before our SNI meeting at six o'clock. Plus, I had to squeeze in a meeting at Lillian's place in Shar-e-Nao.

Before we left, I discovered that we did not have a CD version of the film to take with us to the family's house. We tried radioing a friend to see whether she had the CD but could not get through to her. Instead we ended up getting into Abdul's taxi and going to our friend's house, stopping on the way to pick up some candy for the Aamirs. When we arrived at our friend's house, we found her at home and asked her if she had the CD. She did. We took it and went on our way.

When Heather and I got to the Aamirs' compound, one of the kids came out to meet us at our taxi. "Did you bring the computer?" he asked.

"Yes," we said.

We walked to the gate, greeted the family, and handed them the candy. The entire extended family was at home—including the men. Children were playing in the courtyard and mothers were washing clothes in big plastic tubs. We visited with them and exchanged details about our recent days' activities.

Eventually, I went to the grandmother and gave her the two copies of my children's storybook. I told her one copy was for Aly and one was for the man we recently had met.

"Keep these copies well-hidden," I said. "It could be very dangerous for you." She said yes, she would hide them very well.

The family brought us into the new room and we sat down to tea. We were greatly impressed with the construction work, which the men had completed themselves. The room was well built and clean, with several *toshaks* bordering the walls. The walls were painted pale pink, and the floors were covered with nice red carpets.

"Would you like to see the film?" we asked. "It's kind of late and we may not have time to finish it. What do you think?"

They were insistent. "Yes, we want to see it. Yes, please show the film."

Heather and I set up my laptop, but we could not get the CD to work. I was accustomed to playing DVDs on my computer. Since the film was on a CD, we had to do a few things differently to get the movie to play. At this point, I truly did not believe we would be able to show the film that day, but Heather got the computer working properly after about fifteen minutes.

Once we had the film playing, we realized that the volume was not going to be high enough through my laptop speakers for a room of twenty people. I would have to go back to Wazir to get bigger speakers. Aly offered to ride with me in the taxi. I told him no, but he pleaded, so I brought him along.

On our way back to Sherpur, I noticed that as we passed the Taliban checkpoint, Aly sank down in his seat to avoid being seen, which I thought strange. Aly had never acted fearful of being seen with me before. The Aamir kids roamed around with Heather and me all the time. They normally chased our taxi whenever we left their house. They would grab our hands and walk down the street with us, begging to ride in our taxi.

At one point, Aly motioned to a man riding away from the Aamir compound on a bicycle. "That's my relative," he said. It was the man for whom I had copied my storybook. I found it odd that he had not greeted us when we first arrived. And why wasn't he staying at the house for the film? He had expressed interest in Jesus, and he had asked for my book. Why was he was leaving the scene?

Heather: After Dayna left to go get the speakers, the family continued to watch the film in complete silence. The volume was very low, and they all seemed to be straining to hear, even the children. The atmosphere was markedly different from what it had been the last time I showed the Aamirs the film. *This family certainly seems intrigued with the story of the life of Jesus,* I thought.

Once Dayna returned with the speakers, it wasn't twenty minutes before the first CD finished playing and we had to insert the second. We experienced difficulty getting the second CD to play, but after working on the machine, we were able to get the picture to the screen. Dayna left a few minutes later to meet our taxi driver, Abdul, so she could make it to Lillian's house in Shar-e-Nao in time for her meeting.

Meanwhile, I sipped tea and sat with the Aamir family during the rest of the film. We finished just before six o'clock. I had arranged for Abdul to pick me up at 5:30 so that I could go back to the house in Wazir and pick up our Waco guest before going to the SNI meeting. I chatted with the family for a few minutes, using some vocabulary sheets I had brought in Dayna's computer bag.

The grandmother and the men told me they were going to discuss as a family what they had seen and how they wanted to respond. I explained the risk of following Jesus: "It is dangerous for you to follow Jesus. It is dangerous for me as well, but it is more dangerous for you."

They nodded, apparently understanding what I said.

I packed up my things, hugged and kissed the women, and stepped out into the courtyard.

part two

REFORM SCHOOL

seven

IN TALIBAN HANDS

Dayna: After the Taliban police picked me up in Sherpur, nearly two hours passed before they intercepted Heather on her way back to Wazir for the SNI meeting. I sat alone in the back seat of a Taliban sedan outside of what I presumed to be a Vice and Virtue building. An armed Talib stood beside the car. My mind raced. I imagined being interrogated and remembered the whip lying across the lap of the Talib who had gotten into the back seat of my taxi in Sherpur.

I had been whipped before. One afternoon I was walking to a meeting in Wazir with some other foreign women when a white Toyota Corolla station wagon stopped beside us. A man burst out of the vehicle and began whipping us. He cracked me on the back twice.

The children on the street yelled, "They're foreigners! They're foreigners!"

One of the foreign women walking with me yelled, too. "We're foreigners!" But the men did not seem to care.

Stunned, we continued walking briskly toward our destination—another foreign friend's house—and were met at the door by the foreign men, who had heard the commotion. They stepped outside to talk to the Taliban.

"Don't you have whips to beat your women?" the Talib who whipped us asked, sneering. "Women are not supposed to be in the bazaar." We had never heard of such a rule and assumed it was an excuse to attack us.

Sitting alone in the sedan now, I began to wonder whether the Taliban police might torture or beat me during interrogations. Would they ask me to renounce my faith? Would they demand I give them the names of any Afghans who had asked me about Jesus? I tried to prepare myself mentally for any physical abuse I might have to face. I did not know whether I could handle torture, but I prayed God would give me the strength and courage to bear whatever lay ahead.

As I contemplated these difficult questions, I tried to maintain my composure and act as if the arrest were just a big misunderstanding that I expected to be resolved any minute.

At one point, most of the Taliban guards milling around left the scene and headed to the mosque for evening prayer. A single armed Talib was left standing next to my vehicle. After a while I rolled down the window. "Can you take me to a rest room?" I asked.

"Why did you wait until now?" he responded nervously, noting the absence of all the other men.

"Well," I answered, "because I need to go now." He reluctantly walked me through the compound past all of the Taliban trucks to a rest room. The guard seemed anxious, as if he thought I might try to escape, which I did consider. But I imagined myself breaking away from the man only to be gunned down as I ran.

When Abdul, our taxi driver, showed up in front of the government building some time later with Heather and a couple of Taliban, I experienced great relief. I wished Heather could have gotten away—especially since she had the film about Jesus in my computer bag. But when I did see her, a lot of tension left my body. I felt less vulnerable with Heather there and thought it less likely the Taliban would commit rape or any other horrible act against us now that we were together.

Some men led Heather over to my vehicle and put her in the back seat with me. A Talib with a large nose got into the front seat and began rifling through Heather's cloth backpack—they had already taken my computer bag off of her shoulder. The Talib chatted blithely with us as he proceeded to take everything out of Heather's bag and put it aside for safekeeping. He left her with the bag itself, a pencil case, a calculator (he took the instruction manual), some money, and her office identification.

From me the man collected some computer disks containing e-mail from my family. He pulled out a photograph of me dancing at an Afghan wedding and looked at it with interest. I was a bit embarrassed, but at last he put it back in my purse. He also left my passport. This Talib turned out to be one of our interrogators.

"Will you please call our boss?" we pressed. "He lives in Wazir. He's at a meeting there right now. Can you take us to our boss, please?" He said he would try to get permission.

Heather turned to me and said, "Well, the worst thing they can do is kill us."

Some minutes later a station wagon pulled up. Out of the back seat several Taliban dragged a man whose hands were tied behind him.

"Isn't that a man from the Aamir house?" I asked Heather. It was. The police had captured a sweet man who wore a prosthesis. Heather and I became very concerned. What if they took the whole family? What would happen to the Aamirs? Eventually the guards put the man into the trunk of a green sedan. We were horrified. What would become of this poor man? Our hearts broke for him.

Minutes later a driver got into our car, and we followed the green sedan to another building. We stopped. At this location the guards pulled the Aamir man out of the trunk and took him inside. We never saw him again.

Our car proceeded down the road a bit farther to what looked like a government compound. We parked and several armed men escorted Heather and me through a doorway leading into a courtyard. We stood there a moment while the men seemed to argue about where to take us next. Then they gestured for a woman to join us.

The men led us through a gate off the courtyard where we confronted a sea of faces behind a barred window. Hundreds of people stood behind the glass. From a distance, I thought the prisoners were women and imagined the men were going to lock us into the packed room. Closer up, I saw the prisoners were boys.

Next the men led us through a curtained-off area, and we approached some stairs leading down to what appeared to be a dank, cement basement. *Surely, they won't send us down there,* I thought. To my relief, we were told to walk forward. The men called a woman toward us and then gestured for us to follow her.

We followed the woman through still another gate and entered a dirt courtyard with a tree in the center. Prayer rugs hung over the limbs of the tree, and about thirty girls and young women were chatting in small groups around the yard. All activity came to a standstill when Heather and I walked in.

It was nearly dark. *"Khaarijee,"* the young women whispered. More tension left my body. I was so relieved to see the women and utterly grateful to be out of the sight of all of those men.

The woman we followed into the courtyard, Mariam, was the female overseer of what we were told was an Islamic school for ladies. Later we discovered the truth: It was a prison. The women did receive Islamic instruction, but they had not ventured into this compound of their own volition. Some were assigned years-long sentences for crimes that included things like working, running away with a beloved to get married, refusing to marry a Talib, and masquerading as a man to get away from an abusive husband.

Behind the courtyard was an Islamic reform school for boys where the Taliban were training 1,500 students.

A few doorways opened onto the women's rectangular courtyard. On one side, catty-corner to the gate we had just entered, was a small cement staircase leading to a single room. Mariam, a petite, attractive Pashtun woman in her thirties, took us inside.

Some of the Afghan women appeared to be staying in this room. By the light of a single, dangling bulb, we observed pillows and dirty *toshaks* pushed up against the wall and some bags in the corner. The Qur'an, along with other books and papers, rested on a makeshift shelf—a piece of wood rigged to the wall with string and nails. Arabic calligraphy art decorated another wall, and a coat tree draped with burqas and sweaters stood near the door. The floor of the room was covered with a dirty, red-and-white piece of plastic and a thin green carpet with black stripes. Both floor coverings were worn through with holes.

As we looked around, a small crowd of young women gathered at the room's large window; its vertical glass panes were standing open. *"Faarsee mayfaamee?"* one asked. Do you speak Farsi? Another remarked, "They look like dolls."

Mariam fed us a bite to eat, and the Afghan women crammed into the room to talk with us. Others remained at the window staring. Most looked like they were under the age of twenty-one. Their dresses and head scarves were threadbare and torn. Many of the women wore thick black eyeliner. They smiled and looked at us with curiosity.

"Who are you?" they wanted to know. "Where did you come from? Why are you here?"

We told them we had been to visit an Afghan home and that the Taliban had brought us to their school. The women tried to comfort us: "You poor girls!" they exclaimed. "Do not worry. It was probably a mistake."

"You will be out of here tomorrow," Mariam assured us. "They will not keep you here long." We knew the matter was more complicated.

That evening the Afghan women slept outside in the courtyard because of the heat. Some slept by the tree; others slept on a concrete slab at the end of the courtyard to the left of our room. To make their beds, the women spread out dusty burlap sheets and then put *toshaks* and pillows down. They covered themselves with soiled blankets.

As the nights became cooler, most of the women moved into a large room just off the concrete slab. This was the room, we learned, where the women had their lessons each day and drank their tea. The bathroom, which we all shared, was situated at the top of another small staircase in the corner of the courtyard between our room and the women's room. On the opposite end of the courtyard, to the right of our room, was a concrete area and a freestanding water faucet. A concrete sidewalk surrounded the whole courtyard.

Our first evening, Heather suggested the two of us stay up all night and pray. We imagined we would be questioned the next morning, and we had no idea whether any of our friends knew where we were. Heather kept looking at her watch. "I'm sure they know something is wrong by now," she would say.

We tried to put the anxiety out of our minds and pray. Most of the time we prayed for the Aamir family, especially for the man whom the Taliban had locked in the trunk of the green sedan. "Lord, let him be released," we prayed. "Don't let the Taliban beat him or kill him."

Throughout the night we sang songs to God, and as we sang, I felt myself relax inside. I began to experience the peace and comfort of God in a deep way. He was in control. Things would work out. We were going to be okay.

Late in the night, one of the girls came to the window. "Your singing is beautiful," she whispered. "Keep singing."

eight

ARROWS BY DAY

Heather: Saturday morning, the senior Talib with the large nose who searched our purses and confiscated our property came to our room with two other men. They wanted to ask us some questions. We kindly refused.

"We do not want to answer any questions until we get permission from our boss," we stated.

Even a note from our boss—indicating he knew our whereabouts and the circumstances surrounding our arrest—would be acceptable. We also told the men we would not answer any questions without a translator. Too much was at stake for us to rely on our elementary language abilities. The men listened to our requests and offered to see what they could do.

Several hours later, the senior Talib returned to our room, this time with six men. One he identified as our English translator, though the man's English was rudimentary at best. The senior Talib also informed us that he could not—or, perhaps, would not—get a letter from our boss. Regardless, we were told we had better start answering the Taliban's questions.

"If you do not answer our questions," the senior Talib remarked coldly, "it will be very bad for you."

We did not seem to have much choice but to comply. Who knew what the senior Talib's statement truly meant? On certain issues, I was prepared to stand my ground—even to get beaten—but not this time. Not on account of having no note from my boss. Dayna and I conceded to answer the senior Talib's questions and did so for seven consecutive hours. For three days the Taliban drilled us with little reprieve.

During those first three days, the men conducted the questioning in our ten-by-twenty-foot room off the Afghan women's courtyard. When the men entered, we quickly wrapped ourselves in our *chawdurs* and stood up in a customary show of respect. Meanwhile, the Afghan women would flee from the courtyard into their room for the duration. They were not allowed to be outside while the men were in our room questioning us.

Between six and ten men would come to our room each morning and stay there all day. None of us had enough space to move, and the summer heat was oppressive. The walls and carpets were filthy. Flies would come in and out of the window. Meanwhile, Dayna and I would field a grueling and sustained barrage of questions.

Usually the senior Talib and the chief prison commander—the *raees*, or boss—would lead the questioning. At first, the senior Talib's tough, stoic demeanor stood in sharp contrast to the heavyset boss's jolly, friendly personality. It was not long, however, before the boss proved himself to be manipulative.

Early on, the boss and his interrogators tried to get us to sign our names to answers written in Afghan Farsi, or Dari, potentially in an effort to frame us. The Taliban took this approach: An interrogator would write a question out in Farsi. We would state our answer in English. A translator then would write our answer in Farsi. It was this answer the boss wanted us to sign.

I refused. In my mind, it seemed foolish to sign anything that I could not read or understand. I would only sign my name next to my own handwriting in English. How were we to guess what an answer written in a foreign script might say? For all I knew, the Taliban might write out a preposterous confession and wave it in front of the world as justification for convicting us of a high crime. I determined that the Taliban were not going to win this war of wits, not with our fate—and the fate of our Afghan friends—hanging in the balance.

Dayna and I developed this system, which the boss ultimately accepted: An interrogator would write a question in Farsi. The question would be translated and written in English. Dayna and I would write our answer in English. Someone else would write out a Farsi translation of our answer, and we would sign the English version. With every word I wrote, I tried to anticipate how my answers might be altered or misconstrued. I tried to cover all the bases necessary to protect both our friends and ourselves. The process was extremely laborious, and at times it took hours to answer only a couple of questions.

Just two days into our detainment, a Talib brought a tape recorder attached to a microphone into our room.

"Speak your answer into this microphone," he demanded.

We might have presumed that the boss did not want to fool with the tedious business of writing out questions and answers when he could finish his job quickly with a tape recorder, but he never communicated this logic to us. In fact, no one ever explained what exactly would be done with the recording of our voices. How were we to know where the tape might be broadcast? Perhaps the tape would be manipulated and spliced to convey something that would suit the Taliban religious police. Under no circumstances would I allow my voice to be recorded.

"I am sorry," I explained. "I will not speak into that microphone. I do not know what you plan to do with the tape. You could change my answers to say anything you want."

The boss pressed the matter: "We just need your answers on tape." But he never gave me a sufficient explanation as to why. I refused to move on the issue.

Several days into the interrogation process, the boss took what I perceived to be a more cunning tack in his effort to record our answers on audiotape. By this time, Dayna and I no longer were being questioned in our room. After those first three days, a Talib would come daily to the courtyard, escort us to a nearby office building, and lead us upstairs to the boss's office. There we would sit on brown velour couches, and a low-ranking Talib would serve us tea with hard sugar candies. The boss frequently took his position behind a large wooden desk in the corner while we were questioned. At other times he sat on one of the couches glaring at us with suspicion—or what seemed to me to be ill intention.

"After you have written your answer," the boss instructed us on this particular day, "please read it back to us *very loudly*." I was amused at his assumption of our naïveté. It seemed obvious the men wanted to tape our answers—what else could they have in mind? I refused point-blank to read my answer loudly, and on this point I did not intend to budge even if it meant getting beaten. "I will only write my answers," I stated flatly.

My resistance clearly frustrated the boss, but I would not yield. When the men found they could not get anywhere with me, they began to pressure Dayna. In general, Dayna was more obliging during interrogations. She tended to take the Taliban at their word, while I was inclined to disbelieve everything they said. This discrepancy in our per-spectives created real discomfort for Dayna at times. Whenever the men saw I was not going to bend on a given issue, they pushed her. Dayna found herself in the unpleasant position of wanting to obey the Taliban's requests but not wanting to go against my intuition and firm positions. In the end, Dayna always supported me, and I was grateful.

A day and a half after our arrest, four of our SNI women coworkers were brought to the courtyard. They arrived on Sunday afternoon.
Kati Jelinek and her roommate, Silke Duerrkopf, a bespectacled, artsy
woman in her thirties, came in first. When they walked through the
gate, my heart sank. The ordeal had expanded beyond Dayna and me.

At the same time, Kati and Silke were our first connections to the
outside world, and I was relieved to see them. Kati hugged us, and for
the first time I broke down in tears.

"We are so proud of you," Kati said lovingly.

Half an hour later, we heard another knock on the rickety wooden
gate. This time, Diana Thomas and her roommate, Ursula Fischer,
walked in.

"What in the world is going on?" I wondered.

Diana, the fifty-year-old Arab Australian nurse who originally
accompanied me to the ICRC hospital in the spring, smiled warmly.

"I prayed I would get to see you today," she said, remarking that
she was glad the Lord had answered her prayer, though in an amusing
manner. She hugged Dayna and me and told us she was happy we were
not hurt.

Ursula, a fashionable, subdued woman in her forties, greeted us,
too. She had only just returned from a break in her home country of
Germany.

Our friends encouraged us and informed us that many people
were praying for our quick release. Sadly, they reported that Peter
Bunch, our Australian coworker, had also been detained. A few days
later, we learned that a total of eight foreigners were imprisoned. We
gathered the eighth person was likely Georg Taubmann, our leader,
who was the only married detainee.

None of us knew where Georg and Peter were being held, and we
did not see them for weeks. Eventually, we learned that the two men
spent a week and a half in a wretched, insect-infested Vice and Virtue
prison before being brought to our compound. Once Peter and Georg
arrived at the reform school compound, the boss put them in a room
below his office. The four SNI women slept in this same room for the

first ten days of interrogations before being moved into the courtyard we shared with the Afghan women.

Dayna and I were kept separately from the other SNI women at first because the Taliban did not want us comparing notes. We compared notes anyway. Even though the other four were sleeping in a separate building, they spent their days in our courtyard, and every now and then, our overseer Mariam would let Dayna and me visit with our friends.

In total, interrogations lasted for about three weeks. The sessions were most intense during the week and a half Dayna and I were separated from the other SNI women, and on the whole the interrogation process itself was chaotic. It became a running joke with all six of us, the foreign women, that almost every time we were questioned—or so it seemed—we had to fill out a form giving our father's name, our grandfather's name, our province, and our village. Diana, who did not know her grandfather's name, took to filling in a different name each time the information was required. No Talib ever noticed.

One Taliban translator heavily involved in our case was a young man named Karim. A slight, fair-skinned Pashtun in his late twenties, Karim became our friend and was on our side. He spoke excellent English. His gentle presence during questioning brought us great relief. Eventually, we started referring to Karim as our "Taliban angel friend."

Karim coached us through the interrogations. He would escort us from our room to the boss's office, all the way whispering about what we should and should not reveal. "Whatever you do, do not ever say you have given anyone a Bible," he once advised.

Frequently, he softened our answers in translation. "What you said was very dangerous," Karim would say, "but I changed it." When other translators were going to be present, Karim forewarned us: "Be careful what you say. They will understand you. But do not worry, I will be with you."

Karim was not naive—he knew the risks involved in helping us. But he believed that we were being treated unjustly. We had come to

Afghanistan to love and serve his people, and in his eyes we were like his sisters. We learned much later that many people prayed we would have an ally within the Taliban, an inside connection. Karim was the answer to those prayers. Again and again he risked his life for us. He risked discovery, and perhaps execution, and no one ever asked him to do so.

As much as Karim advised us, I knew I could not lie to the interrogators. I was not going to help the Taliban develop their case by giving them unsolicited information, but if they asked the right specific question, I would have to answer truthfully. Our goal was not to deceive but to provide as little information as we could and make the Taliban draw their own conclusions. While remaining truthful, we gave vague answers as far removed as possible from the people involved in the situation at hand. If the interrogators wanted a certain answer, then they would have to ask a specific question.

For instance, Dayna and I did not know whether the Aamir family had confessed to seeing the film on the life of Jesus. Having heard nothing of their fate—whether they had been harmed or even killed—we desperately wanted to protect them. We knew that the less the Taliban believed the Aamirs had seen of the film, the better it would be for the family, so we tried to withhold on the subject as much as we possibly could. Instead of saying straight out that the family had seen the entire film, we truthfully stated that we had experienced computer difficulties on the afternoon we visited the home, leaving it up to the Taliban to determine how much of the film the family actually viewed.

The Taliban were not satisfied. They came back later and told us the family had discussed the content of the film with them. "The family says they have seen this film twice. They described the entire movie." The interrogators never asked with whom the Aamirs had watched the film the first time.

Then the boss asked directly, "How long did the family watch the film this second time?"

"For more than an hour," I replied.

"Kha," the men said. The answer satisfied them. It was as if they were congratulating themselves for finally having asked the right question. We had completed the round of questioning, but we did not feel good. We wondered what would happen to a family who confessed to having seen a film about the life of Jesus not once, but twice.

When we left that particular session Karim chastised us for having admitted too much. "Why did you confess to showing the film for more than an hour? That is very harmful for you. You should have stopped answering after you described your computer problems."

At such moments I found myself wondering why Karim was trying so hard to help us. His assistance, though greatly appreciated, was unsolicited, and I struggled at times to believe he was truly an ally in this whole business. I wondered on occasion if the Taliban was using Karim as an inside source to gather more information from us.

Another difficult series of questions had to do with the origin of the actual "Jesus" CD. As best we could, Dayna and I wanted to protect the foreign friend from whom we had picked up the film on the day we showed it. When the boss asked us where we had gotten the CD, we evaded and answered indirectly. "It came from Pakistan," we replied. This was true. "Someone brought the CD in from Peshawar," we added in the next go-round on the same question.

"Who brought the CD into the country?" the boss demanded. I said, "Perhaps a language teacher who used to work in Pakistan." I was not sure. Our uncertainty about the CD's origin, and our unwillingness to confess the name of the last person to have the "Jesus" film in hand, enabled our interrogators to discern holes in our story. They dug deeper into the language teacher theory, and before we knew it we were in a huge mess.

After exchanges like these, I left the interrogations deeply disturbed. How do I maneuver through these tricky questions? How much do I share? When should I be straightforward? When should I remain vague? On these points I truly wished I'd had some training.

Dayna and I lied outright about one thing. We stated that the Aamir family had never shown any interest in learning about Jesus. We claimed all initiative in showing the film as our own. We apologized for having caused so much trouble both for the family and for the Afghan government. It was our fault, not that of the family. "Please forgive us," we petitioned.

I struggled with the decision to lie for the Aamirs. I still struggle with it. Reading scripture, I understand lying to be wrong. But how do I respond when I know people might die based on the way I answer a question?

At the time, covering for the family seemed the right thing to do. We had seen one of their men put into a trunk and taken away. We knew family members might be tortured or killed because of their inquiries about Jesus. I had to balance the ethical principle of always telling the truth with the fate of someone's life—an issue I had never considered or faced before. In the end, I did what I thought best at the time. I wanted to protect our Afghan friends who were innocent of any wrongdoing. And I wanted any blame or punishment to fall on us.

Later in the questioning, signs pointed toward our having been set up on the day of our arrest. Our interrogators seemed to possess foreknowledge of our plans on that day, Friday, August 3. During one session, a Talib told us he had been waiting outside the Aamirs' home for hours while we were inside with the family. We later found out two or three Aamir men initially had been arrested but then were released; and we did not hear another word about the family from any of our contacts in prison. If the family had not been cooperating with the Taliban, then the religious police no doubt would have made a point to punish them harshly as an example to all Afghans. For the family's sake, Dayna and I very much hoped that we had been set up. We never found out what happened. We prayed the Aamirs were safe.

Regardless of what actually happened between the Taliban and the Aamirs leading up to our arrest, because I decided to lie for the family, I had to ask myself: Was I willing to take the punishment for the Aamirs? Was I willing to die in the place of these Afghans who as far as I knew merely had exercised their inalienable right to freedom of conscience?

Originally—according to some language that we understood to be written into one Taliban edict—it did not appear that Dayna and I would be sentenced to anything worse than a five-year prison sentence for sharing our faith with the Aamirs, even if we had taken all the initiative as we claimed. Our SNI coworkers, of course, had not been with us at the scene the day we were arrested, making the specter of a harsh sentence for our group more remote. But as our interrogations progressed, I quickly realized that we were in deeper water than we had first thought. Death began to seem a real possibility. And it terrified me.

I do not remember the first time I felt afraid. I recall that during those early days in prison my heart felt peaceful. I knew God was with me wherever I went; he would not fail or abandon me. Daily I spent time with God in prayer, worship, and reading the scriptures. This time was life to my soul. I felt strengthened and comforted by Jesus.

Gradually, however, over the course of the initial three weeks, fear gripped me. We were under tremendous pressure. The interrogations took all of my mental, emotional, and physical energy. We had no idea when we might be released or when we might be able to contact our loved ones. It appeared the Taliban wanted to convict us of a high crime and make an example of us before a watching world. I broke under the strain.

I cried almost daily in the courtyard. Mariam, our overseer, comforted me and begged me not to cry. The boss even came to the yard to check on me. We were their guests, he claimed. He wanted us happy and healthy.

"Do you need a doctor?" he asked one day. I suggested the Taliban let me call my father; that was the only medicine I needed. But the boss thought my request too steep.

Much of my distress stemmed from concern for my parents. Here I was in a Taliban prison after my mother had begged me not to go to Afghanistan. My younger sister had just passed away one year earlier. Before coming to Afghanistan I acknowledged I might face persecution, imprisonment, suffering, and even death as inevitable aspects of the normal Christian life. To the best of my ability I faced these prospects where I was concerned. But the arrest had happened so soon, and what would become of my family should they lose a third child? I worried that my dad might suffer a heart attack.

In the face of death, I grew faint. I was not confident that I would give up my life for my Afghan friends. "Lord, I'm not there yet," I wrote in my journal. I was so disappointed in myself. Why was I falling apart? "Lord, change me!" I wrote. "Let me be so free that I could lay my life down for my friend [and] even my enemy."

When I later learned that Taliban officials were talking about the death penalty as a sentencing option in the media, it confirmed my worst fear. The Taliban announced that they were going to try us in the Supreme Court of Afghanistan under Sharia law, and my heart sank further. To our knowledge, the Taliban had never gone to such extremes to punish foreigners. As the aftermath of the September 11 terrorist attacks on America unfolded in Kabul, fear nearly wiped me out. My heart physically hurt with the pressure and pain. I felt as though I were suffocating. "Oh, God," I cried. "Why don't you do something? I feel like I'm dying."

I wrestled with God. I did not understand why he was letting everything crumble around me. I could not grasp why after spending only four and a half months fulfilling my destiny in Afghanistan I might lose my life. I was not ready to die, not at the age of twenty-four. "I have only just begun to serve you," I prayed. "Would you allow it all to end now?" I was so confused.

I often have wrestled with God, and in doing so have learned a great deal. By asking tough questions about issues or conflicts, I have come away from various trials in life with a deeper understanding of both God and myself. I have not always gotten clear answers from God, and in those cases, I was able to declare, "Jesus, I love you. I trust you. I am going to follow you even if I do not understand."

But to come to that point of surrender and healthy resignation, I had to have started with the presupposition that God is good, that God's ways are higher than mine. Without such a foundation, wrestling with God becomes an excruciating ordeal. You have nothing to stand on. Such was my experience for the better part of my captivity in Afghanistan. I fought hard with God, and I lost.

Only two weeks into the ordeal, I wondered how our situation could get any worse. Did God hear my prayers? I cried out like the psalmist David: "Listen to my prayer, O God. Do not ignore my cry for help! Please listen and answer me for I am overwhelmed by my troubles. My enemies shout at me, making loud and wicked threats . . . My heart is in anguish. The terror of death overpowers me. Fear and trembling overwhelm me. I can't stop shaking. Oh, how I wish I had wings like a dove; then I would fly away and be at rest!" (Psalm 55:1–6, New Living Translation).

David's heart encouraged me. It helped me to know that men of faith also struggled and spoke honestly with God. When life closed in around David, when he was being attacked from all sides, he never withheld his feelings from God. He was honest about his pain, his struggles, and his fear. As I read almost daily from the Psalms, I understood what I read in an altogether new way. Until prison, never in my life had I faced literal enemies, nor had an actual battle been waged against me. Through our daily interactions with the Taliban, I confronted both phenomena.

The other SNI women tried to encourage me. They would pray with me; some would hold me. Diana suggested that I closely study Psalms 27 and 91. In Psalm 91, I read: "Because he has loved me, therefore I will deliver him; I will set him securely on high, because he has known My name" (v.14, New American Standard).

"Though a host encamp against me, my heart will not fear," stated Psalm 27. "Though war arise against me, in spite of this I shall be confident" (v. 4, NAS).

Nevertheless, I did not feel confident. In the midst of chaos and ever-deteriorating circumstances, I lost touch with these scriptural truths.

Over the next weeks and months, I tried to hold on to God. I looked up verses in the Bible that described God as my shield, my defense, and my refuge. I meditated on the miracle-working power of God and the sufferings of Christ. I was reminded that Jesus, who had died on the cross for me, understood my pain. I was not alone. I read about the persecution of the early church in the New Testament Book of Acts. My experience was not so different from that of others who followed Christ throughout history. Many were imprisoned and even killed for their faith. Despite our uncertain fate, I caught glimpses of hope. God was working out a beautiful plan for my life and the nation of Afghanistan, and I was grateful to be a part of it.

Ultimately, though, my struggle with fear and my inability to break through the despair strained my friendships with the other SNI women. We fought among ourselves and tension escalated. At times I endured deep rejection, and so did they. For two weeks I stayed away from the daily worship and prayer meetings we held in our room. I felt hypocritical worshiping God with the others while our relationships were under duress. Instead, I spent honest time alone with God praying for deliverance from the fear.

nine

REFORM SCHOOL UNIVERSE

Right now one of my best time passers is fly killing. We ordered some fly swatters last week, and we kill an average of 200 flies a day. It helps me keep my hand and eye coordination at peak level.
—LETTER TO A FRIEND, AUGUST 21, 2001

Dayna: On our first full day in prison, Saturday, August 4, the boss began ordering meals for Heather and me from the Herat Restaurant downtown. "You are our guests here," he told us.

For that day's lunch Mariam brought in Kabuli palau, the oily Afghan rice dish with meat, raisins, and carrots. After several meals in a row from the restaurant, we told the boss to quit placing orders. We did not feel right about receiving special treatment. Mariam—or her alternate, Lumya—would bring in bread and several bowls of food usually oily vegetables, for the women to share at lunch and dinner.

We wanted to eat what the other women were eating, and this arrangement suited the boss. His money was running thin.

On that first day while the senior Talib was trying to locate an English translator and—we hoped—a note from our boss, Heather and I wrote a song called "Fear Not." We incorporated several verses of scripture, particularly a passage from Isaiah that was special to Heather. "Fear not, I am with you," the song started. "Fear not, you are mine." Then a verse picked up:

When you walk through the waters they will not overtake you;
When you walk through the fire you will not be burned;
When you go through the valley, I will be with you:
You are mine.

"Do not let your heart be troubled," went another one of the lines. "Do not let it be afraid." We often sang this song to encourage ourselves.

Late Saturday night the boss came to our room with a few of his right-hand men. They brought in plastic sacks and seemed excited. The boss wore a big smile. "See, your friends know where you are. We have had contact with them." He told us that our boss had brought these gifts for us. Later we found out an Afghan brought them on Georg's behalf.

In the bags were a couple sets of clothing, underwear, bottled water, jam, butter, cake, cookies, and plastic ware. We gave the jam to the Afghan women the next morning. We wanted them to have a special treat, but we also expected to be released soon. Our Taliban interrogators kept telling us, "It will only be two or three days. You will be okay. It will be over soon." Mariam, too, would tell us, "It won't be long before they let you go."

In the beginning, the interrogators wanted to put together our profiles. They asked Heather and me questions about our families, and since both of us had divorced parents, the subject of divorce came up for discussion. The men were intrigued that we did not agree with divorce. A couple of times they even complimented us on our morals.

"But what about you?" the men asked. "Are you nuns? Do you not want to be married?"

I explained that in our culture our parents did not arrange our marriages for us. "We are waiting on God to bring the right person." They nodded but looked puzzled.

By this time the boss had found us another translator, Noorahmed, to replace the first translator. Noorahmed lasted only a couple of weeks.

One day he said to me, "You should become a Muslim. You will be happy if you become a Muslim."

I said, "Thank you, but I love Jesus. He changed my life, and I am very happy."

"How did he change your life?" Noorahmed asked.

"I did many bad things when I was younger. I did not obey my parents. Then I asked Jesus to come into my life, and he gave me a new clean heart. He changed me. Now I have a good relationship with my parents."

One morning Noorahmed brought in a note he had written to Heather and me. He did not give the note to us, but he read it to us aloud. In the note Noorahmed encouraged us to be strong and not to be afraid. "I do not expect anything from you, but I want you to know I am going to help you." We never saw him again.

Sunday afternoon, August 5, all of the Afghan women ran to the courtyard gate. Heather and I were sitting on the cement steps outside our room after a grueling day of questioning.

"They are bringing in foreigners!" the women exclaimed. In walked Kati and Silke. We ran over to them and hugged them.

Diana and Ursula came next. Mariam separated Heather and me from the others, but we learned later what had happened.

An emergency SNI prayer meeting had been scheduled for 2 P.M. that day. Kati had gone to the street kids project beforehand to collect some things. Everyone anticipated that the SNI facilities would be searched. In fact, a cadre of Taliban showed up at the project while

Kati was still there. The men told her they wanted to bring her into custody to question her. She said she needed to return to her house first, and the Taliban conceded.

When they all got to the house, the men followed Kati inside and arrested Silke, too. Fortunately, Silke was able to grab a substantial amount of cash before she left. This cash lasted us the three and a half months we spent in prison.

We learned some weeks later that our leader, Georg, was passing by Kati and Silke's house while the Taliban were inside. When Georg stopped to see what was happening, a couple of Taliban roughed him up and pushed him into their vehicle. Kati and Silke never saw Georg, and, in fact, it was some time before any of us SNI women even could confirm Georg's arrest.

Meanwhile, Ursula and Diana had gone to the SNI office in Shar-e-Nao to get money out of the safe. There was quite a lot of money in the office, since SNI was about to start a large project at the refugee camp in Herat. When the women arrived, they saw that the Taliban had barricaded the compound's front gate. A Talib assured Diana and Ursula that he would try to find a key. In the meantime, the women stood outside the gate and waited.

As the women were waiting, an armed Taliban guard fired a shot in their direction as if to intimidate them. Soon afterward, Diana realized that no one had gone to fetch a key. In fact, she recognized, the Taliban likely were preparing to arrest them. She and Ursula decided they had better leave the scene, but as they turned, another Talib made a gesture as if he was going for his whip. The women decided it would be wise to stay put.

At that time Diana sent out a call on her handheld radio. "We are outside the office," she said. "They're here to take us." A Talib took the radio out of Diana's hands as people began responding to her call.

In the midst of the radio episode, Diana spotted her countryman Peter Bunch and an Afghan man approaching the gate in one of the organization's vehicles. Suddenly, she heard a skidding noise and thought, *Oh, good. They saw us and got away.*

But moments later Peter drove up—he could not leave the women there. When he came to a stop, the Taliban instructed Diana and Ursula to get into the vehicle. Then the Taliban themselves climbed in and told Peter to drive. The whole group went together to the reform school prison compound. On their arrival, Diana and Ursula were brought back to our courtyard, Peter was taken away—eventually to a Vice and Virtue prison, we later learned—and the vehicle was confiscated.

At some point, SNI's sixteen Afghan employees were rounded up and arrested, too. We found out later that all remaining foreign SNI workers fled the country the next morning, Monday, before dawn.

Interrogations proceeded apace once the other four SNI women were brought to the prison. By that time we were being taken to the boss's office each day for questioning. The sessions were very draining; in particular, grappling with the issue of truth-telling took a large amount of emotional energy.

Neither Heather nor I wanted to lie, but we were decided about generally denying the Aamir family's interest in Jesus to protect their lives. I did not have trouble justifying the lie, given what could happen to the Aamirs if their interest in Jesus were exposed. Rather, navigating the ripple effects of this general lie is what created stress and difficulty.

"We have found these folders of copies in the Aamir house," the boss announced one day. He meant the copies of my children's storybook that I had handed to the grandmother on the day of our arrest. The boss asked who had given the family the copies.

"I did," I confessed.

I claimed I made the copies of the book on my own initiative, which was a reach. I had initiated making copies in the sense that while declining to give Aly and his relative the book, I had offered instead to make copies. But by omitting the fact that the family members ever asked me for the book in the first place, I felt I was riding the line on truthfulness.

When the boss asked us whether we had shown the Aamirs the film about Jesus, Heather and I tried to protect the family by asserting simply that we had experienced computer difficulties that day. The implication, if the Taliban chose to read our answer this way, was that because of our difficulties we had not shown the whole film. What the Taliban chose to conclude was their business, of course; but I would have felt more comfortable telling the boss flat out, "We showed the whole film."

Similarly, when the boss wanted to know where our "Jesus" CD came from, I would rather have told him directly from whom we got the film. Instead, we tried to protect our friend by giving answers as far removed from the actual hand-off as we could and, in the process, became entangled in a Q-and-A about an unnamed language teacher who used to work in Pakistan.

I did lie outright on a specific point once and carried a lot of guilt over it. "Did you ever give an *injeel* [New Testament] to anyone?" an interrogator asked. One family came to mind, but I answered, "No." I was afraid of drawing another Afghan family into the ordeal. I could imagine the questions: Who are they? Where do they live? Even so, afterward I deeply regretted lying. I wished I had said, "Yes, I've given an *injeel* to one family," and then just not said to whom.

One day we were up in the boss's office, and he asked me several questions about my computer: Where did I get it? Was it mine? I wrote out a more forthcoming set of answers than I had for the whole duration of questioning. The computer was mine, it was a gift from my mother, and so on. I handed the paper to him. Then someone translated it.

"I am sick of you lying," the boss shouted abruptly. "You must start telling us the truth. All these things you have told us are lies!" He ripped up the document, crumpled up the pieces, and threw the wad on the floor. I sat there, dumbfounded, and proceeded to write out the same answer again.

Later, our translator, Karim, told us, "Do not worry. Their seniors instructed them to put pressure on you. Do not get nervous. Do not be afraid."

Every morning, we woke up nervously wondering whom among

our acquaintances the Taliban might bring to our courtyard next. Perhaps a day or so after the other SNI women arrived, a guard came in with our egg lady, Leena, and her asthmatic mother.

Leena, crying uncontrollably, was nearly hyperventilating. She threw herself on the ground, weeping. Her mother tried to comfort her, but to no avail.

I went over to Leena, hugged her, and tried to get the story out of her. She cried out, "My two little children! Dear God, dear God!" Apparently, she had locked the children up by themselves in her mud room while she went out to sell eggs. She was desperate to get back to them. They were only two and three years old.

Once she calmed down, Leena told me what had happened. On hearing that Heather and I had been arrested, Leena and her mother went to the Masons' house that day to sell eggs. Of course, by then the Masons had fled the country. When the women arrived at the Masons' house, a strange man came to the door. Not certain what was going on, Leena and her mother decided to wait on the street for Katherine to return. Within minutes, a group of Taliban pulled up in a truck and grabbed the women, deliberately breaking Leena's eggs in the process.

I immediately wrote a note to the boss imploring him to release the women. "We only bought our eggs from them," I wrote. "They have done nothing." Heather and I both signed the note.

Mariam helped plead the women's case, too; but, while Leena and her mother were questioned that evening, they were not released until the following morning. Mariam had tears of joy in her eyes when Leena and her mother left the compound. She praised the boss for having given Leena the equivalent of five U.S. dollars to help her get a taxi home. We, too, gave Leena some money for the eggs she lost during the arrest.

One day we learned that the Taliban had captured all of the boys who participated in the street kids project. We heard it from one of the Afghan girls, whose mother had brought her the news on visiting day. This girl's mother told her that the boys had been taken off the street, beaten, questioned, and accused of being Christians. The news sobered us. We were deeply grieved to learn that these boys had suffered on account of our actions. To our great relief, our Afghan friend told us a couple of weeks later that the boys were back on the street.

The boss finished the bulk of our interrogations after a week and a half, and he came to tell Heather and me about it late at night. We were already in bed. The boss came in smiling and said, "Now you can talk with the other foreign women. Now you can see them."

We were not terribly excited. We wanted to sleep. Plus, unbeknownst to the boss, we had been talking to our friends with Mariam's consent during the day while they stayed in our courtyard.

Nonetheless, with his typical joviality the boss urged us to come with him. We followed him to the other women's room in the office building, where our friends were winding down for bed.

"See, you can talk together," the boss said, grinning. We all kind of looked at each other. He seemed surprised that we were not particularly emotional, but we stayed together and talked. An hour went by.

At some point I went to the rest room, which was down the hall from our friends' room. On my way back, I could hear music being played on the floor above me. In seconds I recognized the melody and realized that the Taliban had searched our house in Wazir. They were playing one of my cassettes of Dari worship songs. I would have more for which to answer.

Interrogations became sporadic for the next week and a half. By now, our four SNI friends were staying in our room off the courtyard. We tried to make light of the questioning sessions. "Who gets to go drink tea with the boss today?" we would ask each other every morning. Going to the boss's office was not so bad—at least in doing so we got to leave the courtyard.

One day the senior Talib said to me, "The Aamir family said you gave them a radio and that you guided them to Jesus radio programs."

I said, "Yes, I gave them a radio and told them about the Jesus programs, because that is what I listen to. But they had a choice to listen to whatever they wanted to hear."

Later that afternoon, our translator, Karim, came to the court-yard to visit us. He looked at us blankly: "You really are guilty. You had those tapes. You guided the family to those radio programs. You really were trying to convert people."

"No!" we replied. "We just shared with them the things that have helped us—to give them hope." It was a sad exchange.

The next day, however, Karim was back on our side, and on the interrogations went.

Our days in the reform school prison began at 4:30 A.M. to the sound of the call to prayer going out over the *madrassa*'s loudspeaker on the other side of our compound. The volume on the loudspeaker was exceedingly high. Audiocassettes of singing and chanting would play for about thirty minutes, and it was difficult to sleep through the sound. Only a handful of the Afghan women would wake up to pray at that early hour.

At 6 A.M. one of the Afghan women would sweep the dirt in the courtyard, and we would awaken again, this time to the sound of the coarse straw broom brushing over the ground. Kati and Silke slept outside, which meant the two of them got swept out of bed every morning. The Afghan women swept twice a day. Sometimes we would sweep for them, and at least once a week we would try to clean all of their dishes at the freestanding water faucet. The women always tried to stop us: "No, do not do that! That is our job," they would insist. But we would continue to help.

Sometime between 6 and 7 A.M., we would hear a knock on the courtyard gate, and Mariam would enter our room carrying flat bread wrapped in a filthy cloth. She would put the cloth down, then put out the bread, a teakettle, and a few glasses. Heather slept through break-fast on some days; her *toshak* was positioned against the back wall some distance from the door.

Right after breakfast, we would hear another knock on the rickety wooden gate, and the young women's teacher would come into the yard. The Afghan women would follow the teacher into their large room by the concrete slab and go through their lessons until 11 or

11:30. The women learned by chanting. Sometimes they would come outside and break up into small groups to chant or practice memorization drills. All of the women would come out into the courtyard at around ten o'clock for a break, at which time the teacher and some of her favored pupils would drink tea.

While the Afghan women were in class, we foreign women would take our showers—or bucket baths. We would carry pink plastic buckets up the staircase in the corner of the courtyard into a kind of foyer area for the bathroom. A dank, dirty concrete room, the foyer contained only a small faucet from which cold water sometimes trickled. If there was no water, then we would go back down to the courtyard and fill our buckets at the freestanding faucet.

The Afghan women typically took their baths in the foyer, and at almost any time of day, you would walk in on women bathing in this room.

Across the foyer was a wooden door that hung off-kilter on its hinges and opened onto a room furnished with a filthy bathtub and a squatty potty—really a hole in the floor surrounded by concrete with places for your feet. The Afghan women tried to keep the bathtub full at all times by stuffing the drain with paper. Floating on top of the dirty water were plastic jugs and cups. The women manually flushed the toilet with water from the tub and washed themselves in lieu of using toilet paper.

I took my bath in this second room. The floor was nasty from the toilet water, and like the Afghan women, I wore plastic sandals when I bathed. The bathroom had no working light—only a tangle of wires where a fixture used to hang—which meant you had to keep the door cracked in order to see. Once while taking my bath I touched the live wires and shocked myself.

"Ohhh!" I cried, and Mariam came running to help. Happily, the incident resulted in some improvement for the Afghan women. Two or three days later, the prison arranged to have the whole light fixture repaired.

Several weeks into our stay, we discovered that we could order items from the bazaar by giving a list and money to Mariam. I usually made the list at noon. One of the first things we ordered was a heating coil to warm our bathwater. We also ordered toilet paper, which unfortunately tended to clog the squatty potty.

We regularly ordered cucumbers, tomatoes, and cheese to supplement our prison diet. At mealtime, Mariam usually would bring in a few bowls of vegetables cooked in grease—okra, eggplant, or pumpkin, for example. Sometimes she brought only rice with a few raisins sprinkled on top, or beans without rice. We would cheer when she brought rice and beans, our favorite meal, which we got every two days if we were lucky. Potatoes elicited cheers, too, but we had potatoes only four or five times. The meat we were given on rare occasions consisted of mostly fat and gristle and usually was served in a greasy broth that tasted like oil. Bread, the Afghan staple, came with every meal.

If we declined to eat a particular prison meal in favor of our hodgepodge of food items from the bazaar, then we would give our portion of hot food to the Afghan women. We offered any extra salad to the poorest girls—those without family to give them money—as the women with family usually were gifted with fruits and vegetables when their relatives visited on Tuesdays.

One day we ordered fly swatters from the bazaar. We could not sit in our room for more than a few seconds without flies landing all over us. At night we noticed that hundreds of flies took to resting on the blue plastic clothesline strung across our room. Once we bought the swatters, fly killing became a sport—we considered it a way of simultaneously passing the time and entertaining ourselves.

I would tear off a couple squares of toilet paper to use as burial cloth for the flies and would wrap up the paper only after retrieving fifty deceased insects. My goal was to kill 150 flies each day. Every now and then Kati, Silke, or Diana would take up the other fly swatter and join in the battle. We would count aloud as the flies dropped dead: "Twenty-three! Twenty-four . . ." Our shenanigans really did help to clear the room of flies, at least for a time. Once we put the swatters to use playing badminton out in the yard with a crumpled-up piece of paper.

I used the mornings to pray and worship God while the Afghan women were in their room with the teacher. During this time, some of us foreign women would sit on the *toshaks* lining the sidewalk out-side of our room. You also could take a *toshak* and move down the sidewalk toward the bathroom, but then you would have to acclimate yourself to the smell. If you stayed too near our room, those inside could hear you singing. I usually took a metal chair to a corner of the courtyard or grabbed a dusty burlap sheet and sat near the tree.

Finding a place to sit quietly did not always come easily, as there were several curious little girls staying in the courtyard with us—the daughters of Mariam and a couple of the Afghan women prisoners. Mariam's two small girls were particularly playful. They would wander up and turn the pages of my Bible or touch my hair. One of the little girls approached me one morning and started making faces in the reflection of my sunglasses. She pulled out the corners of her mouth and stuck out her tongue right up next to my lenses.

Commotion was the norm in our courtyard at other times of day. Often the Afghan women would fight with one another or sit alone and cry loudly. At least twice each day, one of the Afghan women would break down and wail. Usually, if one started, then others would begin to cry, too. Dramatic sessions of moaning and crying would break out and go on for long stretches of time. When the crying would start, we foreign women would remark, "Who do you think that is?" and "I wonder what is wrong." Some of the girls cried more often than others.

I noticed one sweet pattern. Whenever Heather cried, our young friend Nafisa—who had run away from her abusive husband in Herat—would also cry. Once Nafisa threw herself down on the concrete near the women's room, covered herself up with her *chawdur,* and bawled for an extended time. After a while, I walked over to her and asked her what was the matter. Nafisa said, "When Heather cries, it makes me think of my father." She knew how badly Heather missed her parents.

The only real way to have privacy in the courtyard was to do as Nafisa did and cover your head with your *chawdur*. I did this a lot in the mornings and was able to enjoy my quiet time this way with fewer interruptions. I would sing to the Lord and read scripture. Much of the time I would sit still and listen. What was God saying to my heart? I love you. Trust me. Do not worry. Rest. You will get out of prison safely.

These simple things brought me such comfort. I felt secure. The words *I love you* penetrated my heart. They were not just words. One moment I would feel alone. Then I would sense the love of God and realize I was not alone. God really was right there. The simplicity and power of God's presence calmed me. I felt very close to him. Once while praying I had an image in my mind of God, my father, holding me while I clasped my arms around his neck. The picture reassured me that God would not let me go. He would always be with me to comfort me. I did not need to fear.

Every day I would write down what I thought the Lord was saying. In doing so I developed discipline. For years I struggled to keep a regular record of the things God was speaking to my heart, but I could never do it. I prayed for help and still could not seem to make the time. In prison, God answered my prayer. Despite the distractions in the courtyard, I had all the time in the world to spend in prayer, and an entirely different kind of intimacy with God opened up for me. My heart's constant cry to know him better was met with the most beautiful response. God wanted me to know I could trust him and that he had good plans for my life.

After the September 11 attacks on America, and then again after the United States started bombing Kabul, I had to regroup. I asked myself, "What if I die?" God brought to mind something I heard said at a conference shortly before I returned to Kabul in March. At the conference, someone asked Jackie Pullinger, who lived for decades with the poor in Hong Kong: "How did you really make it serving the poor for so many years? What is the secret of sticking it out for the long haul?" She answered something like this: "You have to resolve in your heart that God is good. No matter what happens, you must know in your heart that he is good."

I determined that I would believe in God's goodness. In prison I said, "Okay, Lord. I believe you are good. I trust that if I die right now in this situation, then it must be the best thing for me. If I die, I will be with you. If dying will cause many people to call upon Jesus, then dying would be an honor."

Of course, I did not want to die. I wanted the chance to get married. I did not believe I was going to die based on what the Lord seemed to be saying to me; but I accepted death as a possibility, and I did not fear it. I trusted the Lord with my life. I meditated on this verse from the Psalms: "All the ways of the Lord are loving and faithful" (Psalm 25:10a, NIV).

Once I was asked, "Dayna, do you really think we are going to get out of here?"

I responded, "I am going to believe it to the end. If it doesn't happen, then I just missed God; I didn't hear him. But until then, I am going to believe for our freedom."

Looking at the practical pieces of the puzzle, I could not imagine the Taliban killing us. Our translator, Karim, told us about a decree Mullah Omar had issued in June, declaring that a foreigner charged with inviting Afghans to accept another religion would receive three to ten days in prison and expulsion from the country.

In our case, the Taliban had no evidence that we were trying to coax the Aamir family to change their religion, only that we had shown a film and presented literature. Of course, I realized that the Taliban might not appreciate the difference. Still, I tried to explain my point of view during questioning.

In one session, the senior Talib with the large nose looked at me and said firmly, "Just admit that you were preaching and all of this will be over."

I replied, "I understand why you think we were preaching, but I cannot admit to something I was not doing. To me, preaching would be telling someone they needed to change their religion. I was sharing what I believe, just sharing about Jesus and how he changed my life."

Except for Karim, I was alone during this exchange. On a few occasions, due to physical exhaustion from the pressure, Heather requested to remain behind. I did not mind. During these sessions, the interrogators would ask questions pertaining only to me.

Finally, I knew that if the Taliban harmed us they would be involving three countries—the United States, Germany, and Australia. International opinion appeared to matter to the Taliban. The press, we later learned, had spotlighted our case. The boss seemed overly concerned about our condition. Frequently, he came into the courtyard smiling and asking about our health: Were we eating? Were we happy? Diana fasted from food quite a lot in order to draw closer to God, and this practice made the boss nervous. He did not want to appear to be mistreating his prisoners in the eyes of the world.

I gained a great deal of strength from the other SNI women—they believed we were going to get out of prison alive, which helped sustain my hope. From the minute they walked through the courtyard gate, our friends began encouraging us with scriptures. Diana believed Heather specifically would benefit by reflecting on Psalms 91 and 27. These psalms gave me confidence too. I read them aloud, and verse 14 of Psalm 91 specifically touched my heart: "'Because he loves me,' says the Lord, 'I will rescue him'" (Psalm 91:14 NIV). That is, God would save us and get us out of prison simply because we loved him.

Later, Diana encouraged us with the story of Shadrach, Meshach, and Abednego from the Book of Daniel. King Nebuchadnezzar tried to burn these three young men in a furnace, but God rescued them, and they came out unharmed without even the smell of smoke in their clothing. We believed God likewise would rescue us and that our prison experience would not leave us damaged in any way.

Several weeks into our imprisonment, Georg was able to sneak notes to us through Karim. The notes would include scriptures like

Psalm 118:17: "I will not die but live, and will proclaim what the Lord has done." Georg sent the verse for Heather, but we all clung to its promise.

He also sent Psalm 55:18: "He ransoms me unharmed from the battle waged against me, even though many oppose me." Kati later used this verse to write a worship song that we sang often in our second prison.

Once our SNI friends were allowed to stay with us in the courtyard, we began to hold regular worship meetings in the mornings and evenings. Without these times of worship, I likely would have fallen into despair. Yet as our time of captivity dragged on, I was able to maintain my equilibrium as I continued to worship with the others. I do not recall one meeting in which I did not experience the presence of God in a real way.

Our morning meeting started at ten o'clock, since everyone needed time for bathing and washing clothes while the Afghan women were in class. We would begin at ten by sharing scriptures that had encouraged each of us in our private times with God. Then we would sing and pray for about an hour. Afterward, we would pray for a while in a focused way. We usually ended at noon for lunch. Our evening meeting began at seven and usually followed the morning meeting's format.

During our meetings, we prayed a great deal for the nation of Afghanistan—that it would recover from drought, famine, and war. Once all foreigners evacuated the country following the September 11 attacks on America, we began to believe that God had left us in Afghanistan to pray for the healing of the land from inside the country. One of our great joys was that our imprisonment prompted people around the world to pray for the nation, too. We would get letters through various channels from friends saying they were praying for the Afghans even as they prayed for us.

We prayed often for the families of the victims of September 11. We prayed that the other humanitarian aid workers affected by our arrest would be able to return to the country soon and resume their projects. We prayed for our own protection and release. If one of us was sick, we would pray together for that person's healing.

Early on, Diana shared her belief that our imprisonment would somehow result in the saving of many lives. We did not know what this meant, but we did feel called more than ever to pray for the plight of Afghan women. We prayed especially for a change in government that would allow women to return to school and work and experience freedom.

Since we were being held with Afghan women, our compassion for them only expanded. We found it ironic that after going to such great lengths to separate Afghan women from foreign influence, the Taliban would imprison us with the women and allow us to share in their lives. Though the boss certainly tried to restrict our interactions with the women, we recognized our imprisonment with them as a rare opportunity to live up close with Afghans.

We often prayed for the specific needs of the women in our court-yard. We prayed for their healing and peace. We sang songs over the women from our room. If things in the courtyard were chaotic, we often sang a song with the chorus "Come, Lord Jesus," or another one that began, "There is a light that shines in the darkness, and his name is Jesus." One of our favorites started, "Where the Spirit of the Lord is, there is freedom." The chorus picked up, "Freedom reigns in this place, showers of mercy and grace, falling on every face. There is freedom." Sometimes we would break into spontaneous singing. Our hearts were full of love.

One particular morning, I told the others I thought we needed to dance in our room while singing a song with these lyrics: "You have turned my mourning into dancing, You have turned my sorrow into joy." I believed we were supposed to dance as an act of faith, believing that one day the Afghan women would see their hope restored and their mourning turned to dancing. I felt a bit embarrassed suggesting the idea, but the other foreign women were up for it, and the dancing refreshed us. Some of the Afghan women looked on through the win-

window and laughed, but our passionate antics lightened the atmosphere in the yard.

At one evening meeting, Heather suggested we all do an encouragement exercise she used to do with her small groups of college students at Baylor. We spent the time going around the room and sharing about the good qualities we saw in one another. The exercise left all of us feeling loved, strengthened, and appreciated.

On another occasion, Heather asked me to introduce a song we had sung one day at Leena's mud house on the outskirts of Kabul: "Holy Spirit, come. We have need of thee. For you are the one who sets the thirsty free. We are dry, but you are our supply. Oh, come and fill us now."

On many evenings we sang about the cross of Jesus: "Nail-pierced hands, a wounded side, this is love, this is love." As we sang to God, we would bow down in our little room. Remembering what Jesus endured helped us not to lose heart.

One night more than a month into our imprisonment, we held our evening worship meeting in the dark—for some reason the electricity had gone out in our room. We were all feeling strained due to the events of those days, and during our time of singing, I believed God wanted me to introduce a new song specifically for Heather. In the moonlight I saw her sitting with her head down. The words to the song, a prayer to God, were: "I need you to hold me like my daddy never could, I need you to show me how resting in your arms can be so good."

The song touched all of us, particularly Heather, and I was so thankful for the opportunity to help my friend in a small way. We had experienced some tension between us. At times I felt hurt and rejected, as did she. After many of my attempts to comfort her had failed, to be able to give her even the small gift of a soothing song meant a great deal to me.

ten

LOVE AND WAR IN REFORM SCHOOL

Great qualities of Afghan people: hospitable, resourceful, extremely strong in the face of great suffering, [able to] find joy in the midst of great pain.
—JOURNAL ENTRY, REFORM SCHOOL PRISON

Heather: No matter how tough prison life became, I reminded myself that God was fulfilling my heart's desire to live with the Afghan people. Among the women in our courtyard, we witnessed love and cruelty, both in great measure. The Afghan women looked after one another, and they brutally cut one another down. They tended to one another's wounds after beatings, and they inflicted wounds. Mariam embodied the contradiction.

Mariam was a complicated, passionate character. It was almost as if she had two personalities. A teacher in the days prior to Taliban rule, Mariam was motherly toward us all. The Afghan girls loved her. Often they would lie giggling in her lap and play with her hair. In true Afghan form, Mariam would serve us black tea several times each day. As foreign women, we were her guests, and she hated for us to be upset. The same rule of hospitality, however, did not apply to her own people. Mariam routinely walked around the courtyard with a short, hard rubber hose and beat the Afghan girls who misbehaved or fought with one another. At times she even tied the girls to the tree in the courtyard as discipline for unruly behavior.

Shortly after the boss concluded our interrogations, he forbade us to associate with the Afghan women in our courtyard. We also were instructed not to share our possessions with them, including food and toiletries. Despite the warning, we did both, but with extreme caution. I made it a point to talk with the women only in Mariam's presence. Occasionally, Mariam invited me to join her and a group of girls for tea. I figured as long my interactions with the Afghan women were out in the open, I would be safe. And so would the women.

One day, I turned out to be horribly mistaken. That afternoon our prison's stout stand-up comedienne, Aida, brought me a clean facecloth she thought belonged to one of us foreign women. A girl in her late teens, Aida had the soft, Asian features of a Hazara and long, silky, black hair. One of her legs was shorter than the other, and she walked with a limp. An aid agency had flown her to Germany to receive reconstructive surgery when she was a child.

After Aida delivered the facecloth, I checked with my foreign friends and found it did not belong to any of us after all. I promptly returned the cloth to Aida, who was sitting with another prisoner, Samira, in the Afghan women's room making tea. They invited me to join them. As was proper Afghan etiquette, I graciously refused the initial offer.

"No, thank you," I politely replied. I was concerned that sitting down for tea with Aida and Samira without Mariam present might cause trouble, but the two women pressed the issue. "Please come have tea with us," they urged.

I decided to ask Mariam for permission to sit for tea. Surely, if Mariam approved our interaction, I would bring no misfortune to my

Afghan friends. Permission was granted. Without hesitation Mariam exclaimed, *"Bishee, bishee!"* Sit, sit!

I returned to Aida and Samira and for twenty minutes drank tea, chatted about nothing of significance, and played with Samira's two-year-old daughter. As soon as I left, Mariam picked up the rubber hose, went straight into the room, and mercilessly beat the women. We heard bloodcurdling screams coming from inside.

"What is she doing?" I said aloud, and stormed back over to the women's doorway.

"Mariam," I exclaimed, "if someone has committed an offense, it is my fault. I have sinned. You should hit me. Do not hit them!" Mariam let out a patronizing laugh and pinched my cheek. "No, no. You did nothing wrong," she cooed. "They are just being punished for fighting."

This lie infuriated me. My heart broke over the injustice. The more I tried to plead on behalf of Aida and Samira, the worse their circumstances became. Mariam returned to the room, shut the door, stuffed the windows with pillows and blankets, and continued to beat my friends. The screams were almost unbearable. Samira's little girl witnessed the entire episode.

We shared lighter moments in the courtyard. Mariam sometimes would tell wildly humorous lies to make sure that we foreign women did not become upset.

At dusk one evening, I was lying down on a *toshak* near our room praying when I noticed a creeping shadow moving along the wall. "What is that?" I said aloud. Then I recognized the shadow and jumped to my feet. When I looked down, I saw a scorpion crawling near the *toshak.* I jumped up and ran to our room.

Mariam saw me, hastened to the *toshak,* and killed the scorpion on the spot.

"Don't worry," she said, flashing an unctuous smile. "It was only a worm."

"That was not a worm!" I insisted. "I saw it!"

She patted my cheek. "Oh, you saw it."

Afterward one of the Afghan girls ran toward me with a bowl of water and splashed the water on my face.

"Why did you do that?" I asked. The girl said she was trying to protect me from being cursed by the scorpion I had seen.

One afternoon we foreign women wrote a prison song. Since Mariam and the boss were always exhorting us not to be upset, we set the song to the tune of "Don't Worry, Be Happy." One line went, "If the Taliban put you in prison, say two or three days, but it's forty-five days, don't worry. Be happy."

In the afternoons, the Afghan women occasionally would fill their time by playing games. Early on, I taught them how to play duck-duck-goose. I did not know the Dari words for duck and goose, so at Dayna's suggestion I renamed the game cat-cat-dog—or, in Dari, *peshak-peshak-sag*. The women loved the game and often played it on their own.

One of the Afghan women's games looked fun but very dangerous. A number of the women would grasp the edges of a blanket, put one person in the middle, and then, by jerking the blanket, throw that person up in the air. I warned them that someone might get hurt playing this game, but the women persisted.

One day a few of our group got up the guts to try the blanket-throwing game. Silke got on the blanket first; then, with a little persuasion, Kati tried. Dayna ventured a try, too, but I opted for looking on.

On another occasion, Dayna and I tried to teach the women how to swing-dance. We had only learned how to swing-dance ourselves the evening before our arrest, and the women did not seem overly impressed with our moves. Being without music no doubt hurt our cause.

Though the Taliban outlawed all nonreligious music, the Afghan women—displaying the true heart of Afghan culture—made music on a variety of improvised instruments. In the women's hands, our green plastic washing tubs became sonorous bass drums. Some of the women would turn the tubs upside down and play amazingly intricate beats, while others sang spontaneous melodies over the rhythms.

The women often sang dirges, lamenting their plight as prisoners. One of the most common songs had this mournful lyric: "Mother, mother, why have you let the Taliban take me prisoner? Why did you raise me only to weep?"

Still other women would dance to the beats played out on the washtubs. Mariam's helper, Shalah, was the most exuberant dancer of all. Young and beautiful, Shalah played off her sensuality and often danced provocative routines, at least by Afghan standards.

About nineteen years old, Shalah was the self-appointed leader of the pack of Afghan women. She was one of the few educated women in the prison and sometimes substituted for the women's teacher during lessons. Shalah had a rich inner life, which she expressed through art and writing. Once she showed us a book containing her poems about prison life and sketches of Afghan women—sketches that, of course, were outlawed by the Taliban.

Shalah also assisted Mariam in daily administrative and household chores, including the distribution of food at mealtime. Occasionally, Mariam even gave Shalah the authority to discipline the girls who misbehaved.

Yet for all the favor and recognition Shalah received, she was not without her own struggles. She and her father were both thrown into prison when they refused the marriage proposal of a Taliban neighbor to Shalah. The Talib demanded the father pay a bribe to get his daughter off the hook. Shalah's father, a poor man, did not have the money, so both he and his daughter were arrested. Eventually Shalah's father was released, but her own fate remained uncertain.

Mariam had high hopes for Shalah to marry a blue-eyed mullah, the deputy commander of the compound, who also was a friend of our translator, Karim. We affectionately nicknamed this young, handsome deputy "Big Eyes."

Shalah did not seem overly stuck on the prospect of marrying Big Eyes—she had a number of other ideas. One day before we were ordered not to associate with the Afghan women, Shalah and some other girls joined Dayna and me in our room for conversation.

"You should become Muslims," Shalah announced. "All you have to do is say this." She began to repeat the Muslim confession.

"No, no," interrupted another young woman. "They do not need to change. They are good like they are."

Shalah did not argue. Instead she proceeded to ask us about life in America and casually came around to the subject of suitors. "Do you have any brothers?" Shalah asked Dayna.

"Yes, I have one," Dayna replied, somewhat amused.

"How old is he?" Shalah asked.

"Twenty-five."

Shalah's eyes widened with interest. "Is he cute?"

"Yes," Dayna answered, "I think so."

"Can you tell him about me and see if he would take a pretty Afghan girl as his wife?"

Dayna laughed and told her she would speak to her brother.

Shortly after that exchange, the girls were no longer permitted to spend time with us alone in our room, but they did gather at the window to take a peek inside on occasion.

Our room at the reform school prison was drab and dank. Only a whale-shaped concrete patch covering a large hole in the wall added variety. Silke, an artist, determined that we needed something to spruce up the atmosphere and decided to carve a mural of animals onto our walls. We called our room the Kabul Zoo.

Within a few days, our walls teemed with mammals: An enormous elephant stood out as the focal point; a monkey hung on the elephant's trunk; a camel curved around one corner of the room; a smiling cat sat beside a crocodile. One of Mariam's little girls had put in a request for the cat. *"Peshak,"* she simply said on entering our room one day.

Silke created a tree around a socket in the wall for a wood-burning stove and added an opossum to its limbs. Bats hung from the neck of a lanky giraffe. The whale-shaped patch of cement obviously became a whale. As a backdrop were the mountains of Kabul covered with mud houses.

Silke created this masterpiece using a tool from her manicure kit with which she chipped through an old layer of cream-colored paint. Lime-green paint underneath formed the outlines of the animals. Silke mixed lotion and mud to produce brown paint of varying shades. Then she used her hands or pieces of toilet paper to dab the concoction onto the wall, adding texture to her animals. All of the Afghan women observed the development of the mural with utter amazement. Many of the girls had never seen the animals depicted on the wall. With great difficulty we tried to explain the likes of alligators and opossums.

Taliban officials gave Silke's artwork mixed reviews. When the boss finally noticed the room's altered appearance, he literally jumped back from the shock. Disapprovingly, he reminded us that in Islam— or under the Taliban's interpretation of Islam—images of living creatures were not allowed.

"Our girls cannot pray in this room with pictures on the wall. These pictures are forbidden. We will allow them to remain only until you leave." As he left the room, I sensed we were pushing the limits of his graciousness.

Big Eyes, however, visited our courtyard the next morning with Karim and responded to the mural with great enthusiasm. *"Beekhee!"* Excellent! Big Eyes exclaimed. Completely, totally excellent! He vigorously complimented Silke's artistic skills, and we felt more at ease with our new decoration.

Since I spent a lot of time out in the courtyard, I played often with the Afghan women's young daughters. I would swing the children around and hold them in my lap, and they would put their faces right up close to mine. Mariam's two girls were three and six years old. Then there was Samira's two-year-old daughter. And an Afghan woman we called the "beggar lady" had a girl, Tooba, who was maybe eight or nine. The beggar lady beat Tooba relentlessly, usually with a plastic sandal. We would try to stop the abuse as often as we could, and occasionally we succeeded.

One afternoon while beating Tooba with a plastic sandal, the beggar lady snatched her daughter by the arm and dragged her off the sidewalk into the dirt courtyard area. Tooba was getting scraped up in the process and screaming at the top of her lungs.

I happened to be sitting near the window in our room and, not wanting to waste any time by going through the doorway, jumped through the window frame onto the sidewalk below. Several of us ran to the scene and grabbed Tooba from the beggar lady. We held the little girl for a few moments while she calmed down, and we tried to examine her for scrapes and cuts. But before we could do anything to help her, Tooba jumped up and ran right back over to her mother. She had been warned to keep away because we were foreigners.

I did not find out until my head started itching that all of the little girls in the yard, particularly Tooba, suffered from severe cases of head lice. Diana and Dayna checked me one morning on the steps outside of our room and gave me the bad news.

"Yep," Diana remarked. "You have lice."

Immediately, I was quarantined and not permitted back in our room unless I was wearing my head scarf. To remedy the problem, we placed an order with Mariam for medicated lice shampoo from the bazaar.

The day after I shampooed my hair, my head continued to itch fiercely, so I asked one of the Afghan women, Layla, to check me again. One of the oldest women prisoners, Layla was in her mid-thirties and had been arrested for wandering around town begging. She always wore a head scarf to cover an enormous goiter on her neck and would let the head scarf hang low at the top to cover her eyes. Layla was deeply ashamed, and we never saw her take the scarf off. We never saw her wash her hair. The other women made fun of Layla and usually gave her the smallest portion of food at mealtime. Layla often sat alone singing beautiful, mournful songs.

Layla checked my head for lice after I completed the treatment, and sure enough, she found that the shampoo had done all but nothing to quell the infestation. She offered to help me and spent two hours picking lice one by one out of my hair. She used a little, red fine-toothed comb with a piece of thread interwoven through the teeth. She went through my hair root by root and got most of the eggs out.

Later, after the six of us got to see our parents and diplomats, we ended up with several boxes of more potent lice treatment from Pakistan. You could treat two people per bottle, so one day I lined up eight of the women—including Mariam and Shalah—and shampooed their hair. Many of the women's heads were raw from scratching. One of my young friends—a preteen forced to marry a man in his thirties—suffered so severe an infestation, her hair seemed full of snowflakes. She and the others were grateful to get some relief.

Whenever we gave the Afghan women gifts or shared the treats sent in packages by our diplomats, we had to act secretively. One night I snuck a toothbrush to my young friend Nafisa.

Nafisa, nineteen years old, fled her home city of Herat in western Afghanistan two years after her family married her off to an abusive husband. She pulled a daring, if creative, stunt to make her escape, masquerading as a Talib in order to travel to Kabul. Her disguise consisted of her husband's clothing and turban, and she painted her eyes with thick, black eyeliner. Without a beard, Nafisa was able to pass herself off as a preadolescent boy. Her muscular frame and dark body hair lent an air of authenticity to her character.

Hopping from vehicle to vehicle, Nafisa traveled hundreds of miles to make her way to Kabul. The rugged and strenuous journey, however, destroyed her health and she ended up in a local hospital. There the doctors discovered the truth about her gender. Her actions were viewed as a high crime, and she was incarcerated in Kabul's most infamous high-security prison. For one year, until someone from a government ministry took up her case, Nafisa lived on two pieces of bread a day in a cell infested with rodents. She received no visits from family or friends. Finally, she was moved to the reform school.

More than any other prisoner, I connected with Nafisa. I respected her fight for freedom, her compassionate heart, and her determination to overcome seemingly insurmountable problems. Though we could not always talk, Nafisa and I would try to communicate in other ways. From across the courtyard, we would smile at each other. Nafisa often signaled with her hands: *I love you*. I signaled back. On many occasions, I wondered how I might bring Nafisa to America with me once we were set free. She had so much to offer and deserved much more than the life apportioned to her.

One pleasant evening when the stars were out and the air was cool, I decided to sleep in the courtyard underneath the tree. I put my *toshak* near Nafisa and some other Afghan women. The yard's single lightbulb, which dangled from a line run between the tree and the roof of one of the compound buildings, burned out that evening, leaving our compound pitch black. I knew Nafisa did not have any possessions to speak of; she had no family in Kabul to bring her soap or shampoo. Since the light was out, I realized I had an opportunity to sneak Nafisa one of our toothbrushes. We had received several in a package from our diplomats.

I went to our room and got the toothbrush. Pretending I was going to get a drink of water from the courtyard faucet, I tiptoed past Nafisa's *toshak* and threw the toothbrush to her. Then I quietly slipped into my bed. Moments later, something landed on my head. Nafisa had thrown me her beaded hair accessory as a gift of gratitude. As I dozed off, she crawled over to me and said: "Thank you so much for my toothbrush. I have never had one."

As frequently as we could, we provided medicine to the women who were sick or injured. Khalida, probably in her mid-thirties, arrived two weeks after we did. She had married off her daughter to a Talib, who ended up abusing the young girl. Khalida attempted to help her child get away and got caught. Khalida loathed the Taliban.

In an effort to reform Khalida's strong will, Mariam insisted she do her prayers five times a day. The Afghan women prayed in response to the call to prayer from the *madrassa*'s loudspeaker, and on Thursday evenings, Mariam led the women in Qur'anic memorization drills. Khalida insisted she could not bend down to pray due to arthritis in her knees. To us, however, it appeared Khalida did not particularly want to pray.

Mariam and Khalida fought constantly over the prayer issue. One evening the argument got out of hand, and Mariam reported Khalida to Taliban authorities. A Talib came to the gate to get Khalida that night. As instructed, she put on her burqa and left the courtyard with Mariam. An hour later, Khalida returned, clearly shaken. The next morning she was escorted out of the compound again; and when she returned this time, Khalida could barely walk.

Immediately, the other prisoners gathered around Khalida and draped a burlap sheet over the clothesline in the courtyard to prevent us from seeing the extent of her injuries. Some of the Afghan women went back and forth to the water faucet dampening rags. Later I stole a private moment with a few of the women and learned that the Taliban had beaten Khalida with pieces of wood on her feet, wrists, and back. For weeks Khalida limped on a swollen, black-and-blue foot. To help alleviate the pain, we often snuck her Naproxen tablets by dropping them off on a barrel by the water faucet.

One night we heard a horrifying episode transpire on the other side of our courtyard wall. Except for Silke, who was sitting outside on the steps, we were in our room laughing and playing cards that evening. At some point, Nafisa walked across the courtyard and told us to be quiet. *Why do we have to be quiet?* I wondered. *Are there men in the courtyard?*

I looked outside to see what was going on. All of the Afghan women were sitting in the courtyard in silence. Some were crying. We listened. Somewhere nearby a whip was being cracked. We could hear a man groaning and then the sound of a group of men roaring with laughter. The laughter sounded unlike anything I had ever heard before. It was a deep, brutal, inhuman sound—the sound of evil. As the whip cracked steadily, I quietly began to sing a song as a prayer: "There is a light in the darkness, and his name is Jesus." The man's groans grew weaker. Finally he cried, *"Bass, bass."* Enough. Enough. And there was silence.

Moments later an eerie, beautiful sound rose above the courtyard walls. The tormentors were forcing the beaten man to sing the woes of prison life. He sang for twenty minutes. All of us wept. The broken man's voice was one of the most beautiful sounds I had ever heard.

Somehow out of his suffering had come true sweetness. The atmosphere in our courtyard became subdued for several days.

When Mariam heard us talking among ourselves after the beating, she approached with a smile and said, "Don't worry. The Taliban were just performing a drama for our entertainment. The man was not actually tortured."

Her lie was so repulsive, it did not even merit a response.

Though I did not trust Mariam, I relied on her presence as a means of protection. During interrogations I insisted Mariam accompany us whenever we were escorted to the boss's office; and after interrogations, I refused to leave the courtyard for any reason without her. The Taliban could put us in a truck and take us anywhere, and no one would ever know. If the Taliban planned to kill us, then they likely would say they were taking us to the Herat Restaurant to serve us a beautiful meal.

About two weeks after our arrest, the boss agreed to take all of us to our houses in Wazir to pick up extra clothing and toiletries. We had eight outfits among the six of us. Kati and Silke desperately needed to feed their dogs. After a good deal of pressing, the boss finally gave in. Diana and Ursula were fasting, and the boss agreed to take them along only if they would eat. They would not eat, they told him; the rest of the group would have to return to our neighborhood without them. In the end, the boss let them come with us anyway.

Taliban guards collected us from our room late at night. They always worked in the night hours. If they wanted to talk to us about something after questioning, they came to the courtyard at night. If they were delivering packages from our embassy, they came after dark. When they came to get us for the trip to Wazir, it was pitch black outside. I was nervous before we left and insisted Mariam come with us. This was the first time we had left the prison compound since our arrest.

What seemed like a whole battalion of armed Taliban acted as our escort. The men put the six of us plus Mariam into two vehicles. Ursula, Diana, and Silke were put in one; Dayna, Kati, Mariam, and I in the other. Already the trip looked like a bad idea. Why would the boss put Dayna and me—the two accused of the most serious violations—into one vehicle and most everyone else into another? I imagined the worst.

Then the men drew curtains over our windows, causing me to grow even more anxious. I could not figure out why the men needed to pull the curtains. It was totally dark outside, and we were draped in our *chawdurs*. I thought: *They could do anything they wanted behind these curtains and no one would ever know we were in here.*

Meanwhile, Kalashnikov-toting Taliban jammed the back of each truck, and several men piled into our front seat. One guard set a whip on the dashboard and turned on some religious music. Karim got in with us, which calmed me a little.

We entered Wazir, and immediately I could sense a dramatic change in the atmosphere of the neighborhood. There were no foreigners going house to house, as we used to do before curfew. I did not see any aid organization vehicles out on the streets. The neighborhood was dead quiet.

Kati and Silke's house was our first stop. Ten to fifteen Taliban took Kati and Silke inside their home while we waited in the truck with several armed guards. Fifteen minutes later, two more vans of armed men pulled up in front of the house. All of the men got out and went inside.

Why did it take all of those men to guard Kati and Silke as they simply packed a suitcase? Another fifteen minutes passed. I became very agitated. What were all of those men doing? Did they tie our friends up? Were they raping or killing them? I was so nervous I began to shake.

"Mariam," I asked. "What is wrong? Why aren't they coming out?"

"Do not be afraid," Mariam soothed. "These are Taliban. They are good men."

She then spoke to a guard standing outside the truck. He sneered at me, and a devious smile played across his lips. He pulled back the trigger on his gun, cocked his bayonet, and started cackling. His ploy worked—I was terrified. I believed these men would have no qualms about hurting us. My fear continued to escalate. Where were our friends? Wouldn't they have come just to tell us they were on their way and not to worry?

By now nearly forty-five minutes had passed. "Under no circumstances will I go inside our house if those girls do not come back," I told Dayna.

Finally, we heard the dogs barking, and Kati and Silke came out with a suitcase. Apparently, the ordeal took so long because the Taliban could not find the keys to the women's bedrooms. Taliban were living in the house by that time.

"Get a grip," I told myself. "They did not kill Kati and Silke, so maybe they really are just taking us to our homes."

We went next to our house. About fifteen armed men went inside with Dayna and me. We noticed that a Talib was living in the *chowkidar*'s room. Dayna had our keys, so we went right in. Mariam came, too. So did Karim and Noorahmed, our second translator, who soon afterward was dismissed.

The boss and his men were insisting we would not need much. "It should only be two or three more days, *Enshallah*," God willing, they kept saying. I did not believe them, but I did not think I would need months' worth of supplies at that point, either.

We stopped first at Dayna's room. It appeared someone had broken into the house through her balcony door. She grabbed some clothing, makeup, her Bible, and some books.

The men puzzled over Dayna's photographs, pointing to different people and asking about them. They asked about her books. Karim wanted to know whether he could borrow some of Dayna's books one day and whether he could hear her play her guitar in the future. Noorahmed asked Dayna if she would read any books on Islam if he could get them for her.

"Sure," she replied.

"You are good, clean girls," Noorahmed noted. "You really should be Muslims."

By the time we got to my room, the men were yelling, "Hurry up! We have to go. It is late." The atmosphere was so chaotic, I ended up leaving essentials behind. I did not think to get my money, passport, or airline ticket. Other than a couple of family pictures—which later greatly helped me endure the absence of my loved ones—I left most of my photographs behind. I did not think to get an extra pair of shoes. I brought a lot of clothing for the Afghan women, but nothing I really could use the rest of our time in prison.

I did get permission to take my reference Bible. The men flipped through the pages to make sure the text was in English, then they let me take it. I also grabbed a packet of mail from my father containing some sensitive e-mail printouts. When I went to put the packet in my bag, a U.S. newspaper article fell out: "Taliban Single Out Non-Muslims." It may have had to do with a Taliban decree requiring Hindus and Sikhs to wear identity badges. One of the men called Noorahmed over to translate. Noorahmed passed off the article as insignificant and threw it on the floor. Later, at the compound, I spent hours chewing up the pages of sensitive e-mail and contact information in the packet and flushing them down the squatty potty. I did not want the papers falling into Taliban hands.

Our last stop was the bathroom. Looking for items I could bring back to the Afghan women, I emptied our medicine cabinet. Dayna grabbed a large supply of toiletries along with some towels.

On our way out of the house, the Taliban instructed us to make a list of the items we removed and sign it. Dayna handed the men her set of house keys. Then the men loaded us up in the truck and we proceeded to Diana and Ursula's house.

After Diana and Ursula had been gone for a while, we heard Diana yelling from inside the house. When Karim came back to the truck, he said, "Miss Diana is a very bad woman. She called us all liars and thieves."

Apparently, the women refused to give the Taliban their house keys on the way out. At some point, we learned, the boss spit on one of their carpets. From then on, we adopted a new name for the boss: "Carpet Spitter."

KABUL GORGE: *The ruggedness and beauty of the Kabul gorge capture the attention of all who pass through it. Just beyond the pinnacle, the capital city spans out at an elevation of 7,000 feet.*

KABUL CITY: *The capital city Kabul, devastated by twenty-two years of war, is a constant reminder to its people of the hardships and suffering they have endured. Mud houses built on the side of the mountain, often without electricity and running water, provide shelter for the city's poorest of the poor.*

LANDSCAPE: *The rugged landscape of the Kabul road near the oasis village of Sirowbi is breathtaking. This is one of the few places on the road between Peshawar and Kabul where a traveler can see lush vegetation as the river winds against the backdrop of the Hindu Kush mountains.*

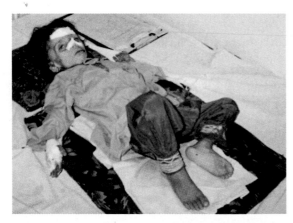

STARVING CHILD: *A four-year-old girl dying of severe malnutrition and amoebic dysentery in an Afghan refugee hospital in Pakistan. Sweltering heat reaching 115 degrees, lack of air-conditioning, and poor sanitary conditions made recovery a slow and difficult process. Heather's encounter with this little girl in 1998 was one of the motivating factors in her decision to return to help the Afghan people.*

OUR HOUSE:
Our home, situated in a heavily populated expatriate and Taliban neighborhood, became a benevolence center for dozens of widows and children who came daily.

DAYNA WITH STREET CHILDREN: *Dayna with a group of children whom she befriended and consistently helped. The child standing in the back is actually a girl dressed in boy's clothing—not an uncommon practice in Afghanistan.*

HEATHER WITH CHILDREN: *Heather with a pair of street children during a visit to their home.*

REFUGEE CHILDREN: *Refugee children flock to the side of foreigners who come to bring aid. For these precious children, foreign aid is often their only means of survival in the harsh, unrelenting conditions of the refugee camps.*

GROUP OF YOUNG AFGHAN GIRLS: *This group of beautiful young Afghan girls maintain their joy despite the Taliban law prohibiting girls from attending school or working.*

TWO GIRLS: *A pair of Afghan girls. Their piercing eyes and beautiful smiles reflect the strength and vigor of the Afghan spirit.*

SMILING BOYS: *These smiling Afghan street boys grab onto a passing car loaded with foreigners, hoping to get some money while their picture is taken.*

KIDS IN A TRUCK: *A handful of children from the nomadic Kuchi tribe piled into a cargo truck driving from Kabul to Peshawar through the Khyber Pass.*

STREET BOYS AT THE SHELTER FOR KIDS PROJECT: *Many of the street boys gathered daily at the project, Shelter for Kids, where they were provided a warm meal, an opportunity to learn various job skills, and a safe area in which to play.*

WOMEN IN BURKAS: *Under the Taliban regime, Afghan women were forced to wear the head-to-toe coverings, hiding them from the view of men. The small mesh piece over the eyes impaired vision and hindered the ability to carry out daily activities. Only young girls and elderly women were exempt from this law.*

PATIENT ON THE FLOOR: *Lack of financial and medical resources and poor sanitary conditions left this patient on the floor of an overcrowded hospital in Kabul. Medical care in Afghanistan is among the worst in the world.*

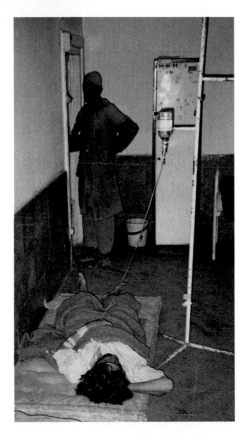

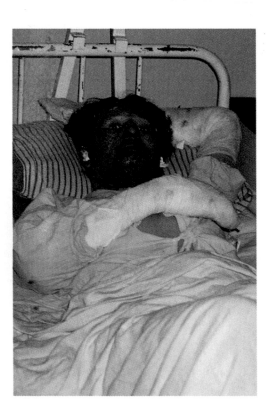

BURN VICTIM: *People such as this one, suffering from severe third-degree burns, are not an uncommon sight in Afghanistan's hospitals. Often young women set themselves on fire in order to escape a life of poverty, rejection, and abuse.*

PRISON #1: *Our prison, located at the headquarters of the Ministry for the Promotion of Virtue and Prevention of Vice. Our room, approximately 10 × 20 feet, connected with a larger compound housing thirty female Afghan prisoners. We lived here for six weeks until just after September 11. The elephant drawing is the remains of an elaborate mural of animals drawn on our wall by Silke, a German artist and fellow prisoner. The Taliban painted over all the other animals when we left.*

REUNION WITH OUR PARENTS: *After we landed in the C-130 aircraft at the military base in Islamabad, Pakistan, the long-awaited moment finally arrived. With tremendous joy we hugged our parents, Nancy Cassell and John Mercer, and celebrated our freedom from Taliban captivity.*

DAYNA AND HEATHER ON THE PHONE WITH THE PRESIDENT: *The evening of our rescue, November 14, 2001, we received a phone call from the President of the United States, George W. Bush. We were incredibly honored and excited to talk with him.*

IN THE OVAL OFFICE: *We receive a tour of the Oval Office from President Bush.*

DAYNA AND HEATHER WITH FRIENDS: *Thanks to the generosity of our church in Waco and their contacts, we were able to renew ourselves during a five-day trip to the Virgin Islands with two of our friends one month after our release from captivity.*

The next day Mariam allowed me to give out my clothing to the women who did not have extended family. Nafisa got one of the outfits. Shalah picked out a Kuchi dress, even though she did have family. Dayna gave Mariam a bottle of shampoo for everyone to use. Mariam used the shampoo often, but we never saw the bottle in the hands of the Afghan women.

THE WORLD OUTSIDE

Dayna: Our first contact with the rest of the world came in the form of a package courtesy of our embassies in Islamabad, Pakistan. The package's arrival was heralded by the boss's late-night knock on the courtyard gate. We came to recognize the knocks of pertinent parties. The boss knocked firmly, whereas Karim had a much softer knock than anyone else. Usually the man who brought our food at mealtime knocked as if an army were about to storm the courtyard.

The night of August 18, the boss and some of his sidekicks came into our room carrying a box and a black plastic backpack. The boss was grinning ear-to-ear. He put the parcels on the floor and proceeded to unpack the items one at a time, almost as if he were the giver and not merely the bearer of the gifts. He took out chips, cookies, shampoos, conditioners, deodorant, brushes, lotions, razors, soap, scented shower gels, medicine, jam, and cheeses.

Then he said, "Well, Mr. Georg and Mr. Peter do not need these." Out came a stash of feminine supplies. The boss relished the joke. He could not quit smiling.

Mariam told us afterward that when he first sorted through the package, the boss had seemed somewhat mystified by feminine packets. "The men do not need these," Mariam said by way of explanation. The boss blushed.

In fact, we noticed something humorous about the products a few days later. One brand was called Always, and the other Trust.

"Wow, a message from God!" we joked. But the coincidence was neat, especially since no note had accompanied our package. We decided "Always Trust" would do for a clandestine communication.

As we sorted through the gifts, Heather noticed packages of M&M's and Oreos included in the parcels. Those treats were her favorites, and when the boss unpacked them, she knew her dad had been involved in assembling the package. She was greatly encouraged.

Before the boss left, he told us: "Do not give any of these things out to the other women." He did not want the Afghans spoiled by Western luxuries, he said. We did not obey fully. The next day we passed out bowls of M&M's as a lunchtime dessert so our Afghan friends could try them.

Silke spent hours making a card for each embassy to thank our government officials for the parcels. On the cards, we were depicted in our small room opening all of the gifts. Sadly, none of the cards was delivered. First Karim came to the courtyard and told us that tea had been spilt on the card for the German embassy. So Silke patiently produced a fourth card. Then some men came to our room and asked us to write down and sign a list of the items we had received.

"The Taliban are doing this so they do not have to send the cards," Heather remarked. She was right. Our signatures, not the beautiful cards, were all our embassies received as evidence that the gifts had been delivered.

About a week after the embassy package came, a couple of the Afghan girls approached me in the bathroom. "Can we have some soap?" they whispered.

I went back to the room, got them a Dove bar, and carried it inconspicuously back up the bathroom stairs. As I started down the stairs, I took a wrong step and fell hard, smacking my side against the edge of the cement staircase so loudly that everyone heard it.

"Aaaagh!" I cried. The fall knocked the wind out of me. All I could do was lie on the sidewalk and continue to groan. I could hardly breathe.

Diana, who was an orthopedic nurse, came running over to see about me. She prayed aloud, asking Jesus to touch me, and I began to relax. Seconds later, Heather was at my side holding my hand. We had not spoken since the day before due to some strain between us, and I was grateful she was near.

"It is so good to see you, Heather," I said.

Mariam called in the prison compound's doctor-in-residence, but Diana told him she had everything under control. Helpful as he was, the doctor made a few outdated suggestions, and Diana wanted to keep hold of the reins when it came to our health. She put me on observation every half hour for the next several hours and was concerned about possible damage to my spleen.

Later that evening, the doctor came again to check on me and found me not well. I could not move, breathe, cough, or laugh without a great deal of pain, and my asthma had started acting up. Diana thought I might have suffered a fracture, but she could not tell without an X ray.

Interestingly, the boss gave permission right away to have me checked out. He proceeded to round up a cadre of right-hand men to take Diana and me to the hospital and then back to my house in Wazir to retrieve my asthma inhaler. The next day we understood why the boss had been so amenable: Representatives of the International Committee of the Red Cross arrived at the compound to examine us.

My trip to the hospital commenced, as usual, after curfew in the late hours of the night. We left around 11 P.M. Our party included Diana and me, Mariam, the doctor, the boss, and several armed guards. Our vehicle formed a caravan with the requisite black pickups—one in front of us and one behind. The boss was driving us.

We drove through the city past Wazir to a Soviet-era monstrosity of a building reported to be the best hospital in Kabul. The boss pulled up right next to the front door, almost as if he were making sure to avert any attempt we might make at an escape. The hospital was all but deserted. We passed a couple of doctors and empty beds in an emergency room area and boarded an ancient elevator equipped for an elevator man. We got off several floors up and found the doctor we needed. He knew some English. There were no patients on the floor, as far as we could tell.

Diana shuffled the men out of the room so I could remove some clothing in preparation for the X ray. The doctor came back with a lead covering and took a frontal X ray, which came out showing I was fine. Diana suggested a lateral X ray, and the boss became irritated. When the doctor from our prison compound supported Diana's request, the boss relented. The second X ray did not take very well, but the boss insisted we had no time to do another. Diana pressed. The boss rebuffed her and told the hospital doctor not to listen to her. Meanwhile, the hospital doctor prescribed some pain medicine. The boss offered to pay for it, but we already had medicine back at the compound.

Next our group headed to Wazir. When we got to my house, the boss pulled out a big box of keys belonging, I assumed, to all the houses the Taliban had seized. I recognized my key chain, and we broke the seal on the front door to get in. I could not see into the living room because the doors to the different rooms were locked, but I could see that the foyer and hall were dirty. In a bucket in the downstairs bathroom lay a dead mouse, already smelling.

I opened the door to my bedroom and confronted a disaster. Clothing and papers and knickknacks were all over the floor. I dug through my drawers to find my inhaler and, for the other foreign women, some socks. Nights at the prison had become cooler. I secretly took some more makeup, as my supply at the prison had nearly run out. Then I grabbed my pillow—the pillows at the compound were hard as rocks—and a green fleece blanket, since the prison blankets were rank. The kitchen was locked, and as there was no hope of identifying the kitchen key among the dozens of others in the key box, Diana and I had to forgo retrieving food items.

I asked the boss if I could take another Bible since we were short one in the prison, but he said no. I would not be permitted for reasons having to do with the Taliban's inventory records on the house. Then I asked the boss about playing cards, explaining that the cards would help us pass time at the prison. The other women had begged me to bring some back.

The boss and his men looked at one another. "Yes, you can take that."

I grabbed four decks, which we wore to pieces in the following months. Back at the courtyard, our friend Shalah told me that any Afghan caught playing cards would be slapped with a three-month prison sentence.

The following day a Talib with the Ministry of Foreign Affairs named Abdul Gaffoor Afghani—we called him, simply, Afghani—came to the courtyard and told us in flawless English that representatives from ICRC had arrived at the compound to see us. We told Afghani we were not going anywhere without permission from our boss.

"I have been lied to several times," Diana quipped. Afghani left to see what he could do.

"I have had a victory," Afghani said when he returned. "I have gotten permission for you and the two foreign men to meet together." We were overjoyed.

A woman and two men from ICRC were waiting for us in the boss's office. The woman was an administrator; one of the men was a doctor; and the other man was the leader of the delegation. Another foreigner accompanied the group as a translator.

We sat down on the boss's familiar couches, and then Peter and Georg walked in. We had not seen the men at all since before the arrest more than three weeks earlier. The only word we had gotten from Georg at that point was a note encouraging Diana to quit fasting. As we suspected, the boss had made him write it.

Georg approached each of us and shook our hands. He looked very bad. His face was pale and drawn. Yet even in his apparent state of ill health, Georg was the perfect diplomat and leader, graciously thanking the ICRC guests for coming.

The ICRC delegation was very interested in our overall treatment, living conditions, health, and diet. After asking us some questions, the doctor explained that he wanted to examine Peter and Georg first and then examine us in our room. The boss—via Afghani's translation—replied, "No." A male doctor would not be permitted either to examine women or to enter an area of the compound where Afghan women resided.

The head of the delegation seemed somewhat irritated but maintained his composure. Apparently, the delegation originally had been granted permission to bring a male doctor in to examine both men and women. Yet to comply with the boss's strictures, the ICRC leader radioed a highly qualified female Italian nurse to join us.

When the man pronounced her name, we recognized it immediately. He had contacted the Italian nurse from the ICRC hospital where Heather volunteered before we were taken. This was the nurse who had been helping us try to find a home for Lida, the girl with cerebral palsy. When the nurse arrived, we greeted her but pretended to have no acquaintance with her. She did the same. Simply seeing her comforted us.

Throughout the meeting, Heather seemed to be very tired. She held my hand and did not look very well. In a free moment, the male doctor asked some of the others if Heather was okay.

When we had finished answering questions, the Italian nurse and the female administrator accompanied us back to our room for our examination. After we sat down, the administrator handed me a note.

It was from my mother. She wrote, "I'll be there as soon as they tell me to come." I was surprised. My parents' loving commitment deeply touched me.

In our meeting, we told the administrator we needed new blankets and complained about the dreadful bathroom conditions and infestation of flies in our room. The woman gave us some ICRC forms for letter writing and assured us that the Taliban would pick up our letters the following day for mailing. From that point on, she said, ICRC staff would come to visit us on a regular basis.

At the Italian nurse's suggestion, I followed her back to the office building so the male doctor could examine me. I was suffering a lot of pain from my accident the day before, and the boss granted the doctor permission to see me. Squeezing my side—a painful experience on my end—the doctor determined that I was badly bruised. I had not broken anything, he said, but my side would hurt for several weeks. In fact, it was six weeks before I could lie down without the support of extra pillows. For two weeks I took pain medicine every day.

After the doctor finished, he and the Italian woman asked me several questions about Heather's state of mind. I explained that she was struggling emotionally. The doctor and nurse sent me back to the courtyard to offer Heather the opportunity for counseling during subsequent ICRC visits, and Heather agreed. She thought speaking candidly with someone on the outside about the pressures of our situation would benefit her. But the doctors never returned. The Taliban would not permit them. The closest we got to seeing anyone from ICRC again occurred when the boss allowed a shipment of ICRC blankets to be delivered to our courtyard. There were enough for all of the Afghan women, too.

Heather: When Georg and Peter came into the ICRC meeting in the boss's office, I experienced some relief. Georg was our leader. His presence—and Peter's—provided me reassurance. I was delighted to see them. When Georg came to me and shook my hand, he held it for what seemed a long time. He could tell I was having a rough time. Our eyes filled with tears. I was just so happy to see him.

I listened intently as the various ICRC representatives explained the reason for their visit along with their hopes for future interactions. They were amazingly diplomatic.

On the following day, August 27, Karim visited our compound and told us our parents and diplomats were in Kabul. He had mentioned more than a week earlier that the diplomats arrived in town, but we never saw them. Instead we got the care package, which at least confirmed a rumor that our parents were in Pakistan. Once I saw the M&M's and Oreos, I knew my father was close by.

Throughout the day on the twenty-seventh, we held our breath. Would we see our parents? Morning. Afternoon. Evening. "Well, there is still hope," Dayna kept saying. This was her prison refrain.

After dark, Afghani came to get us. Afghani initially impressed us with his polished manner. He was very smooth and had the air of a real diplomat.

We were taken in shifts by nationality to the boss's office. The Germans went first and met with a representative from their embassy in Islamabad, Pakistan. When Afghani came back, he took the Australians. I just about died waiting, but Afghani explained that by going last Dayna and I would have more time than the rest of the group. If this was the case, I was willing to wait as long as was necessary. We were the only ones with parents there to see us.

For the first time in a while I fixed my hair and put on makeup. I wanted to look somewhat refreshed so my dad would not be worried about me. My Afghan friends commented on my improved appearance. "Your eyes look beautiful," remarked some of the girls.

When the time came, I could hardly get to the boss's office fast enough. As I walked into the room, my dad was the first person I saw. He stood in the center of the room wearing khaki pants and a light jacket. He clapped his hands when he saw me, and his eyes watered with tears. He looked like a little boy whose only dream had come true. I ran to him. I could not believe I was seeing my father again. He had traveled so far. We wept together and hugged for several minutes. He drilled me with questions concerning my health, and I suggested we take a seat on the couch.

"Heather," my dad assured me, holding my hand, "there are people on all levels of government working on your case. Your situation is a priority. People are working hard. I am going to stay in Kabul until I can take you home. Do not worry. You are coming home."

He told me our detention had become big news in the United States. "Dan Rather went to your mother's house," he explained. "Matt Lauer called her looking for an interview."

This news shocked me. Why did our nation care so much about two young aid workers in Afghanistan? Still, after living for weeks in an information vacuum, I was comforted to think that people outside were taking an interest. I hoped the pressure of media attention would encourage the Taliban to act favorably toward us.

The U.S. consul general to Pakistan, David Donahue, sat in the room with us. Donahue, as we affectionately called him, became a champion for us in the months ahead. A keen, persevering man, he stayed close to our parents for the duration of our captivity, applying all of his gifts as a negotiator at every available opportunity. In the midst of what became an international crisis, Donahue interacted with the Taliban with great grace and wisdom. We later learned—and were utterly thankful—that Donahue and the whole embassy staff in Islamabad worked around the clock trying to secure our release.

We only saw Donahue three times. He had been trying to gain access to us for some weeks and rejoiced with us at this first meeting. He told us he was on hand to facilitate relations with our parents, provide whatever information he could about the Taliban's legal system, and ensure that our needs were met. He asked basic questions about food and our living conditions. I told him I needed lice medicine and that we badly wanted books to help us pass the time.

Dayna: Draped in a borrowed black *chawdur,* my mother sat down in a chair beside me in the boss's office and proceeded to fill me in on the latest information: The television show *Good Morning America* had called my father. She also told me we were at the top of prayer lists all over the United States, which greatly encouraged me.

I was startled by how high-profile our case had become. I hoped the attention would lead to a speedy resolution of our plight, but I particularly felt pressure when I considered having to give interviews after our release. Some days later I told my mother that, oddly, I almost felt more anxious about facing the press than I did about our current straits in Afghanistan.

"The media says you have written a confession letter," my mother remarked in this first meeting. I explained that we had written down the things we did on the day of our arrest—things like going to the Aamirs' house, drinking tea, and showing a film. We had apologized for causing problems for the country. But we had not confessed to a crime.

Had I heard talk of a trial? my mother wanted to know. We had not been told anything about a trial on our end, and I dismissed the idea as mere speculation on the part of the press. Some news stories mentioned the death penalty as a sentencing option in our case, my mother noted, but she urged me not to worry about these claims.

My father, I learned, was prepared to fly to Kabul the minute I said the word. I told my mother to please thank my dad, but I did not want him to leave his job and spend all of the money such a trip would require. At that time, my dad's presence did not seem necessary.

My mother also shared the devastating news that one of our *chowki-dars* had been taken into custody. She thought the Taliban arrested our night *chowkidar,* but later we found out they had arrested Khalid.

Chris and Katherine Mason barely made it out of the country two days after our arrest, my mom reported. Two of our friends with another aid organization also evacuated to Peshawar because of their association with us.

Just a few days after this first meeting with our parents, the Taliban expelled the remaining Christian aid organizations from the country. Karim first gave us the news, then my mother mentioned the expulsion order during our parents' next visit. She said the Taliban gave the organizations seventy-two hours' notice to get out.

Heather and I struggled with real guilt after getting the news. Had we caused well-established humanitarian groups to lose the ground they had been working to gain for decades? Had we been reckless during a season when the Taliban were tightening the vise on religious minorities? The news was difficult to stomach. We prayed God would open the door for these organizations to return.

On August 30, Diana had a birthday and turned fifty-one. Her prayer was to be able to eat with Georg and Peter. Ursula wrote a note to the boss days in advance asking his permission to share a meal with the men. We did not expect to hear from the boss—often our requests went unanswered. But at about ten o'clock the night before the birthday, we heard his knock on the gate.

"You can meet together at six o'clock tomorrow morning," the boss announced. He told us he was consenting to the meeting without permission from his seniors. In other words, he was doing us a big favor, or so he wanted us to think.

The next morning, a Talib led us to a conference room in the office building where Peter and Georg stayed. We were given more than an hour with our two friends. The Taliban brought us a cake that we had ordered from the bazaar. We carried our breakfast food—jam, cheese, cookies, and our morning bread. The atmosphere was light and optimistic.

Peter told us in his thick Australian accent that he had been wearing the same clothes for three weeks. Ursula often joked that we needed a translator to understand Peter through his brogue.

Heather: For Diana's birthday dinner we ordered a meal from the Herat Restaurant, and on a lark we asked whether we could eat with the men in their room again that evening. At the last minute, the boss approved. Karim and one of his friends ate with us while the boss came in and out. Georg thanked the boss profusely for his graciousness.

When we returned to the courtyard at nearly ten o'clock, we celebrated Diana's birthday by holding a big dance with the Afghan women. Mariam was gone that evening, and her stand-in, Lumya, an aged lady with few teeth, treated us leniently. Some of the girls got out the washtubs and put on a big production, while Lumya attempted to quiet us down. The boss would never permit such a commotion, and if he heard us, we no doubt would face some consequences.

More than thirty of us lined up along the wall in the women's large room and created a dancing circle. The Afghan girls kicked off the celebration by throwing confetti on Diana. Then, while some of the girls played out complicated rhythms on the tubs, others took turns showing off their dancing styles. Shalah demonstrated her dance moves (provocative by Afghan standards), which by that time I had mastered; the dance involved a lot of clapping, shoulder shaking, and finger snapping.

Silke entered the circle and performed a kind of slithery dance combining what looked like karate and ballet. Aida, our resident comedienne, got up and did her famous Talib impersonation, donning the outfit Nafisa had used to escape from Herat. For stage makeup, Aida used the soot off the bottom of a cooking pot to make a black beard and wore dark eyeliner.

Dayna danced furiously with Talib Aida, raising her eyebrows as if to flirt back and pulling out every Afghan move she had up her sleeve— mainly upper-body movements. The girls erupted with laughter. By the end of the evening, we all were in high spirits. Perhaps our circumstances might take a turn for the better, we thought.

Late the following evening, one of our prison guards delivered letters to Dayna and me. Our parents had sent them via the foreign ministry. We were so encouraged to receive any bit of communication from our loved ones, and I eagerly opened the letter from my father.

As I was reading, Dayna gasped, "Oh, my gosh!" Dayna rarely became unsettled, so I looked up.

"What is it, Dayna?" I asked. "What does it say?" She handed me the note. I read: "There is going to be a trial. It's serious, so be prepared."

Immediately, I realized our position had become much more precarious. Why did the Taliban want to put us on trial? To me it seemed the Taliban wanted to appear just in the world's eyes while severely punishing us. A trial would add legitimacy to the sentence handed down, and no one would be able to dispute it.

I started to cry. I had been so encouraged after spending time with my dad and Donahue. ICRC had come; we had gotten to enjoy time with Georg and Peter. After daring to hope for the first time in a long while, I could not handle another blow: the idea of a drawn-out legal process. It was simply too much.

I cried for a long time. The man who did our shopping at the bazaar came to the courtyard several times to see about me. The Afghan women were concerned. Mariam tried to tell me everything was okay and not to be upset, but I became furious. "I am not playing that game," I said sharply.

The next day Dayna and I met with our parents again. We understood we were meeting with our parents in five-day cycles for half-hour visits. The diplomats were not permitted to join us.

Without hesitation, I asked my father what he knew of the trial. I wanted to know what was really going on—no more sugarcoated talk.

"It is not going to be like a Western trial with a lot of witnesses," my dad said, trying to comfort me. "You will be offered legal representation. We do not know much now, but we will find out more in the next few days."

During that same meeting, I told the boss that my father would be having his sixtieth birthday in two days, on September 3. I would like to see my dad on that day, I said.

"*Enshallah, Enshallah,*" replied the boss. God willing, God willing. Over the course of my imprisonment at the reform school, I had come to discover that a response of "*Enshallah*" often indicated that my wish would not be granted.

September 3 came and went, and I did not get to see my dad. Nevertheless, I assembled a birthday present for him. The gift consisted of a stick of gum, a jalapeño pepper, a roll of Life Savers, and a beautiful card Silke had made, depicting the Kabul Zoo mural in our room. Silke sketched the card using the nubs of some colored pencils she had collected when we all went back to our houses in Wazir. Inside the card I tucked a letter and then slid both into an envelope. I tied the items together in plastic, using pink toilet paper for a ribbon. The Afghan women were fascinated by the gift and passed it around for a showing.

I gave my dad his present when I saw him at our regular meeting on September 5. As we talked, he left the gift sitting in his lap. When the boss gave the signal that our time was up, my dad fumbled at the card with his fingers. The boss gestured to Karim.

"He wants to know what you have," Karim said.

"It is a birthday present from my daughter."

Then the boss gestured, and a Talib came over and plucked the card from my dad's hand.

The boss infuriated me. He had no compassion. I spoke unashamedly about his injustice.

"You will get it back on Saturday," the boss rebutted. I did not believe him, and besides, Saturday was three days away.

"It is his birthday present!" I replied in Dari with a harsh tone. "You would not allow me to see him and now you are taking away his gift?" The boss was unmoved.

Karim and the boss convened for a moment. Then the boss instructed Karim to read the letter. Karim approved it and handed the letter, along with the card, back to my dad.

I later learned that the boss had returned the card only to placate me. As soon as my father left the building, one of the boss's men came and took the card and letter away a second time, promising to return them both. My dad never saw that part of his present again.

the hall, we noticed that the door surrounded by the shoes now stood open. A mob of people, most of whom appeared to be foreign reporters, pressed up next to the door waiting to enter the room. We scanned the crowd for our parents and, to our relief, spotted them, along with Donahue and the German and Australian consular officers.

We entered the cramped room and made our way toward several rows of chairs arranged toward the front. The chairs faced a hardwood desk belonging to the chief justice. On the wall behind the desk hung a large framed prayer mat flanked by swords and a whip. In the front left-hand corner of the room stood a bookshelf lined with ornate leather-bound books. We passed a table displaying more heavy books on the way to our seats.

The eight of us sat in the first two rows of chairs. Our parents sat directly behind us so that we could hold their hands and pass notes. Donahue sat with them. Meanwhile, behind us the room was packed to the gills with reporters.

Eighteen justices sat in chairs forming a horseshoe around the chief justice's desk. Most of the justices were elderly, white-haired men. Their faces wore grave expressions. Some massaged their prayer beads during the proceedings.

Once we sat down we were handed forms to fill out. As usual, there were places for each of us to fill in our name, father's name, grandfather's name, country, province, and village. In keeping with her practice, Diana filled in yet another name for her grandfather.

Next we identified ourselves by nationality for the chief justice, Mullah Noor Muhammad Saqib. The chief justice was a young man wearing an enormous turban and a long, dark, unkempt beard streaked with henna. His countenance was solemn. Though his eyelids seemed to droop, his manner was sharp and discerning. He had an air of sophistication and composure, and as we understood, he commanded great respect among his peers.

The proceedings opened with a prayer, after which the chief justice delivered a prepared speech in Pashtu assuring us that we would be given a fair trial and extolling the Islamic judicial system. His

"Th
mission
We
with sh
mother
very ha
You tak
very mu
My
Tho
some st
Kar

Dayna:
came to
permiss
call fron
We
We had
gular bu
we were
We cou
walk be
"Do
"Th
sons du
We
reached
The boy
learned
Kar
before h
dad. Wh
be marr

Heather: At 2 A.I
"Diana, what
"That was a b
Adrenaline co
the courtyard. Re
exploded one aft
through the air. W
started to cry.
Immediately, l
her first day in Afg
what would becor
I went to the
someone's attentic
banging. She was
ling me. But at tha
an open courtyard
taking the necessa
Karim finally
his clothes wrink
awakened.
"Karim, pleas
underground."
Karim laughec
bombed the airp
explained. "Do not
An ordinary pa
not faze Karim. N
Afghan prisoners,
I had never heard a
Everyone's see
making me feel ve
the necessary step

Pashtu, Diana later told us, was flawless, but he used a translator who in time proved to be inept, at least in the minds of a reporter or two. One spectator injected his own much-needed translations into the dialogue that ensued between the chief justice and our group.

The chief justice began by asking us if we had a lawyer. We were all aghast.

Dayna: "They didn't even tell us there was going to be a trial, and now they want to know if we have a lawyer?" I whispered to Heather.

Heather & Dayna: "How are we supposed to get a lawyer when we barely have contact with anyone on the outside?" Diana fired off.

Georg complained to the same effect. "We were never allowed to talk with anybody from the outside about anything, just about how we are doing and what our health is."

"Now you are informed," replied the unflappable chief justice. He told us we either could defend ourselves or hire a lawyer. The attorney could be Afghan or foreign, Muslim or non-Muslim.

Heather: "Your excellency," I said, standing, "can you please explain to us the process by which we appoint a lawyer? As far as I know, none of us are familiar with the legal process in Afghanistan, so we therefore don't know how to go about this."

Heather & Dayna: A vague, unmemorable answer came back through the translator.

Donahue and his Australian and German counterparts complained about being denied access to us. For weeks they had tried to get in to see us before they were finally permitted a visit. If they were not allowed to see us, how could they help us find a lawyer?

Some in our group took advantage of the public setting to announce that they had no idea why they had been detained in the first place.

"I don't even know why I need a lawyer," Peter complained. "I have only been questioned once."

My mother a
feeding us? Del's
grateful he had c

When we al
the attack on M
Karim informed
make mention o
happens to Mass
month max."

"A month!" I

Dayna: As I talk
eavesdropping fc
conversations wi
been having to e

"Did you g
brought?" my mc

I told her I di
this new one was
course, but wear

My mom re
rate press report
rect quotation. .
mother as I exite
closely.

Our parents
Karim came to c

Two planes l
and New York Ci
The account wa
about a plane cra

Karim went
thing to do with
We did not unde

I trie

I
need
at tha
ents
satisfi

Dayr
in the

"
"They
with
ing tc

B
Karir
Karir

H
was c
meek

C
go ba

K
consi
tion
go it

Hea
think
thing
be ov
wasn
overv
frail–

K

Heather: "I heard what happened in America," I told my dad.

"You did? Well, you could not have written a worse script. But don't worry. You're going to be okay. We will all be okay."

Finally, someone was admitting that our situation was serious. Not that admitting it made the experience any easier, but at least I felt understood. I deeply appreciated my dad's optimism. Hearing his voice, I gained strength.

"I want you guys to leave immediately," I insisted. "I want you to get out of Kabul. You must stay safe."

"Well," he said soberly, "we are being evacuated."

It occurred to me that whatever had happened in America must have been more serious than what Karim described. Why else would my parents be forced to leave? My dad offered no information.

"You know I wouldn't leave unless I absolutely had to," my dad assured me. "We have no option at this point. I will go to Pakistan and stay there. I will be there when you get out. Do not worry. For our sakes, please do not worry."

He said they were leaving letters and money to be delivered to us the next day.

Before I passed the phone off to Dayna, I spoke with my mother and Del. Though my mom wept as she talked, she still sounded hopeful. Del was steady and optimistic. Were they really convinced my circumstances would be resolved? Or were they simply telling me what I wanted to hear? I chose to believe the former.

When I said goodbye, I was not certain whether I would ever see or talk to my family again. As our captivity continued, I wondered many times if that phone conversation had been our last.

Dayna: When my mother got on the phone, she encouraged us to rethink the decision to hire a lawyer. She thought it would be more expedient for us to defend ourselves, especially considering that Mullah Omar would have the last say on our sentence.

She wrote an e-mail to my father after the call: "I just spoke with Dayna. We were going to try to keep the news of the attacks in the

U.S. from them, but they knew about it I think . . . [S]he knows we are going back to Islamabad. I didn't tell her that [all foreigners were] going, too."

My mother told me leaving Kabul at that moment was the hardest thing she had ever done. "I feel like I'm deserting them," she wrote later in another e-mail update. She promised to stay in touch through a contact in Kabul. She said she would leave some jam, soup, and other essentials to be delivered.

"Do not worry," I told her. "God will take care of us. Just keep praying."

As Karim and Big Eyes escorted us back to the courtyard gate, Heather asked the men some questions about the previous night's bombing. Big Eyes proceeded to share stories about his own personal experience of war.

"I have grown up fighting all my life," he said, standing at our gate. "I have seen war, and I love war. I love fighting in the name of God. I love *jihad*." He talked about fighting against Russia and other "infidel" nations, or countries that do not embrace Islam. His forthrightness shocked us.

"What are we?" Heather asked.

"Well," he replied with a startled look. "You are our guests. You are our guests because you came here to Afghanistan to help our people. And you will be fine if America does not attack Afghanistan. But if America attacks, it will be very bad for you."

Heather: On returning to the courtyard, all I wanted to do was go to sleep. What a distressing day. I longed to close my eyes and forget about it. Now that I knew my family was safe, I would be able to sleep. But at ten o'clock that night, Karim returned.

"I will take you to a secret meeting with Peter and Georg," he explained.

We welcomed any contact with Peter and Georg, but this meeting was scheduled for an unusually late hour. When we got to the men's room, we understood the reason. Revising Karim's original report,

Georg informed us that two planes had flown into New York City's World Trade Center towers and another plane had hit the Pentagon. A fourth plane crashed in Pennsylvania, he said. The death toll numbered somewhere around six thousand.

Unbelievable. Within seconds two planes had become four, and four hundred casualties had become six thousand. In my heart, I guessed the perpetrator likely was Osama bin Laden, which meant the Taliban and Afghanistan would pay heavily.

Karim, who was in the room, continued to insist that Afghanistan was not behind the attacks. Georg seemed somewhat relaxed, but I could read his face. Unless we got out of the country soon, we would be caught up in a sea of potentially deadly consequences. Georg did say he believed that America would not retaliate without doing extensive research and assured us we should not expect an immediate response.

SEPTEMBER 15, 2001

Heather:

> Oh Lord Jesus, I struggle so much with fear here. Every moment
> of every day I battle the fear that either a [Talib], a bomb from [the
> Northern Alliance], or an angry [terrorist] will kill me. I want so
> much to live and proclaim the miracles you have done. Oh Lord, I
> beg that you might spring open this door and let us go free alive
> and unharmed . . . You alone can rescue us. Please rescue us soon and
> save us from violence and revenge.
> —JOURNAL ENTRY

SEPTEMBER 17, 2001

Dayna: In the days following the attack on America, we learned that many top Taliban officials were evacuating Kabul. Several reportedly went back to their home village of Wardak, located on the road to Ghazni toward the south. Mariam, also from Wardak, sent her two daughters home. The boss began releasing some of the prisoners.

The woman we called "beggar lady" got to leave with her daughter, Tooba. A teenager was released in order to marry. She had been arrested for running off with her beloved in order to get away from a man to whom she was engaged. Now she was being made to marry that man. We put together a little makeup package for her, using some gifts that came in one of Donahue's packages. Two more girls who had been taken for interacting with men unrelated to them also were let go.

We were so happy to see the women released. The Afghans wailed when the time came to say goodbye. They always cried when others got released, wishing they, too, could go free.

In the midst of the departures, we had the sense that something was about to happen to us. The boss seemed nervous about keeping us at the compound. There was talk of moving us to a safer place. We did not understand the Taliban's intentions.

On the morning of the seventeenth, Mariam came to me while I was praying in the courtyard. "You need to start getting your things together," she said.

Heather: I was sitting across the courtyard from Dayna. Mariam approached and asked me, "How would you like to go to Wardak?"

"The Taliban are moving us today?" I asked.

"Yes, go pack your things." The idea of Wardak appealed to me slightly. At least we would be out of the city if America bombed. I casually collected my possessions, expecting that the move, like many things about life in Afghanistan, would take hours. Then an abrupt knock came at the door.

In walked the boss. "We are taking you to a nice place today," he said, noticeably anxious. "You will be very comfortable there and much safer. But you have to hurry."

"Are we going to Wardak?" I asked.

"No, just beyond Wazir, over the far side of the mountain."

Now I was not so excited. One place in Kabul would be no safer than any other. I wondered where they truly were taking us.

Everyone packed frantically. We ended up leaving much of our food behind. But if we were going to a nice place, then perhaps we would not need all the extra food.

We had scarcely any time to say goodbye to the Afghan women. More than anything, before I left I wanted each of them to know she was loved. They all came out of their lesson to see us off. I cried as I hugged them. "I love you," I whispered to each one.

When I reached Nafisa, my heart sank. How could I say goodbye to this precious girl? I hugged her. "I love you, Nafisa. I will never forget you. I would take you to America with me if I could." We pulled back and looked at each other. Tears ran down our cheeks, and we made the sign we had used across the courtyard when forbidden to talk. We each covered our heart with our right hand and smiled.

I found Samira and her little girl in the bathroom. Samira was bawling. We embraced, and I prayed for them. Meanwhile, Dayna and the others went down the row of Afghan women hugging and kissing them goodbye.

Living with these women had become my great joy and a source of strength. As we walked out, I stood at the gate waving as long as I could.

part three

WAR GAMES

first, then the boss told them we were all standing outside ready to go.

"Do not worry," the boss kept saying. "We are taking you to a nice, comfortable place in Kabul. You will be well looked after. You will be safe there." We wondered where such a place might be, but we believed the boss could be telling the truth. Maybe he planned to take us to Wazir and put us up in one of the foreigners' homes the Taliban had confiscated.

Instead, our caravan of vehicles set out in the direction opposite of Wazir, eventually turning into a desolate section of town. Dust coated the buildings. Many of them looked abandoned. We pulled through the gate of a large compound. Barbed wire topped the high wall bordering the property. Several guards were stationed at the gate. We thought, *Surely we're just making a stop on the way to our destination.*

Once inside the compound, the boss told us we would be getting out here. We were astonished. If the boss had lied about taking us to a safe, comfortable place, what might the Taliban really be planning to do with us? We cautiously unloaded our bags.

Guards led Peter and Georg away. Big Eyes escorted us—the women—through a rickety wooden courtyard door not fitted properly on its hinges. A chain and padlock were fastened on the door. Two feet of barbed wire ran around the top of the courtyard's mud brick wall; this wall also served as the outer wall to the whole compound.

The wooden door opened onto a dusty wasteland. Rocks covered the ground, and there was nothing green to be seen. A silver water pump was positioned in the center of the yard. A couple of broken metal chairs languished nearby. Shoved up against the wall opposite the courtyard door was a soiled *toshak*. To our left stood four wooden posts wrapped with burlap. Inside the enclosed area was a mountain of feces.

Is this supposed to be our outhouse? we wondered.

A two-story, concrete prison building formed the right-hand wall of the courtyard. Rusty bars covered the windows. A set of windows on the ground floor was bricked up. Pieces of concrete that had fallen off the building were strewn over the ground below.

Two women jailers greeted us. "Welcome," they said, and showed us to a room the size of a large closet just inside the building.

"Put your bags in here," we were told. We stood at the entrance to the room and looked in. The dusty room contained a bunk bed and a desk, affording only a sliver of standing room. One small window let in precious little light.

"So this is where they are putting us."

We laughed anxiously. "Out of the frying pan and into the fire," someone muttered.

As we stood there, we noticed some Afghan women and children peering at us through a barred door several feet away. We found out later that the women were imprisoned for transporting weapons across town. Someone had hired the women to do it. Now they were stuck here.

Ursula was sick the day we arrived and needed to lie down. The jailers brought a corroded metal bed frame out into the courtyard and placed a *toshak* on top of it. The legs of the bed were secured precariously with ropes to the bars on one of the ground-floor windows.

In the courtyard, Big Eyes and some other men were wrapping up the details of our handover to the authorities at this prison. The men in charge wore especially large turbans. Our boss from the reform school was not in the party.

Heather: I approached Big Eyes and began asking him to please identify the prison and these men.

"This is Commander Najib," said Big Eyes. "He is in charge of the prison." In front of us stood a healthy-sized man in his late thirties or early forties. He wore a large, black turban. His beard was dark brown and pointy toward the bottom. He had an olive complexion, round eyes, and a prominent nose. He looked stern, as if he had just completed an important business transaction.

We greeted him warily.

I turned to Big Eyes. "You are a Pashtun," I began. "You told us that, as a Pashtun, you would take good care of us. You promised you would not harm us because we are your guests. As a Pashtun, you must treat your guests with respect."

Big Eyes nodded in agreement. Overhearing the conversation, Najib spoke his own words of affirmation.

"Oh, you do not have to worry," he assured me. "You will be my guests. You are our guests, and we will take care of you." In time, Najib proved himself kind and gracious; he did take care of us.

Heather & Dayna: Meanwhile, another man who we later learned was Najib's superior, Sonan, walked onto the scene. The men talked briefly, and before Big Eyes left, he assured us he would return regularly to check on our conditions. We never saw him again.

The moment Big Eyes walked out of the courtyard, we sank. We felt betrayed, depressed, and sick over our circumstances. Foreigners and Taliban were fleeing the city. The United States might start bombing at any moment. Who could guess whether our governments knew where we were? We were terribly anxious.

Someone suggested we sit in the courtyard and sing worship songs to encourage ourselves.

Heather: I went to Najib and asked him for permission to sing so that we would not start off burning bridges with these new Taliban. Najib consented.

Heather & Dayna: Once we began to sing, Sonan—a stocky, youngish man—quickly intervened.

"Please," Sonan said. "You sing loudly. People will be able to hear you over the wall. You can sing later once you are inside, after your room is ready." Workmen would have us a large room prepared before nightfall, he promised.

The news of a large room marked an upswing in the mood of the group. Of course, time would tell whether Sonan was speaking the truth, but not much time was necessary in this case. A crew of men soon arrived and began knocking the bricks out of the ground-floor windows. We had never seen Afghans move so quickly. The men swept all the dust and rubble out of the room and carted it away; they measured the windows for glass and within an hour had returned with brand-new panes.

We learned from the Afghan women prisoners—two young women and one elderly—that men had come the day before and cleaned out the room, which to that point had served as a storage area. The young daughter of one of the women told us that before we arrived the men had carried weapons out of the room.

This piece of information worried us. Were we being held at a military installation, a prime target for U.S. bombers? Later, a guard denied that weapons were being stockpiled at the compound, but we knew that the room directly above ours contained at least ammunition. We could hear bullets drop and roll on the floor over our heads late at night as the prison guards prepared their guns.

Najib, our new boss, ordered us a nice lunch that first afternoon. We were served rice, meatballs, potatoes, and yogurt, an excellent meal by any Afghan's standards. Late in the day men carried in some worn, dusty carpets for our room. We cleaned the floor as best we could before the carpets were laid. The men moved *toshaks* into the room to accompany two sets of bunk beds. Close to eight o'clock, the men brought us blankets. The women prisoners sewed the *toshaks* and blankets, we learned, using brand-new fabric.

"They sure went to a lot of trouble for us," we observed. "Maybe this will not be so bad after all."

Our second prison, what we later learned was a high-security intelligence prison, proved a happier arrangement in some respects than the reform school prison. We did have a bathroom, and we did not have to share it with thirty other women. We met with Peter and Georg nearly every day. Privacy was still hard to come by, but at least we were not dealing constantly with people and clamor.

The metal door from the courtyard into the prison opened onto an entryway. Just off the entryway to the right was the closet-sized room where we put our bags after arriving the first day. The women jailers used this room when they were on shift. Four women rotated twenty-four-hour shifts; after the United States started bombing Kabul, three women rotated six-hour day shifts. The fourth woman fled the country, we were informed.

From the entryway, a barred door led to a narrow corridor. Turning left on the corridor, we came to our room on the left-hand side.

The doorway to our room was short and wide. We entered facing a large picture window that looked out on the courtyard. Our walls were painted mint green. Against the right-hand wall, the two sets of bunk beds were lined up head-to-foot. We put a *toshak* against the left-hand wall. A tall metal cabinet stood in the front left-hand corner; we used it as a combination pantry and medicine cabinet. We placed a second *toshak* in front of the window and a third *toshak* to the right as you walked in the door. We had just enough space in the center of the room to spread out a *destarkhaan* during mealtime.

Out in the hall to the left of the room was a small table where we set our heating plate for cooking. A four-tiered metal shelf—where we kept pots, plates, and metal bowls—stood to the right of our door. The prison supplied our cookware, utensils, and the heating plate.

The heating plate plugged into a precarious socket, which dangled by a cord from a nail in the wall. Live wires ran out of the socket, and the holes in the socket were cracked and melted, presumably due to electrical fires. The fuse box in the hallway looked worse, amounting to a tangle of live wires interlaced with plastic bags. It, too, apparently had experienced a couple of meltdowns.

Silke took on the job of electrician. Almost every day, something in the socket next to our room went awry, and the heating plate remained cold. Silke would take her manicure kit to the scene and use her implements—previously employed in the business of mural carving—to make sense of the mess.

Across the hall from our room was a small storage room. Several weeks into our stay, Najib had the room cleaned out and a *toshak* brought in for a colorful, but soon-to-be-released, prisoner—British journalist Yvonne Ridley. Yvonne never ended up staying in the room, though Ursula and Silke slept there on occasion. Apart from a picture of a mosque painted on one wall, the room was sparse. A plank of wood covered a large hole in the cement floor. When left uncovered, the hole became an entranceway for mice.

The window in this storage room looked out toward the men's courtyard, a less barren plot of ground than ours. Springing up from a patch of garden were red, pink, and white roses, flowers famously tended and appreciated by Pashtuns. On occasion Taliban guards would pick the roses and put them in the barrels of their Kalashnikovs.

Our bathroom was situated at the opposite end of the hallway. When we entered the tiny room, we faced a sink. The sink turned out to be cosmetic, not that it brought any sense of aesthetic comfort—it was not attached to a water line. On the right was a porcelain squatty potty that we flushed manually using buckets of water we would carry in from the pump in our courtyard.

We set up a cleaning rotation for the bathroom. Whoever had bathroom duty would clean the concrete floor with soap and water and then sweep the water down a hole in the floor. We cleaned the sink and toilet with bleach and emptied the sack of toilet paper hanging on the wall. We did not want to flush paper since at the reform school prison our paper flushing had clogged up the plumbing.

We washed dishes and clothing in the courtyard next to the pump. A laborious activity, washing clothes at least anchored our daily routine. We ordered washing powder every week from the bazaar. Wringing out thicker items, such as sweaters and towels, required two people when we were involved; the Afghan women, however, had strength to wring such garments and linens without assistance.

When we first arrived at the prison, the bathroom door was bereft of a lock. This turned out to be a problem. The four children staying in the prison with their mother—one of the three women arrested for weapon smuggling—were a pesky lot. One of the little boys would stand outside the bathroom while someone was inside and flick the light switch on and off. Sometimes the children would open the door while one of us was bathing. We complained to a prison deputy, and Najib had a lock put on two days later.

The only thing we complained about that Najib neglected was an enormous wasps' nest located just outside our bedroom window. The wasps were loud and sometimes got inside the building through a small hole. A few of us got stung.

Heather: I got stung just days before our departure. It became a running joke among us that all health travesties seemed to happen to me. I barely missed being stung by a scorpion, I contracted a stubborn case of head lice, and I got stung by a wasp.

The wasp inflicted the sting as I was sitting on a *toshak* near the window making a card for my mother's forty-eighth birthday. I was trying to apply some of Silke's fabulous card-drawing techniques. Just as I moved my leg to readjust my position, the wasp stung me. I have a minor allergic reaction to insect bites and stings, and the back of my thigh swelled up and turned purple. The sting looked like a gigantic bruise.

Heather & Dayna: To the left of the bathroom door—on the same side of the corridor as the small storage room Najib fixed up for Yvonne—was another small room, this one meant to be a bedroom for the Afghan women prisoners. The room contained a bed frame usually piled with the Afghan prisoners' ancient, mildewing *toshaks* and filthy blankets. Unlike us, the Afghans were not given new bedding. Also in the room was a small shelf where the women would keep extra bread or rice.

The room smelled foul, especially if a breeze was blowing in from the outside and carrying the bathroom stench with it. When we got to the prison, the Afghan women inmates were keeping their *toshaks* out in the hallway to escape the odor. Eventually, Najib ordered the room to be cleaned, but the smell lingered.

We called this room the "spare room," because for most of the nine weeks we lived in the prison, we did not share our corridor with

Afghan prisoners. The three women and four children who greeted us when we entered the yard that first day were gone in two weeks. Two more women and a ten-month-old baby joined us for several days in early October around the time the U.S. bombing raids on the city began. Days before our departure, another woman showed up. Then we were gone.

We often used the spare room as a private prayer room. A mouse lived in a hole in the wall underneath the bed. The mouse would travel back and forth from the hole to the shelf, pilfering pieces of bread. One night the six of us agreed to hold an all-night prayer vigil for Afghanistan and the rest of the world in light of the pending war. Each of us signed up with a partner to use the prayer room for different time slots. The two of us—Heather and Dayna—took the 2 A.M. to 4 A.M. shift.

We had a great time until the mouse showed up to raid the shelves. The mouse would hit the bed on its way to the hole and make an awful racket. In an effort to avoid a face-to-face encounter with the mouse, we ended up cutting our time short and finishing our shift praying quietly in our bedroom.

On the floor above us were a prayer room for the men who worked at the prison, a "pharmacy," though ammunition was stored there, and Najib's office. All of the rooms looked out over our court-yard, which meant we had to wear our *chawdurs* whenever we ventured outside. Taliban officials could see us washing our clothes in the yard, pumping our water, and spending time in quiet reflection. Sometimes men would spit or throw water from the prayer room window into the courtyard. Najib often would call out to us from his window and ask us what we were doing.

Dayna: One time I was sitting in the courtyard writing in my prayer journal, and Najib called down from his office asking me how I was and what I was doing. I would often take a chair and sit in the corner of the courtyard, facing the wall to be alone. Mice would come out of a hole in the wall and rummage through our trash, which—with much nagging on our part—was collected once a week. As long as the mice stayed outside, I actually thought they were cute. I honestly thanked God they were mice and not rats, even as I thanked him for clean water to drink and the freedom to go outside. I tried to remain positive and keep the perspective that, for an Afghan prison, our conditions were not so bad.

When Najib called to me this particular day, he saw that I was writing.

"What are you writing?" he asked.

"I am writing what I think God is saying to me."

"Well," Najib inquired, "what is he saying?"

"He tells me that he loves me, that I'm going to be okay and not to worry."

"Ah, but what does God say for me?"

"I don't know," I said. "I will ask him."

Heather & Dayna: Though he was a youngish middle-aged man, Najib behaved toward us in a paternal way. He had nine children. On a few occasions, Najib took weekends off and went back to his village to spend time with his family. When he returned from one of these visits, he brought us a cloth sack full of almonds. His wife and sisters-in-law had collected them for us and offered us greetings, he said.

"Do you know how to open the shells?" Najib asked.

We did not know, which prompted a chuckle from Najib. He went out into the yard, collected some rocks, and came into our room to show us his method. We were to set the almond on one smooth rock and smash the nut with the other. Often we pulverized our almonds, leaving them all but dust. Eventually, though, we got the hang of shell cracking and used the almonds as a nice garnish on many of our dishes.

Najib told us he had lived in Pakistan for twenty years and moved to Afghanistan less than two years earlier to plant an orchard. He had just planted a thousand trees.

"I came here because it is peaceful," he said. "And now we are at war." We were deeply saddened for Najib. He just wanted to live, work, and care for his family, but it was not to be.

Najib's personal cook prepared our food. Every morning at seven, someone would come to the door with bread and ask us what we wanted to eat that day. Before the bombing started, the women jailers would interact with the guard for us. Once the jailers stopped sleeping at the prison, we took the morning bread from the guard and put in our own menu requests for that day.

Trying to figure out what we wanted to eat every day took time. Diana, usually the only one awake when the guard came, would go out and give him our order. Diana knew only a little Dari, and many times the guard would ask her, "Can you go get Dayna-jan to come explain?"

At lunch and dinner, Najib's cook would come down to the gate himself and hand the food over to us. The women jailers took the food from him at lunch. After the bombing started, we collected the food in the evening, as the jailer on duty would already be gone. The cook would give us the pot, his hands always black with soot, and ask, "How was your lunch?" or "Did you like what I made you last time?"

We would encourage him by saying, "We enjoyed it. Thank you."

Sometimes when we met the cook at the gate, he would take a spoon and sample the meal to show us that it was truly tasty—and that it was not poisoned. He wanted us to know that he, too, would eat his own creations.

One day the cook asked us if there was anything else we wanted to eat besides his regular fare. Given the limited selection of ingredients we could obtain in Kabul, we could only think to suggest that he try making macaroni instead of rice. The cook had never heard of macaroni, but one of our women jailers told him where he could buy it. In turn, we proceeded to give him the recipe.

We explained that he needed to boil water and then place the macaroni in the water for approximately ten minutes. Afterward, he could pour out the water and the macaroni would be ready to eat.

What we received was a more complex version of the dish. The cook did bring us macaroni, but the pasta was floating in a pot of oil.

Apparently, he had boiled the macaroni in oil and failed to drain it. To an Afghan, a meal is not a meal unless it is prepared in oil. We did not put in a request for macaroni again.

One day we gave the cook a pair of socks and some sugarcoated almonds as an appreciation gift. He accepted our offerings graciously, and from that time on we had a friend in the cook.

In addition to our hot meals, Najib brought us fruit, vegetables, and yogurt from the bazaar on the house, so to speak. At the reform school prison, we paid for these items out of pocket. By the time we got to the intelligence prison, our money supply had diminished significantly, and we were grateful for Najib's generosity. All of us were sharing Silke's money at that time—the money she had managed to collect from her house the day she was arrested.

Shortly after our arrival, we learned that in the midst of America's war on terror the dollar had dropped to nearly half its value, which forced us to scale back on our spending. We cut out jam, cheese, bottles of cola, and other luxuries, and reduced our shopping list to bottled water, cleaning supplies, and medicine. After our lawyer started making trips in from Pakistan, we received care packages from our parents. When these goods would run out, we resorted to buying cheese once in a while so that we would have protein at breakfast.

One of the delicacies sent in by our parents was coffee. We tried to maintain a two-cups-a-day rule. We ended up stretching the rule to allow for three cups a day. We would usually have one or two cups at breakfast and then one or two cups around three o'clock in the afternoon. The afternoon coffee ritual helped break up the day, providing a welcome rest from mundane activities.

To pass time in the afternoons—and to quench the nagging anxiety about how and when we might ever be released—we played cards, exercised, and read books. Most of us collected some of our own books on the trip to our houses in Wazir. Kati and Silke brought page-turners like John Grisham's *The Firm* and *The Chamber,* for instance—though *The Chamber,* about a man sentenced to death, was a bit too intense for us given the pressure we were facing. Donahue brought us a cache of books at the reform school prison before evacuating to Islamabad. He and our parents retrieved these books from the dusty shelves of the library at the American Center/GSO/Club compound, which the United States closed along with its embassy compound in 1989.

Among the books the diplomats brought us were some Reader's Digest fiction anthologies; a book authored by Geraldo Rivera in the mid-seventies called *Special Kind of Courage: Profiles of Young Americans;* Elsie Reif Ziegler's *Light a Little Lamp,* which told the story of a woman reformer working with refugees in Chicago; and many others. Our parents sent more books in with our lawyer later, including *The Horse and His Boy* by C. S. Lewis and a biography of Benazir Bhutto, the former prime minister of Pakistan.

Dayna: A Reader's Digest book, *They Beat the Odds,* told stories of individuals who persevered through serious trials. One man survived a plane crash in Alaska and endured subzero temperatures for more than a hundred days before he was rescued; another man, already blind, lost his hearing, too. The stories challenged me to make the very most of our prison experience—to enjoy life and live it fully. Our circumstances could have been so much worse.

Heather & Dayna: In between nerve-splitting bombing raids, we tried to maximize the small pleasures. Sometimes we would read while soaking our feet. Our feet became severely chapped over our prison stay. We soaked them often. We would heat up water in one of the green plastic washtubs, sit together, soak our feet, and read. Then we would scrub our feet and moisturize them with lotion or Vaseline. We ordered the Vaseline from the bazaar; it was cheap and came in a plastic bag. We transferred the bagged Vaseline into an actual Vaseline jar and a canister for cream. We would pass the jar and canister around during our morning and evening worship meetings and tend to our feet then.

Dayna: Diana made our daily shopping list for the women jailers. At the reform school prison, I made the shopping list and then communicated it to Mariam, who would write the list in Farsi, which uses the Arabic alphabet. Since two of the women jailers in this prison could not write, Diana would make the list. Being from an Arab family, Diana could write Arabic script. Kati happened to have a Dari schoolbook with her, and Diana would use it to look up any vocabulary she could not recall. Then she would spell out the words in script.

If Diana had trouble communicating with the guard who was taking the list, I helped her. Heather spoke good Dari by this point, but she usually was asleep when Diana was dealing with the guard in the morning. Kati's Dari was very good, but she tended to intervene in complex situations involving Najib or other Taliban officials. She was a brave straight-talker. I preferred helping out with day-to-day communication needs. Confronting or dealing with authority figures made me nervous.

Heather & Dayna: Four women jailers looked after us up until the time when the bombing started—Sweeta-jan, Maria-jan, Rohena-jan, and Trinaa-jan. After the bombing commenced, we heard that Trinaa-jan had left the country. Of the remaining three, we were closest to Sweeta-jan and Maria-jan.

Maria-jan was six months pregnant with twins when we arrived. She wore her hair down under a small head scarf, and she wore makeup. Maria-jan was very poor; she lived on the side of the mountain with no electricity in a two-story mud house. She had been married off at thirteen and would tell us how scared of her husband she used to be in those early years. Now things between them had improved.

Maria-jan had several children, including a daughter who wore a prosthesis. The prosthesis did not fit her daughter's leg properly, and Maria-jan would often tell us that her girl was bleeding and in pain.

Before the Taliban came to power, Maria-jan's house was rocketed during some cross fire between warring Mujahideen factions. That day she returned to the house after work—she was working in the same prison—and found two of her children dismembered.

Maria-jan was not afraid to ask us for things. We gave her some clothes, tea, sugar, and money. Diana, petite in stature, offered one of her dresses to Maria-jan to take to her daughter. Maria-jan was thrilled to receive the dress and decided she would claim it for herself. She badly needed new clothes. On her next several shifts, Maria-jan wore Diana's colorful dress with the purple sweater she daily used as a cover-up.

We always shared our extra food with the women jailers. By the time we got to the prison, the women already had gone two months without salary and needed any help we could offer them. Najib, struggling financially himself, understood his employees' dilemma and on one occasion paid some of their wages out of his personal income. He often brought them gifts when he would return from visiting his village. The women jailers thought highly of Najib and treated him with reverence. They would sit down to tea with him, clucking, "*Amir Saeb, Amir Saeb.*" Commander Sir. Commander Sir.

Sweeta-jan, an educated widow, grieved over her dire circumstances. She had little at home to eat. After the bombing started, Sweeta-jan said, "I wish America would just come and kill us all. It's better to die than live hungry." She had tears in her eyes. We rarely saw her cry.

Sweeta-jan was short and stout. Most of the time she smiled and made jokes. She patted and comforted us. She was always trying to help. "Let me pump water for you," she would say, or "Let me wash your clothes for you." We never allowed her, but she always offered. She was very active and frequently cleaned the hallway. She was older than Maria-jan, maybe in her forties, but she looked much older than that. Her skin was worn and leathery. At the corners of her eyes she had prominent crow's-feet.

Heather: Surprisingly, Sweeta-jan had no gray hair. She wore her long hair up in a bun most of the time. One day I started pulling out some of my gray hairs, and she gasped, "Do not pull out your gray hairs! More will grow back!" Sweeta-jan mothered me. One of her daughters was my age—twenty-four. Whenever I got upset, Sweeta-jan would come and take care of me. "Do not be upset," she would say softly. Unlike Mariam's exhortations, Sweeta-jan's encouragement actually diffused my fear.

One day some weeks after the bombing had started Sweeta-jan made me afternoon tea. We sat down together in the spare room for conversation. I was barely making it emotionally. Tensions with the other five women were high. Planes dropped bombs on the city both day and night. The political situation in Afghanistan was deteriorating rapidly. Progress on our case seemed to be at a standstill. I knew it truly would take a miracle to get us out of the country alive, and I was hardly able to hang on to the promises of God for our deliverance.

Suddenly, a series of explosions erupted nearby. The whole prison shook, and my body vibrated with every boom. I jumped to my feet, and my tea went flying. I was soaked through to the skin and covered in tea leaves. That was it. I started shaking and crying. My nerves were shot.

"It is okay, Khatera-jan," Sweeta-jan said lovingly, calling me by my adopted Afghan name. "The soldiers are just testing their guns."

Najib came in to investigate the commotion.

"Sir," I choked, "you said you would tell us the next time the guards tested their weapons. You said that they would not shoot their tanks inside the compound."

Uncertain what to do with me, Najib reassured me that he would address the issue and have the tanks removed from the compound. I had a hard time believing him.

For the next hour, Sweeta-jan held me in her arms and stroked my hair. "Do not cry. It will be harder if you cry." She told me she loved me like her own daughter. Her tender voice comforted me. At that point I just wanted to know that I was loved and that someone cared enough to hold me.

Heather & Dayna: Sweeta-jan was on shift our first night at the prison. She told us she doubted we would be kept at the prison more than a week or so. People sent to this prison were usually on the verge of being released, she said. After a week had come and gone, we let this hope die.

Sweeta-jan served as a source of information. She loved to read and often read a newspaper to keep updated as best she could on the details of the war. She also owned a radio and would bring news when she came in for her shift.

Heather: A few days after we arrived, Sweeta-jan reported that she had heard my father on Pashtu BBC radio offer to take my place in prison. Sweeta-jan spoke both Pashtu and Dari. She did not want to tell me about my father's offer, because she feared I would become upset. Instead, she mentioned it to Georg as he and Peter were leaving our courtyard after visiting us. I overheard the conversation and managed to pull the information out of them. It bothered me that they pampered me. Though I greatly appreciated Sweeta-jan's kindness and compassion, I did not appreciate information being withheld, especially when it related to me.

When they told me about my father's offer, I was deeply grateful. Though I would have never permitted him to take my place, it was just like my dad to make such an offer. He would give his life for me without a second thought.

Heather & Dayna: Sweeta-jan's uncle, it turned out, was the carpenter Kati hired two days before our arrest to teach at the SNI street kids project. This same man had done some of the work on the interior of our house in Wazir—he built a cabinet in our kitchen, he made a table for our living room. He was also one of the sixteen Afghan SNI employees the Taliban rounded up following our arrest.

When we first arrived at the intelligence prison, Sweeta-jan told us that the sixteen Afghans were being held in the men's compound.

Georg and Peter were kept in a tiny room—two by three meters—on the upper floor of one of the buildings. Our sixteen employees stayed on the lower level of a second building directly across the men's courtyard.

The dungeonlike area where the sixteen stayed was the vilest part of the compound; men put there were beaten severely. Sonan, Najib's boss, inflicted brutal beatings, we were told, using a steel cable to strike the men's heads with repeated blows. Georg and Peter ordered medicine from the bazaar to treat the Afghan men, many of whom had suffered at the hands of Sonan.

Prisoners would be put in the dungeon early in their incarceration and then moved up to a higher floor whenever the authorities deemed it time—that is, whenever the prisoners came up with the means to pay a bribe, we understood. One afternoon, Georg and Peter saw our employees being led out of the dungeon and then out of the compound. It seemed the sixteen were being released. Later we learned the authorities had taken the men to the city's most infamous prison, Pul-e-Charkhi.

We found out over the course of our stay that along with the sixteen SNI Afghan employees, our *chowkidar,* Khalid, had been imprisoned. On hearing of our arrest, he had refused to abandon his post at our house in Wazir. Eventually, the Taliban found him there, loyally guarding the property. We were heartbroken over Khalid's detention, and in the weeks following, prayed a great deal for him and his family.

A prisoner from Kandahar informed Georg that the SNI projects in that city had been utterly ransacked. Georg was devastated, as were the rest of us. We prayed that God would restore double to SNI and the other aid organizations that lost everything.

Najib permitted us to visit with Georg and Peter daily for the first three weeks of our incarceration. He then reduced the visits to every other day. Najib's brother, a high-ranking prisoner at the compound, befriended Georg and, toward the end of our stay, smuggled in a radio for Georg along with a camera and a roll of film. Once Georg got the radio, we started getting reliable information on a regular basis. He would come to our room and report the news first thing. He might leave us detailed letters regarding current events tucked under a *toshak*.

At first, Najib sat with us during the meetings. Though Najib did not speak English, he wanted to supervise our conversations. He never knew his brother had smuggled Georg the radio and camera. Najib was a Talib commander, after all, and there were limits to his leniency.

One time we learned that Sonan had rebuked Najib about the coed meetings in our room. Apparently, Sonan suspected some funny business. He reprimanded Peter and Georg in accordance with his assumptions. "This is a prison, not a house to be married," he snapped. We all laughed at the absurdity of the statement.

fifteen

PROCEEDINGS

Heather & Dayna: "I have good news for you!"

The day after we were moved to the intelligence prison, Afghani's deputy—a short, stocky Talib wearing a white turban—arrived at our courtyard. The deputy was a young man, perhaps in his early thirties. He told us we were to come with him right away. A delegation of high-level Pakistani officials had requested to see us.

We threw on our *chawdurs* and piled into Najib's van with Georg and Peter. Finally, things seemed to be moving in the right direction. We knew the United States would probably bomb Afghanistan soon, and we anticipated the meeting with the delegation would yield news concerning our release. We did not expect to remain in the intelligence prison for long. High-level Pakistani officials asking to see us could only mean progress, or so we hoped.

Driving a black Mercedes, the deputy led our two-vehicle caravan through the city to the Ministry of Foreign Affairs building, where Afghani awaited our arrival. The deputy and one of his armed guards escorted us to an executive conference room on the building's top floor, and instructed us to sit down. We sat in padded wooden chairs at one end of a long conference table. Large picture windows lined one wall, overlooking a courtyard and garden, and from the room we could see one of the main streets running through Shar-e-Nao.

As we waited, we were served high-quality tea in fancy teapots. We drank from china teacups with handles and spooned in sugar from a sugar dish. Georg encouraged us to pray with the person next to us.

Nearly half an hour later, several Pakistani officials entered the room. They were courteous and polished, and their demeanor was grave. The officials asked us questions about our health and the way we were being treated. Georg did most of the talking.

The two of us told the officials that our parents were in Pakistan awaiting our release, and the men offered to take written messages back to Islamabad on our behalf. We dashed off quick notes. Then the officials brought out several beautiful packages wrapped in shiny metallic paper and tied with pink bows. These gifts—a variety of sweets and delicacies—were meant as tokens of encouragement and support from the Pakistani people, the officials said. The men heartened us, saying that they were discussing our detainment with the Taliban. We graciously expressed our thanks.

After thirty minutes, the meeting ended and we were ushered out of the conference room. Georg told us that one of the men had remarked to him that our situation looked hopeful and that we might be released soon, which encouraged us. Otherwise, we left the Foreign Affairs building with no concrete information about our plight, nothing on which we could stand. We were thankful the men had taken the time to meet with us, but we came away disappointed.

Nearly a week later, no progress had been made on our case, while the atmosphere in Kabul seemed to be heating up. The Taliban were testing weapons around the city, and we heard that demonstrators burned a Pakistani flag to protest that country's cooperation with America in its war on terror. We became increasingly concerned that our lawyer, Atif Ali Khan, might not venture across the border after all.

We discussed various courses of action and decided to petition the court to allow us to defend ourselves. By defending ourselves—and not having to wait on a lawyer—we figured we would be able to move things along with greater agility. Georg wrote a letter of request to the chief justice concerning our change in strategy. He even wrote a letter to Mullah Omar himself, pleading for our pardon and quick release. We needed to get the ball rolling.

The courier of these letters was Karim, our faithful translator from the reform school prison. Karim also worked as a translator for the justices while they were reviewing our case. Apparently, the boss at the reform school never told Karim we were being moved to the intelligence prison. To find us, Karim had to appeal to one of his contacts in the prison system. When our friend finally arrived, we were overjoyed to see him.

"Are you healthy? How are you?" he asked. "Do not worry. Najib is a good man, and he will take good care of you. I will come to see you when I can." Unlike other Taliban officials who made similar assertions, Karim kept his promise.

On September 24, Karim delivered Georg's letter to the Supreme Court requesting we be allowed to move forward and defend ourselves. We got an answer the next day when Afghani arrived at our prison with some letters, money, and items that our parents had left for us before being evacuated to Islamabad nearly two weeks earlier.

"Your lawyer is on his way," Afghani announced, smiling. "You will be going to court soon."

Our reaction to this declaration was mixed. We wanted to get the court proceedings over with before the United States started bombing Afghanistan, and we knew we did not have much time. But we did not know whether a lawyer at this point would expedite the process or bog the proceedings down. We hoped our lawyer would be able to work quickly; at least he finally was on his way.

Afghani's deputy and another Talib came to see us a few days later. By that time, demonstrators in Kabul had burned buildings and cars inside the old U.S. embassy compound to protest America's imminent attack on the country. The demonstration did not help build our confidence that we would be given a fair trial.

When the deputy and his helper came in, they pulled out a Polaroid camera. As ambassadors for a regime that disallowed pictures or representations of living things, the men told us they needed to take our photographs for the court's records. Not only that, we had to pay for these pictures—1,500 rupees in total, or twenty-two U.S. dollars. The men made us pose in a chair in front of one of the courtyard walls. None of us enjoyed the exercise.

The next morning Afghani came back, this time with our lawyer, Atif Ali Khan, and his assistant, Bismillah Jan. The meeting was very brief. Atif introduced himself and greeted us with cordiality and respect. Bismillah, several years older than Atif, smiled graciously and seemed to be a kind, collected man. Atif told us he would meet with us again the next day.

On September 30, we joined Atif and Bismillah for another round of official proceedings at the Supreme Court building. Najib loaded us up in his van that morning, but Silke stayed behind. She was ill and did not feel like she could attend. For some reason, even as we all climbed into his vehicle, Najib did not notice Silke's absence.

Again we drove through the city to the government compound. This time no caravan of Taliban trucks accompanied us, nor did a crush of journalists assemble at the gate vying for photographs and sound bites. The front steps were clear of mayhem as well. Without ceremony we followed Najib and a few armed Taliban guards into the building.

We were not permitted to wait in the same room with Peter and

Georg this time and instead were directed to a plain room with *toshaks* while the men were led down the hall. No one took note of our group's diminished number.

After several minutes, a few Taliban officials came to our room with sheets of paper. Yet again the government required our name, our father's name, our grandfather's name, country of origin, and so on. "Ughhh," we whispered.

After one of the officials finished passing out the paper, we asked him for an extra sheet. We needed it for Silke, who was ill, Kati explained. She told the man she had been given written permission to sign the information in Silke's place. The official hesitated but seemed amenable. He said he would talk to his superiors, and the men quickly left the room.

Within moments Najib entered. "Why didn't you tell me she was not coming?" he asked in an exasperated tone. "We cannot continue with the trial without her. Somebody will have to go back. She has to be here."

Kati stood up and left with Najib. We waited in the room. Kati returned with Silke twenty minutes later.

Once Silke had filled out her information, the guards led the rest of us into the courtroom. As before, the eighteen justices were sitting in their horseshoe. We took seats in the front of the room facing the chief justice's desk and the wall adorned with the prayer rug, whip, and swords. Though sparsely attended compared to our last visit, the courtroom was nearly filled, this time mainly with Taliban officials.

After we sat down, a Talib passed us a heavy green book, which appeared to be a courtroom register. The book was open to a page covered with our very expensive Polaroid photographs. They were not even good photographs. We all looked gaunt and unhealthy. Atif's picture appeared with ours, along with photographs of two witnesses, in this case Taliban officials. We each were instructed to place our thumbprint alongside our photograph and sign our names.

Heather: My picture looked particularly bad. My cheekbones jutted out, and dark circles underscored my eyes. Dayna and I joked about how sickly I appeared. I knew I was not underfed, but for some reason no matter how much I seemed to eat, I was losing weight. Later I discovered the problem—worms.

Heather & Dayna: "This is your lawyer," announced a Talib translator. "Do you agree to have him?" He gestured toward Atif.

Each of us replied according to the formality required: "Yes, my name is Dayna Curry," or "Yes, my name is Heather Mercer, and I agree to have Atif Ali Khan as my lawyer."

Then the translator turned to Atif. "Do you agree to represent these eight people?" he asked, naming each of us.

"Yes," Atif replied. "I agree to represent them all."

Next the prosecutor read the charges—in Dari. Atif did not speak Dari, only Pashtu, the language of the Taliban. None of us spoke Dari well enough to understand the charges. At times we could pick up bits and pieces of meaning, but not enough to grasp the substance of the text.

Atif interrupted the prosecutor. "I do not understand Dari," he remarked politely.

The prosecutor explained that the charges would be read out in Dari and a written translation provided to Atif later. We assumed that the prosecutor presented the charges in Dari for the Afghan media present in the room—that is, so the charges could be broadcast over the radio. We also wondered whether the Taliban wanted to ward off any objections we might raise to the charges if we were able to understand them while they were being read.

"You have up to fifteen days to present your defense," the chief justice stated at the end of the proceeding. He insisted the pending war would not affect the progress of our case.

Atif and Bismillah accompanied the eight of us back to our room in the intelligence prison. To our delight, they came bearing Oreos, Sprites, and Cokes. Such treats became regular accessories to our consultations with Atif and Bismillah. One day they brought us Chips Ahoy and Mars Bars. Another day Bismillah carried in a more nutritious snack—a big carton of grapes. On all of their trips to Kabul, the men delivered packages from our parents containing jam, peanut butter, candy, coffee, and other food products. We were grateful for these delicacies and recognized our unique position in having a whole team of people working diligently to secure our release.

"What was the reason behind your choosing me?" Atif asked as we partook of the refreshments that first afternoon. He was a slight, very young-looking man with light skin and a short beard, which he seemed to be growing out. "I am not the most experienced lawyer you could have chosen."

We were honest. "Really, you were our only option," we told him. "You know Pashtu, you know the Pashtun culture, and you have studied Islamic law. You were also educated in the West."

"Well," he responded, "while I am not the most experienced, I believe that with my background in Islamic law and our good relationships with the Taliban, we will be able to provide you a good defense."

Bismillah had contacts at significant levels of leadership within the Taliban administration. A Pakistani national, Bismillah grew up in the Pashtun tribal areas of Pakistan near the Afghan border. He always wore a brown, wool hat of the sort characteristically seen in northern Afghanistan. He smiled and shook his head in agreement while talking to us, often adding *"Enshallah"* to his statements in a positive tone— unlike the boss and his men at the reform school prison. We were grateful for Bismillah's assistance. His relationships would enable him and Atif to start off on the right foot as they built our case.

While we sat together, Atif—a devout Muslim—told us that by defending us he wanted to do something great for God. He said he wanted the world to see Islam in a better light. He wanted to show the world that Muslims and Christians could work together. Atif presented himself in a friendly, professional manner and seemed confident all would go well.

"I will give you my best," he promised, smiling. He assured us the Taliban would treat us fairly. We were not certain we believed him.

Atif went to the court building the following morning to pick up an English translation of the charges, but no translated charges were ready. In fact, they were not ready for four days. Instead, Atif and Bismillah resorted to collecting a written copy of the charges in Dari. Bismillah did his best to translate the Dari charges into Pashtu, and then Atif translated the Pashtu into a sketchy English.

Meanwhile, we worked with Atif individually reviewing the lines of questioning our interrogators had employed. Each of us wrote out statements describing for Atif the events leading up to our arrests. We felt encouraged that we were getting somewhere on our end with the process. Now if only the court would do its part.

On October 4, the court finally provided us with a very poor English translation of the charges. Atif gave each of us a copy and instructed us to notate inaccuracies. Our names and our fathers' names were listed at the top of the first page.

The overarching charge was that we had spread the "abolished Religion of Christanity" among Afghans. Though very difficult to follow, the translated text stated that the two of us were arrested while inviting an Afghan family to accept Christianity. The storybook copies and CD were mentioned as evidence, and our apology for causing problems in Afghanistan appeared. The charges further alleged that we visited the family in the name of our organization—particularly in the name of the street kids project. The organization and its projects were fronts for preaching, according to the charges. For our actions, the text concluded, we were subject to punishment under Islamic law.

sixteen

BOMBS, BIRDS, CATS, AND MICE

*I bought eight little birds and will release them today after a meeting
we are going to have with Mr. [Atif Ali] Khan to discuss your case.
All of us will be there, including the three consular diplomats. The
press will likely be there after the meeting so they will see us release
the birds. Of course, this is symbolic of you guys and your release to
freedom soon.*

—LETTER TO HEATHER FROM HER FATHER,

OCTOBER 7, 2000

Dayna: After we finished notating our copies of the translated
charges, Atif and Bismillah left us. It was evening. As was my custom,
I went outside to spend some time praying and worshiping God. I sat
in one of the broken chairs near the courtyard gate.

These times of quiet in God's presence brought me the strength
and peace I needed to endure the strain. As I reflected on my life, I was
able to let God heal me of deep hurts and open my eyes to his goodness. Many evenings I thought about a man with whom I had shared
some of my life in Kabul. We had decided to part as friends, but I
missed him very much. At one time, I had wanted my friend to ask me

to leave Afghanistan and date him in America. I had not enjoyed a deep friendship with a man in eleven years.

From our time together, I learned that I really could remain pure in the company of a man. We laughed, prayed, and reached out to the poor. I cherished our time. I thought my friend was a gift from God, and I did not want our relationship to end. When we parted ways after a couple of months, my heart was broken. Perhaps my friend had only been a gift for a season, I thought. I spent many days and nights crying over the loss and wondered how I would ever get over it.

During my evening quiet time in prison, too, I would sit in the corner of the courtyard and cry, telling God how much I missed my friend. I would ask God to please come close to me and heal my heart. I would discipline my heart and say, "God, you know I would love to be with this man again, but I trust you. I want your will for my life." My heart ached, but I kept asking God to touch me.

On the evening Atif and Bismillah left with our notated copies of the charges, I had not been out in the courtyard long when I heard footsteps. The gate opened. Najib and another man were leading a woman wearing only a head scarf into our building. I could not see her face. Another prisoner, I guessed. Some days earlier, guards had put two young Hazara women, one with a ten-month-old baby, into the spare room on our hallway. The women were arrested for interacting with some strange men—men not related to them—in connection with a carpet purchase, we were told. Perhaps this new woman was brought in for not wearing a burqa.

Najib took the woman into the building and I went back to talking with God. Some moments later, Diana called me in to help translate. Inside, Najib and an official who had journeyed from Jalalabad were trying to talk to a very frustrated Westerner. Her name was Yvonne Ridley; she was a British journalist. Heather already had been translating for some minutes when I came in.

"Will you please ask these men where I am and what they're doing with me?" the woman asked.

Yvonne explained that she had been transported to our prison from Jalalabad under the pretense that she likely would be flown out of the country from the Kabul airport. If she did not end up flying out, the men told her, then she would be able to stay with some foreigners in a really nice hotel.

"They have satellite television, access to videos and computers, and all the food they want," the guards promised.

Well, she had been lied to.

"This is the first time I've lost it," Yvonne explained to the six of us. Today, October 4, was day seven of her captivity after being arrested for sneaking into Afghanistan under a burqa without visa or passport. She had come into the country under cover for her newspaper, *The Sunday Express,* to report on how the Afghan people felt about the coming war. She was forty-three years old.

"When can she leave?" I asked the men, acting as translator. "When will you fly her out?" Najib and the official did not give a clear answer. "We will be back to talk with her. We will be back tomorrow." Tomorrow was Friday, the day of prayer, an unlikely day for progress on her case.

Najib went to retrieve a *toshak* and blanket for our new inmate, and Yvonne came with us to our room. Tears streamed down her face.

"They've finally broken me," she despaired. We were her first female company since her arrest.

Yvonne told us she heard about our plight on the radio in Jalalabad. She said she also heard Mullah Omar was asking President George W. Bush to reconsider bombing the country in return for our handover. She remarked that the offer was a pipe dream for Mullah Omar.

"I expect America to bomb this week," Yvonne opined, noting the presence of three thousand journalists in Pakistan positioned to report on an attack. "It's not a matter of if the U.S. will bomb, but when. You must brace yourselves for it."

Yvonne proceeded to enumerate the dreadful details of the September 11 attacks on New York and Washington, D.C. With horror and awe, she described the collapse of the Twin Towers and the sheer desperation of the people who jumped from the upper-story windows to escape fires and massive explosions. Passengers on the airplanes used their cell phones, she said, to call their loved ones and say their last goodbyes before the planes crashed. She talked about the incredible courage of the passengers who took their aircraft down in a Pennsylvania field to prevent the hijackers from using the plane as a missile. She told us of the young man, Todd Beamer, who said to the passengers, "Let's roll," before crashing that plane.

The details overwhelmed us. We were gripped with sorrow. We had known the attack was serious, but now we had images—and they were gruesome. For the first time we could vaguely comprehend the emotional nightmare through which our country was living. Our hearts broke for the grieving families. We were also saddened to hear that some Americans were reacting against foreigners who looked Arab or Central Asian. Fear had taken hold.

I was awake in my bed for hours that night; my heart physically hurt. We had spent a lot of time praying for the American families who lost loved ones back when we first found out about the tragedy, but now we felt the impact of the events in a profound way. How could we dare to hope the President would hold off bombing for the eight of us when so many had died? Action needed to be taken against Osama bin Laden. Our lives were in God's hands. If we perished, we perished.

We gave Yvonne a place to sleep on the floor, making sure she was comfortable, and told her she was welcome to have breakfast with us in the morning at seven o'clock.

The next morning Diana made the grocery list, adding a carton of cigarettes for Yvonne. Yvonne warmed up some water and took a bucket bath. She was covered in mosquito bites and taking medication. Then she asked to borrow some of my makeup so she could feel a little more human.

"Eyelash curlers!" she exclaimed, noticing I was holding a pair. "You have eyelash curlers. How wonderful!"

Officials at the prison in Jalalabad had given Yvonne a little kit of toiletries and a fancy white dress covered in gold sequins and beads. We asked her what she was doing with a wedding dress.

"I thought it was a bit elaborate for prison wear," she quipped.

Najib came to our room that morning with another man. They asked Yvonne for her last name and some other information for prison records. The cook needed to know how much food to prepare, Najib explained.

Yvonne would not cooperate. "I refuse to talk," she said. I was translating.

"I am not going to eat anything until I am out of this place." Yvonne was on a hunger strike. She had threatened to go on a no-bathing strike, but we begged her to refrain—Heather was already protesting our imprisonment by refusing to wash. One dirty person in our confines was enough.

I told Najib, "I'm sorry, Yvonne is not eating, so you do not need this information from her."

Najib was steaming—I had never seen him so upset. "Well," he said, "I will be happy if she dies."

"Oh, okay." I waited to translate until he had walked away.

Heather: Atif came back on Yvonne's first full day at the prison and told us he was taking our notes to Pakistan to prepare our case. He and Bismillah would return in a week and present our defense to the court.

I begged him not to go.

"Please, we have no contact with anyone here. No progress will be made on our case if you leave, and the war could start. You might not be able to get back into the country."

Others pleaded, too. Atif assured us he would be back soon. With tensions escalating, however, I was not so confident.

Before Atif left, I went out to the courtyard to write a note for him to carry to my family. Yvonne was in the courtyard smoking a cigarette. I cried as I wrote. I was upset that Atif was leaving. We could be totally cut off from the rest of the world if he was unable to return.

Yvonne and I talked for a while and she told me crying was okay. I truly was comforted. I never felt like I had permission to cry. Yvonne let me be free enough to cry without trying to fix me. I was grateful.

I asked Yvonne what she would like me to put in my letter so that word of her whereabouts could be communicated to the proper people. I added a brief paragraph about her at the end of the note. When I went back inside the room, Atif was waiting to leave. Najib asked me directly if I had written anything to my family about Yvonne.

"Yes," I answered, and he confiscated the letter. I had invested all that time writing to my family and he was taking my letter away. None of us was allowed to include any news of Yvonne in our notes, Najib said. He told me to rewrite my letter. I replied that I could not remember what it said, so Najib gave the letter back and let me copy the part to my parents.

Dayna: On Saturday, the official from Jalalabad returned to the prison to speak with Yvonne about her ordeal. The conversation proved a less-than-harmonious exchange. Yvonne told us she was going to play it tough. We told her she might end up endangering herself. She did what she had to do to try to get released.

Najib asked me to translate, but I told him I would rather not. He understood and asked one of his men to take my place.

"You can judge a civilization by its prisons," Yvonne announced to the men, "and you people are primitive. This is a revolting prison." The new translator worked out the phraseology for the official.

"We have been at war for twenty-five years," the official replied. "The quality of our prisons is not a priority."

Yvonne was unmoved and continued to decry the conditions. Taliban guards gathered at the wooden gate and peered through the slats to glimpse the shouting foreigner.

Later that afternoon, Afghani and his deputy came by to speak to

Yvonne and deliver letters faxed by our parents. Yvonne was no more cordial than before. Afghani, who spoke fluent English, fully understood her. Lest anyone fail to catch the point, Yvonne spit at the men's shoes.

Afghani came inside and told us about the spitting. He was almost laughing from the shock. "She is a very hostile lady," he exclaimed. "She even spit at our shoes!"

We told Yvonne we did not think our conditions were so bad. "Well," she answered, "you have introduced a very hygienic regime. This is likely the first time that toilet has seen disinfectant in many years." She said she was full of admiration for our routine and the way we had organized ourselves. We had minimized the potential for disease and other health crises, she noted.

Every now and then, Yvonne came into our worship meetings. She told us our singing lit up the place, that our voices made a wonderful, melodic sound—"a heavenly sound," she said.

"When you get out of here," she encouraged us, "you all should go into a recording studio and cut an album by the 'Kabul Six.'" We laughed at the prospect. If we ever were to assemble any songs for a record, we most certainly would not be the ones doing the singing!

Heather: Late in the afternoon, heavy gunfire erupted while we were out in the courtyard. I went into the women jailers' room and got under the bed. I did not know what was happening. The shooting and firing went on for more than half an hour. We later were told a U.S. spy drone had flown overhead. The shooting came from antiaircraft guns on the ground.

I knew the episode meant war was near.

That evening Afghani and his deputy returned to the courtyard to see how we were faring after the shooting. They came with a satellite phone. Unprompted by any request from us, they told us we could call our parents. Silke was particularly grateful; she had not yet received any letters from her family, since no adequate German translators could be tracked down in Kabul. For the duration of our imprisonment, the Germans experienced difficulty when it came to getting their letters. Kati, Silke, and Ursula had to remain incommunicado for long stretches, and it was very hard on them.

The phone call made up for the difficult day. We were given unlimited time to talk to our families. I had not spoken to my parents since just before they were evacuated from Kabul, and I was so grateful for the chance to hear their voices again. We caught up on family life, and I told my parents about Yvonne. My dad said he felt confident the United States would not bomb Kabul while we were imprisoned in the city. My mother, on the other hand, told me to make sure I kept my wits about me because I would need them. Both of my parents reassured me that I was handling the pressure just fine. I felt like they understood me and let me deal with the crisis in my own way. I relinquished the phone greatly encouraged.

Meanwhile, Najib, Afghani, Afghani's deputy, and some other Taliban were sitting in the courtyard. When a newscast reported that an American drone had been shot down, the group cheered. The deputy punched the air with his fist. "Yes," he exclaimed. The report about the drone was later declared untrue.

Before he left, Afghani stated, "I am absolutely confident there will be no bombing by America for the next month. Now, for three months, I cannot tell you. But for one month, I am certain."

The following day, October 7, Najib cleaned out the storage room across the hall for Yvonne. He ended up taking her to a room upstairs that afternoon, however, and we did not see her again. We sent her on her way with a Ken Follett suspense novel to help her pass the time.

That evening I was sitting in the hallway chatting with Maria-jan. One of the two Hazara prisoners had just gone into the bathroom. Suddenly, an incredibly loud explosion rocked the place, and the girl in the bathroom flung open the door. Her face froze in an expression of terror. "Was that a rocket?"

We lost electricity. The two Afghan prisoners went into the spare room and began to cry.

Diana knew right away that the United States had kicked off its bombing campaign. I was not sure. Considering what my father had said on the phone, I wondered if perhaps the Northern Alliance was attacking.

I went into the jailers' room and got underneath the bed. I hurriedly walled myself in with *toshaks,* pillows, and blankets. I had already removed the glass panes from the outside window and from two registration windows that opened onto the entranceway.

I knew that the weight of an explosion could shatter glass into thousands of minuscule slivers. I assumed that if an explosion caused any part of our building to collapse, I would be slightly more protected from debris if I was under the bed. At the very least, the covering provided an element of security. I tried to take all precautions—after all, there was now a war going on.

Meanwhile, I prayed aggressively, trying to keep my focus on God's ability to protect us.

Dayna: I stood at the door to the courtyard gazing at the fireworks show. The Afghan women inside were crying. Silke, Ursula, Kati, and I quietly watched the tracer bullets fly through the air. A red ball would traverse the sky and a red streak would follow it. The whole sky would light up red. The bombing did not seem terribly close, but the antiaircraft guns were loud.

I heard Heather praying in the jailers' room: "Thank you, Lord, for protecting us. Thank you, Lord, that you are in control."

Heather: I remained underneath the bed for some time. I was holding myself together, but with great effort. Lying under the bed was almost like being in a coffin. I would say to myself, "Okay, remember when you built forts as a little girl. You are in a fort."

The whole prison was pitch black. We had a few candles burning in the hall.

Suddenly I heard Diana's voice: "Oh my gosh, she has gone into labor! Maria-jan has gone into labor! There is bombing, no electricity, and we're in the middle of a blinking prison!"

I evaluated the desperate situation and I thought to myself, *I am much better use to everyone if I just stay under this bed. The best thing I can do is not lose it.*

The others assisted Maria-jan.

Dayna: Maria-jan was lying down in the hallway next to the bathroom. Her lower back was killing her. Diana was rubbing her back, trying to soothe her. We had given Maria-jan money for the doctor in the past for regular exams. She was having much difficulty with her pregnancy and was frequently in pain. This episode, however, was different from the others.

I was translating.

Diana said: "Ask her if her water has broken."

I asked her. "Is your water broken?"

"Yes," Maria-jan moaned.

"Ask her how much water has come out. Is it a lot or a little?"

"How much water has come out? A lot?" I asked her.

Quite a lot, Maria-jan indicated.

Diana was exasperated. "No, Lord," she prayed. "I can't deliver premature twins. I can't do this. Please don't let this happen!"

Diana said we would have to try to get Maria-jan some help or get her to a hospital. Diana knew premature twins would die if delivered here. Kati went and called for Najib. Minutes later, Najib and Sonan appeared.

When she saw the men, Maria-jan became defensive. She was embarrassed.

"Tell the boss there is no problem."

I said to Najib: "She has just broken her water. She is going to have a baby."

Maria-jan looked at me. "That is shameful to say." These men were not her relatives. For her to be exposed like this was taboo in her culture.

"But these are your children," I said, pleading with her. "You are in pain. You need to go to the hospital."

"I am fine," she said.

Najib and Sonan asked her directly, "Are you okay?"

"I will be fine," she answered.

Then Sonan commanded Maria-jan to stand up. "Get off the floor!"

She could barely move, but Maria-jan gathered her strength and stood for him at attention.

Heather: The others brought Maria-jan into the jailers' room and laid her out on the bed under which I was lying. We all prayed for her—that the labor pains would stop and that the children would survive. She seemed to calm down. The storm of pain had passed. Her water must not have broken. Perhaps the sound of the bombs jolted her into false labor, we thought. Eventually, the others left the room thanking God.

I stretched my hand up from underneath the bed and grasped Maria-jan's hand. We both cried as she recounted the memory of her children's death during a battle between Mujahideen factions.

"I was at work that day wondering if my children were safe. When I returned home, I saw that a rocket had hit my house. I found my two sons dismembered in my courtyard. Their innards were everywhere. Their eyes were gone. My boys were dead."

"Oh, Jesus," I prayed silently. "When will it be over? When will the people of this nation be able to live in peace, without fear, without war?"

My body was trembling. I wanted to be strong and encourage Maria-jan that we would get through the bombing.

"Would you like me to sing a song about God taking care of us?" I asked her.

"Yes, please," she replied.

I sang in English: "The Lord is my Shepherd. I shall not want. He makes me lie down in pastures of green. He leads me beside the still waters of peace, restoring my soul, restoring in my soul."

As I sang softly, the peace of God calmed my heart. I wondered if the song was helping Maria-jan cope as well. Within minutes, I could hear her snoring. The singing must have worked. She had fallen asleep.

Somewhere between nine and ten o'clock Afghani's deputy arrived with a couple of his men. We expected that someone from the foreign ministry might show up to give us information and to ask us how we were doing.

The deputy came to the door of the prison that night wearing a fatigue vest. In one breast pocket were extra cartridges for his Kalashnikov. In the other were extra rounds of ammunition. He carried a walkie-talkie in one hand and a phone in the other.

I went to the door. "Was that America or the Northern Alliance?"

His response was outrageous: "There is no war. No one is bombing. They are just practicing. Do not worry."

I almost laughed. "Those were bombs. Who is bombing?" I insisted. "Please get Afghani on the phone for me."

The deputy called Afghani and handed me the phone.

"Afghani, this is Heather. What happened?"

The Northern Alliance had attempted to bomb Kabul, he answered, but everything was under control. "You are safe," he said.

I was not reassured. He simply was telling me what he thought I wanted to hear. In fact, we would have preferred to hear that America had bombed the city, since we figured the United States would be aware of our location.

The next morning, one of our lady jailers, Roheena-jan, told us American planes had dropped the bombs not only in Kabul, but also in Jalalabad, Kandahar, and other cities.

Dayna: Once the bombing started, our women jailers stayed with us only from 9 A.M. to 4 P.M. They wanted to be at home at night. Bombing usually began at seven o'clock in the evening and occurred in rounds. The electricity would go out, and we would light candles in the hallway. Later, we ordered flashlights from the bazaar.

We pushed our evening worship meeting to a later hour to compensate for the loss of electricity. Silke wanted more time to read before the sun went down and we lost power. To light our room, we placed a candle on the window ledge. One night Najib came down and asked us to put the candle out. He was afraid the planes would see the light and bomb the building. We chuckled. With current technology, the planes would be able to spot the building candle or no candle. Nevertheless, to placate Najib, Silke usually set a book in between the candle and the window.

In the early days of bombing, Kati, Ursula, and I decided we would rather sleep in the hallway to get away from the picture window in our room. Silke and Diana stayed in the room. Their bunk bed was positioned in such a way that they believed glass shards would fly past them if the window blew. Heather began sleeping in the jailers' room under the bed.

At some point, sleeping arrangements shifted again, and I was the only one left in the hallway. Camping solo did not last long. One night a clattering sound woke me up: Mice were jumping around on the metal shelves near the entrance to our room. I could not bear the thought of mice crawling on me while I was asleep. The mice were the last straw. I went back to sleeping in the room.

At first I tied a *chawdur* to the bed to shield myself from flying glass. I slept on the bottom bunk and tied the *chawdur* on the metal bed frame between the top and bottom bunks. Then Diana suggested using a board from the storage room to make a wall at the head of the bed. We also cracked the window to release pressure so the glass would be less likely to shatter in the event of a close explosion. Finally, Diana ordered thick, clear tape from the bazaar and taped big asterisks over the window to prevent glass from shattering into the room. I stopped using the board at that point.

Since the women jailers were gone at night, we convinced Najib to allow us to lock ourselves in the building. He reluctantly conceded. We explained to him that being locked in from the outside while bombs were dropping would make us very nervous. We might need to get out of the building, we said.

One night several weeks into the bombing campaign, we were having our worship meeting in the hallway when we heard a rattling sound at the door. We knew someone had locked us in. We stopped singing. Everyone became very nervous. Heather went to check the door. As we suspected, it was locked. Then she went to the jailers' room and started calling into the courtyard, hoping Najib would hear from his office.

"Sir, sir—we need more water! We need more water from the pump!"

Heather went to the bathroom and emptied some of our containers so she could have them ready. We always needed water at night to flush the toilet.

A man came down to the door. Kati and Heather went to talk to him. "Let us talk to Najib. We do not want this door locked," they said. Najib came down and a discussion ensued.

Silke looked at me where we were sitting in the hallway. "Dayna, they need you to go and talk to him. He likes you." I got up.

Najib was explaining that he was afraid for our safety. He said something about some Kandahari Taliban possibly coming to the prison to harm us.

"Please," he said. "This is for your protection. I love you as my sisters. We need to do this."

I explained that many of us would be very nervous if he locked us in. "We will not open the door unless you come," I assured him. He gave in.

"Do not even open it to me," he said. "Do not open it to anybody."

After that incident, Heather and Diana wanted to damage the metal loop for the padlock.

"That would be destroying the place," Kati and I said. "It might get us in more trouble."

They came up with another idea and wrapped rope around the metal loop so there would be no room through which to slide a padlock.

At night in our room, we could hear men pacing the floor above us and talking on their radios about the bombing. Georg told us Najib had built a small trench out in the men's courtyard for protection.

One night a loud banging sound in our room woke us up. I froze. *Kandahari Taliban,* I thought. *They are coming to harm us.*

Moments later, we realized that a cat had gotten into our room and was hurling itself against the glass. The cat looked wild. I hid under the blankets. Brave Kati opened the window and let the cat outside.

Heather: Normally bombs would drop for twenty minutes, then stop for a couple of hours, then drop for twenty minutes, then stop, and so on throughout the night. Often we would hear a whistling sound and then an explosion. Sometimes we could hear aircraft overhead, then the whistling and then the explosion. We always heard gunfire.

One night we were having our worship meeting when a bomb struck so close that it blew the doors to the bathroom and spare room wide open. The explosion frazzled us. Dayna jumped into Silke's arms.

Sleeping through the bombing proved nearly impossible. Dayna and some of the others took sleeping pills. I tried the pills once, but they served no benefit. Every night I was so wide-eyed anticipating the next round of explosions that I could not fall asleep. All night long I would lie under the bed in the jailers' room and look at my watch. My stomach would tense up. My body would not relax. I passed the time by singing worship songs, praying, and thinking of my family. I always knew another round of bombing would come. If I could just make it to 5 A.M., when most of the raids ceased, I knew I would be able to sleep for a few hours. Once the day strikes started, I barely slept at all.

By the time we got to the second prison I had deteriorated emotionally. I was exhausted and did not know from moment to moment whether I would be able to keep going. I thought I would rather die than continue on in such pain. I tried to hold on, but the more I tried, the more desperate and abysmal my existence became. I faced a crucial decision: Either I could quit wrestling with God and trust him, or I could continue fighting against fear's unyielding grip on my life and in the end surely die from the anxiety and grief.

I feared that if I gave God the power to decide whether I lived or died, then he would take my life from me. I was not certain God wanted me to live as badly as I did. In the end, the exhaustion served me well. I was too tired to keep wrestling. Though I could not see the way ahead, I chose to surrender to God. I gave up. I threw myself into God's hands.

I wrote: "Lord, all I can do is throw myself in your hands and say have your way. I am utterly desperate and I can do nothing, so I put my life in your hands. By now I've gone numb. It's as though I can't take any more, so I just have to shut down. God, I trust you! Lord, you're my only hope. I resign now and ask for your grace to endure. . . . Oh God, I want to live, but my life is in your hands. If I live, I live for you. If I die, I die for you. In the end, you are in control and you have the last word."

My resignation released incredible freedom. The grip of fear began to loosen. I still struggled, but my spirits lifted and hope for my future returned. At times I even believed we might make it out alive. Even so, I ceased putting my hope in the end result of our crisis. My hope rested in the promise I had for eternity. Whether my natural life ended in prison or not, I knew I would live forever in heaven with Jesus. Though the Taliban could imprison my body, they could no longer imprison my spirit. I experienced freedom within, and I could go on.

While at this major spiritual crossroads, I remembered a dream that I had while traveling to Afghanistan for the first time in 1998. Though we were headed to Kabul during peacetime and my heart was filled with joyful anticipation, in the dream I was deeply afraid. God took me in an elevator to a point above the city of Kabul. I prayed fervently and God told me to look down. The city was being bombed. Then I saw myself walking through the city. God was directing me: Turn left, turn right. The route I traveled was confusing and unpredictable. Each time I took a step, the place where I had been standing got hit with a bomb. War broke out all around me; yet, at every point, I was one step out of harm's way. God was showing me exactly where to go.

When I remembered this dream, I recognized it as a foreshadowing of my prison experience. The recollection helped me overcome fear. I believed God was indicating that I would come out alive and unharmed. After some time I told the others about the dream. They were encouraged and jokingly said, "If anything happens, we will make sure we get behind you!"

We enjoyed some light moments in prison. One night I was reading with a candle in the hallway and writing letters. Everyone else was getting ready for bed. I had some bread beside me on a blanket, along with some cheese for a late-night snack. In the stillness I heard our portable heater slide slightly across the concrete floor.

What was that? I thought. No one else was in the hallway, and I knew the heater could not move on its own. I went to investigate, and when I looked back in the direction of my book, I saw my bread had disappeared.

"Diana, come out here!" I whispered loudly.

Diana came with her flashlight and directed the beam on a mouse carrying a long piece of bread in its mouth. The mouse scampered off and disappeared through a hole in the wall near the bathroom.

Neither of us liked mice and preferred to leave this one alone, but days earlier we had ordered a mousetrap from the bazaar. Diana and I decided to set the trap up. We placed it right underneath the hole near the bathroom wall.

In the meantime, Dayna got up to go to the bathroom. Diana and I laughed and warned her she might run into a mouse. The next thing we heard was a piercing scream.

"It's a mouse! It's a mouse!" Dayna cried.

She ran back into the room and jumped on Kati. Diana and I followed her. We feared Najib would come downstairs to see what all the commotion was about.

"I cannot believe you guys get mad at me," I exclaimed. "This is crazy. You are totally freaking out, and it's just a mouse!" We laughed. Within moments we heard the loud snap of the mousetrap.

seventeen

DAY SWEATS, NIGHT MOVES

Dayna: Atif returned on October 10 with more booty from our parents. In the shipment were five sets of winter Pakistani dresses, two blankets, sweaters, two pairs of black loafers for Diana and Ursula, shoes and a new outfit for Georg, lice shampoo, books, more coffee, peanut butter, several asthma inhalers, asthma medicine, and sleeping pills.

Once I arrived at the intelligence prison, my bout with asthma became an all-out war. Some combination of dust and stress likely aggravated the asthma, but for whatever reason, at the intelligence prison I constantly struggled to breathe. I began having to use my inhaler up to ten times a day. I would wake up at four in the morning gasping for breath. One afternoon the others graciously beat our carpets out in the courtyard and washed the floors to rid our room of dust.

Before Atif returned with the inhalers and medicine, which I had requested from my mother in Islamabad, I took a different medical tack in an effort to solve the asthma problem. One morning Diana woke up recalling the name of a drug that she recognized would treat asthma. We ordered the drug from the bazaar and discovered that she was right. The guard who delivered the drug was very careful to repeat the instructions on dosage until he was confident I understood them. He warned me not to take too much.

The drug did wonders for my quality of life. I took one of the pills in the morning and did not have to use my inhaler all day. On the first day, however, I got a bit carried away. I took the medicine—which is a stimulant—at breakfast, lunch, and dinner and became very wired. In the midst of my delirium, I made another bad decision. Early in the evening I took an Aleve to combat some achiness. Soon afterward my mouth went numb. I tried to sing during our evening worship meeting and slurred my words until I broke out laughing. I did not feel well for hours; the medicine kept me up all night. Fortunately, I had started reading *The Firm,* my first go at a novel in some time, which helped me pass the hours. I sat in the bathroom most of the night reading the book and expecting to vomit any minute.

Another of the pharmaceuticals I had begged my mother to send also came with Atif's shipment—wart medicine. I developed a wart back in the reform school prison, and the doctor at that prison told me stress had brought it on. I loathed the wart. Just as I began taking the medicine, I asked Silke to draw a picture of the wart for documentary purposes. At first she refused—the assignment was simply too ludicrous. But some minutes later she handed me a drawing: I was depicted decked out in my blue Pakistani dress with white embroidered trim—one of my four prison outfits—with my hair tied up in usual fashion. On my wildly oversized thumb, Silke had drawn an enormous wart. She dated the picture and wrote "Dayna's Prison Wart" across the top. I loved the picture and asked Najib if he wanted to see it. He reluctantly nodded and smiled.

One day after the medicine came, Roheena-jan, our jailer, approached me while I was out in the courtyard.

"To get rid of warts," she explained, "you must wait until there is a full moon. Then you must get a broom—a brand-new broom from the bazaar. You must stand in the moonlight and sweep the broom over the wart. Then the wart will fall off."

"Hmm," I said.

"You do not believe that kind of thing, do you?"

Heather: Atif submitted an English version of our defense to the court on October 13 and included a copy of Mullah Omar's decree stating that foreigners caught proselytizing were subject to three to ten days' detention and expulsion from the country. We were now at the seventy-one-day mark. The man scheduled to translate the English version of our defense into Dari was late showing up, and when Atif finally got the Dari copies it was already evening. Atif dropped one of the copies off at the chief justice's home.

That evening, Kabul experienced the heaviest bombing yet. Bombing lasted for hours at a time—there were few intervals of quiet.

I wrote: "Many bombs. Started approx. 7:10 p.m. Raids lasted up to 1 hr. [Two] bombs fell very, very near us. House shook for 5 sec. and front door [blew] open. [Two] other bombs dropped consecutively, also near us . . . Most terrifying so far. God covered us."

The next day, Atif resubmitted the Dari version of our defense to the court and met with the chief justice. The judge explained that he would take his time reviewing the case and possibly hold a session for inquiries before handing down a decision.

Atif came back from the court frustrated. He expected the judge would want to prioritize the case due to the escalating war. Instead, Atif noted a decline in enthusiasm for pushing the case forward. In a wartime atmosphere, the chief justice had other responsibilities and high-level meetings to attend.

Nevertheless, Atif maintained his optimism about our prospects with the Taliban court. "You are not going to be used as pawns in this war," he told us. "The war is a separate issue. The judge does not want to keep you here."

Atif considered the Taliban in a more exalted light than we did. It seemed to us that the Taliban were trying to buy as much time as possible with the court case in order to use us as bargaining chips in the war game with America.

Since the judge would be taking his time, Atif told us he would return to Pakistan until given further notice from the court. "The judge is supposed to call me," he explained. "I will be back as soon as I am contacted."

We pleaded with him, "Please do not go. We need you to push our case forward."

But Atif did not want to push the judge. He thought pressuring the judge would only backfire on us.

I became upset. Bismillah comforted me and assured me he would do whatever he could to help us. He promised to return within days. I appreciated Bismillah's heart. He truly did care for our safety. I believed he would have risked his own security in order to keep our case moving. Still, when the two men left our prison, we had no idea whether we would see them again.

"God truly [is] our only hope," I wrote in my journal.

In our group meetings we evaluated our circumstances and made the following determination: "We cannot put our hope in this lawyer. We cannot put our hope in this court case. We cannot put our hope in the diplomats. We cannot put our hope in parents. We cannot put our hope in the possibility that Mullah Omar might pardon us. There really is no other hope outside of the mercy and grace of God to perform a miracle on our behalf."

Psalm 118:9 became a key scripture for us: "It is better to take refuge in the Lord than to trust in princes" (NAS).

Dayna: Day strikes started on October 15. Georg warned us to stay inside even if the bombs were distant. People die every day from stray gunfire, he told us. Whenever planes flew overhead, all of Kabul erupted in shooting. An antiaircraft gun was positioned in our compound for a period of time, and other guns were fired from surrounding compounds. The Taliban frequently placed weapons in the men's courtyard of the intelligence prison for testing purposes. Georg said the Taliban kept their weapons in our compound because the men believed our presence guaranteed them protection from American bombs. Assuming the United States would be aware of our location and deliberately refrain from bombing it, delegations of Taliban would take shelter in our prison during the raids.

The day strikes further unnerved us—physically we were all affected. The bombs caused our bodies to shake; the explosions stunned us. Antiaircraft fire was loud and startling. Dealing with the bombs nightly took much energy. When the day strikes started, we lost our bearings to some degree.

In part, we lost the security of our daily routine, which kept us anchored. Once the day strikes started, we were forced to come in from the courtyard as soon as the planes flew overhead and shooting broke out. We could not wash clothes or dishes; we could not pump water for the toilet. We would leave our dishes outside and come in until things had quieted down. If I were having some private prayer time in the yard, I would have to cut it short.

Eventually I got used to the planes and the testing and would stay in the courtyard if the bombing and shooting were distant. Others did the same. Sometimes I lingered outside longer than was advisable. One day I saw an explosion across the city. A reddish billow of smoke ascended, and a fire started. Najib told us that a bomb had landed on an ICRC warehouse.

Meanwhile, we continued to pray fervently. We prayed no innocent lives would be taken. We prayed the Taliban would flee rather than go out fighting. We prayed for the strength and wisdom of President Bush. We prayed for Afghanistan's restoration according to Isaiah 61—

that now would be the time of God's favor. At one point we heard that other nations had pledged to give aid money to Afghanistan. We prayed the nations would not shrink back from rebuilding the country and that aid would be given to the poorest of the poor.

Heather: We tended to pray for whatever seemed most unlikely or impossible. We believed God could do the impossible. He could turn these devastating circumstances around for Afghanistan's good. Let the war be the thing that frees, not destroys, the Afghan people. Let there be dancing in streets instead of mourning. Prosper the land.

We prayed for our own situation. We prayed that men in authority would have mercy on us and let us go. To gain comfort, we often wrote songs based on Bible verses. Kati wrote a song after Psalm 86 titled "Hear and Answer Me." The words to the song uplifted us all. One line ran, "Guard my life and rescue me, for I am devoted to you."

Dayna wrote several of her own songs. One, titled "My Times Are in Your Hands," was based on Psalm 31. The lyrics resonated deeply with us: "This waiting seems unbearable, not knowing what's ahead. I'm feeling insecure, this world has nothing to hold on to. But Lord I trust in you."

Eventually, we began toying with an idea Yvonne once mentioned to us—making a CD of worship music. Dayna pressed the idea at first, and later Kati took charge and helped us organize a list of our top fifteen favorite songs. We also talked about making another CD of original songs. We wanted to use the proceeds to raise money to help rebuild Afghanistan and meet the needs of the poor. We also hoped the songs that had given us strength through our captivity would greatly encourage others. Who knew if the project would materialize—but we could dream. Dayna, after all, was from Nashville.

Dayna: I read scriptures on perseverance. "Blessed is the man who perseveres under trial, because when he has stood the test, he will receive the crown of life that God has promised to those who love him" (James 1:12, NIV).

This verse touched my heart. When I read it, I saw that the only requirement for receiving the crown of life was that I love God. If I could just come out of the prison experience loving and worshiping God, then I would be rewarded with a crown. God was only asking me to continue loving him.

I read Romans 5:3–5, and my heart awakened to the enormous privilege of our imprisonment. "[W]e also rejoice in our sufferings, because we know that suffering produces perseverance; [and] perseverance, character." I felt I was being tested as never before, but I had the opportunity to develop character.

Even as I reflected on the romantic relationship for which I still longed, I realized that if God had given me what I wanted—if he had allowed me to leave Afghanistan and date my friend—then I would have missed out on the honor of imprisonment. I actually became grateful that God had prevented the relationship from going forward. God wanted me to walk through this ordeal and come out on the other side with his best for my life—a deeper walk with him.

Heather: In several letters to friends and family, we wrote out a passage of scripture that seemed remarkably applicable and relevant to our situation. We hoped the passage would motivate the many people praying for our safe release and believed the power of prayer would alter the course of our circumstances, enabling us to make it out of the country alive.

The scripture, from 2 Corinthians 1:8–11, read: "For we do not want you to be unaware, brethren, of our affliction which came to us in Asia, that we were burdened excessively, beyond our strength, so that we despaired even of life; indeed we had the sentence of death within ourselves so that we should not trust in ourselves, but in God who raises the dead; who delivered us from so great a peril of death, and will deliver us, He on whom we have set our hope. And He will yet deliver us, you also joining in helping us through your prayers, so that thanks may be given by many persons on our behalf for the favor bestowed on us through the prayers of many" (NAS).

Dayna: On October 21, Atif returned just as he said he would. He and Bismillah came in carrying a box, a suitcase, and two big plastic bags. Among the toiletries and foodstuffs were gifts from NBC—two sets of long johns and a pair of hand warmers for each of us. Najib stood by inspecting the items as we took them out.

Eventually I came to an oddly shaped object discreetly wrapped in many layers of paper.

"What is that?" Najib asked.

"I do not know," I replied. He instructed me to unwrap the item in his presence.

When I peeled back the layers of tissue I saw a portable CD player with headphones. I was amazed. My mother and one of our pastors—also staying in Islamabad—sent the player for our enjoyment along with more than a dozen CDs of worship music.

"There's no way Najib is going to let us keep this," someone remarked.

I turned to Najib and tried to explain what I was holding: "This is music about God and his love. It gives us peace when we listen to it."

Bismillah tried to help me communicate. He and Najib knew each other from Pakistan.

While the two men were talking, I took out a CD, put it into the player, and pushed Play. I held out the headphones to Najib. "Do you want to listen?"

Najib took the headphones and tried to fit them over his turban, but he had difficulty. Without saying a word, Bismillah swept Najib's turban off his head. There was Najib, bareheaded, looking as if he had just gotten out of bed! Najib was shocked and embarrassed at first; then Bismillah assisted him with putting the headphones on properly. Najib listened awhile. He seemed to like the music.

"May we have permission to keep it?" I pleaded.

"Okay," he said. "But do not play it so loud. We do not want anyone upstairs to hear. It must be a secret. You must keep it hidden."

We told Najib we could only listen to the music on headphones and not to worry. Later we put together a schedule of three-hour shifts for the CD player. We posted our schedule on the wall next to our window.

Listening to music—other than what we could produce with our own voices—for the first time in months proved an almost breathtaking experience. The instruments made such a rich sound. I wept the first time I listened. I played Kent Henry's song "I Have Loved You," and felt as if God was pouring out his love on me. The music soothed and refreshed us.

"Is it your turn now?" Najib would ask. "When do I get a turn?"

Heather: After he brought the gifts, Atif left us to try to get in touch with the chief justice. Atif said he would return that afternoon. For some reason he never did.

At 6 P.M., Najib came in and announced we were moving to another prison. He said we would return to the intelligence prison perhaps in some days.

"What?" we exclaimed. "But we are supposed to meet with our lawyer!" We were shaken. The war was weakening the Taliban rapidly, and we expected a move might be in store. But we often prayed that we would not be moved again, fearing the Taliban might take us to Pul-e-Charki, where our sixteen Afghan friends had been transferred.

Najib conveyed that he would send Atif to the new prison—our third prison—the following morning. "Do not worry," Najib counseled. "Get ready. We will leave soon."

Frenetic packing ensued. Since no one knew if or when we would be returning to our hallway at the intelligence prison, we packed all of our things—as much as we possibly could—and took our bags with us.

Najib loaded us into his new van—actually, a stolen van that we learned had belonged to some of our friends. On the side of the vehicle was an aid organization logo, which Najib covered up with a big soccer ball sticker from the bazaar. He drove us through town to what looked like a government office building located next to the Turkish embassy and across the street from the UN compound. We pulled around back. In the yard was a beautiful rose garden.

To get to the entrance, we walked down a sidewalk that ran parallel to the building. From the sidewalk, we could see that the windows to the rooms on the lower level were barred. Most of the windows in the building were blown out. We walked up a small flight of stairs to a barred door leading to a corridor. On the hall were a kitchen, a bathroom, a storage room, and some miscellaneous meeting rooms.

Kati and Silke took a room by the kitchen. The rest of us put our things in a meeting room containing a few *toshaks* and a desk. The *toshaks* were thick and comfortable. One of the windows in our room was covered in plastic; the other window still had a glass pane. Cattycorner to our room was the bathroom. It was in foul condition. Feces caked the toilet. Dayna felt ill for a few hours after glimpsing the sight.

Farther down the hallway, another door led to a basement area where male prisoners were housed. Georg and Peter were taken through this door. We understood the men being kept in the prison were political prisoners and hardened criminals, some awaiting death sentences. In such company, Peter did not like walking to the bathroom late at night while the electricity was cut off for the bombing raids.

We felt vulnerable at this prison—what became our night prison. Our guard was a man, which made all of us uncomfortable. Our room door was without a lock. On our first night, the guard tried to open the door without knocking. I was standing at the door and prevented him from coming in.

"You must knock," I said disapprovingly. He was coming to tell us to put out our candles. The authorities were very nervous that this area of town would be bombed.

Kabul was bombed heavily that night, and Ursula agreed to sit out in the hallway with me. I wanted to get away from the glass in our room. There were a couple of couches in the hallway. Our guard was sleeping on one of them. I got underneath the empty couch; Ursula sat on top.

From his couch the guard struck up a conversation with us—two women—in the pitch-black night.

He asked, "Are you scared? Why are you under the couch? Are your feet cold? Should I get you a blanket?" In Afghan culture the whole exchange was improper, not to mention that the man had asked about my feet. His questions made me extremely uncomfortable.

"No, I am fine," I replied. I was freezing. The floor was ice cold.

Then the man shined his flashlight on us. "I do not like this," I told Ursula. We got up and went back to the room. Though I did not want to be in an open room with glass windows during a bombing raid, at that point I preferred such environs over having to endure this man's inappropriate comments.

After that night, we moved a couch into our room from the hallway and set the couch on cushions so I would have enough room underneath to sleep comfortably. We stacked the cushions neatly on top of the couch when we left the room in the mornings to return to the intelligence prison, which remained our day prison.

One night late in our detainment I was reading the Benazir Bhutto biography with my flashlight while lying underneath the couch. Everyone else had gone to sleep. I wept as I read Bhutto's own story of incarceration—as a young woman she spent six years on and off in prison. I could not imagine six months in prison, let alone six years. I tried to stay awake reading the gripping account, but at ten o'clock I became tired and switched off the light.

During our worship meeting that evening, I had taken prescription medication to rid my body of parasites. After almost eight months in Afghanistan, three of them in prison, I decided it would be wise to clean out my system, and I was halfway through the six-pill treatment. When I swallowed this particular evening's dosage, the pill seemed to become lodged in my throat. I assumed the medicine would dissolve by morning.

Once I turned off my flashlight and prepared to go to sleep, I noticed that the pill had not moved. I swallowed hard several times to clear my throat, with no result. Moments later, I felt a piece of string resting on my tongue.

How did I get fuzz in my mouth? I wondered. *Did it come from the carpet?* I pulled out the string, set it on the floor, and turned my flashlight on it.

"Diana! Wake up! Wake Up!" I screamed. "A worm just crawled out of my mouth! A worm!" I froze, not knowing what to do. Diana came over in a daze and looked at the ten-inch worm moving on the floor. It was still alive!

Diana was aghast. "I have only heard of worms crawling out of people's mouths," she remarked with unbelief. "I have never actually seen it happen." She promptly put the worm in a water bottle for safekeeping.

Immediately, I began to feel movement from one side of my throat to the other. More worms were trying to escape. I had to do something. Diana obligingly ran with me down the hall to the male prison warden's room. I knew the visit was culturally inappropriate, but this was an emergency.

"*Saeb,* sir," I called, knocking on the door. "I am sick. Could you please get me some bread?" My strategy was to eat as much food as possible and push the worms back down my esophagus.

The guard invited me into his room. "No, sir, I am sick," I repeated. "I need some food." Finally, he brought out some cake and tea from the kitchen. I ate as much as I could, and the plan worked. No more worms crawled out of my mouth. The next morning, Dayna showed the bottled worm to Najib and several Taliban guards.

Later, after our rescue, I asked a doctor whether the worms had crawled up my throat to escape the toxic worm medicine I was taking.

"No, not exactly," he explained. "You probably had such a bad infestation, the worm had nowhere else to go."

Dayna: Our first morning in the office building I went out into the hallway to spend time alone with God.

"You cannot stay here," the guard said firmly. "This is a business floor. Men will be coming in and out."

"Well, it's going to be hard for us to stay in this room all day," I replied.

"You can come out after eleven o'clock when business ceases."

I hoped we would not have to oblige the Taliban in this manner every day.

Since we had no idea how long we would be staying at the office prison—we did not yet know it would become our night prison—Diana went ahead that first morning and made our shopping list for the bazaar. One of the high-priority items was a toilet brush. We gave the list to the guard. When he returned with our purchases, we discovered that the batteries we had ordered for our flashlights weren't working, so we sent the poor fellow back to the bazaar to fetch us some more.

In the meantime, we prepared to make renovations on the place. Silke was first on the chore list to have bathroom duty. She courageously entered the bathroom armed with our new toilet brush and some bleach and went to work.

In these first days staying at the night prison, we complained to Najib about the guard sleeping in the hallway. We were offended at having to sleep in such close proximity to a man and share a bathroom with him. The arrangement totally violated the mores of Afghan culture. We were accustomed to women jailers, but in this prison we could hear the guard clearing his throat at night. We would have to pass by him going back and forth to the bathroom.

We also went without a lock for a couple of nights and tried to block our door with heavy bags. Georg arranged for the prison overseer to get us a key. After that, we were able to lock the door from the inside.

On one occasion a high-level intelligence official and his sidekick visited us in our room carrying a video camera. Already dressed for bed, we were astounded that the man wanted to film us. I stood talking to the men at the door, trying to be polite in the face of an enormous cultural breach; but the others were saying, "Tell him to leave!" and "What does he want with us?" The man did not understand English, so I explained that we were tired and wanted to go to bed. One of the guards explained that this was a man of high office. I tried to show the official respect but told him we did not want to be filmed. Finally, we got him to leave.

Georg complained intensely to Najib the following morning. Najib protected the man with a ludicrous excuse. "That was not a video camera," he insisted. "Those were binoculars." We stood our ground and argued that the man in fact did have a video camera. Najib would not budge.

Heather: Najib and Sonan came to the office building that first morning and announced that they were taking us back to the intelligence prison to meet with Atif for a couple of hours. We left our things in the room and got in the van.

Atif did not show up at the intelligence prison until 2:30. He was very upset. Apparently, the chief justice was busy with other priorities. Atif had gone to the court building, even to the judge's home, trying to make himself available to answer any questions the judge might have about our case. Everyone told Atif that, yes, the chief justice was in town, but no one seemed to be able to schedule a meeting for our lawyer.

Further, Sonan had exchanged heated words with Atif, who promptly complained to the court about having difficulty accessing his clients. When Atif returned to Sonan with a note from the court granting permission for our meeting, Sonan allowed Atif only ten minutes.

"They are treating me like a prisoner," Atif exclaimed. "I am not a prisoner, and I will not accept this treatment."

He told us he would try once again to see the judge. If the judge would not see him, then he would leave the next day for Pakistan.

"This case is a mess," Atif said. "I do not know how long it will take to get things resolved."

Though disheartened, I was not surprised by the obstacles Atif faced. Once again it became clear that our only source of hope was God.

Before Atif left, he asked us to go ahead and give him our letters for his return trip to Pakistan. We handed him quite a large stack. Among other things, the letters contained directions to our new prison. We were anxious that the U.S. military learn where we were being kept. I tucked a little map inside one letter just so my parents would be clear.

Najib noticed our exchange with Atif and took the letters. "These will have to be translated and approved," he remarked. This was unexpected. Najib had never checked our letters before. In fact, that day he had come into our room encouraging us to write letters in our usual fashion for the lawyer's trip home. I thought of the map and informed Bismillah that he needed to try to retrieve it from the stack of letters.

That night Najib kept us at the intelligence prison. All of our things were back at the office prison, making the evening less than comfortable. I wrote Atif and Bismillah a letter:

> *Without your correspondence and time to talk we live in a vacuum [without] anyone to communicate with. We are left knowing nothing about our case or the events surrounding us that so terribly affect us. As for you, just one day of such madness is a nightmare, imagine please how for us week after week of such uncertainty and frustration must be.*

The next morning, Atif and Bismillah came to the prison with a satellite phone. We had been granted permission to call our families, Atif said. He was not able to make contact with the judge, however, and wanted to leave town soon so he could cross the border before the blackout and the bombing began.

Dayna and I called our parents in Pakistan. We also attempted to call our pastor back in Waco, and Dayna tried to call her father in Nashville. But we could not get through to America.

"We will have to try something else," I told my parents, referring to the court case. "This will not work." They caught my drift and reassured me that they were doing all they could to secure our release.

"Things are being done on your behalf," my father said. "This should all be over very shortly. You do not have to worry."

"I believe you," I said. "You know more than I do."

As the eight of us were making phone calls, an Afghan prisoner was working to finish translating our letters. He had been translating for Najib and Sonan into the evening on the previous day. We later learned that this translator had gone to heroic lengths to help us. Georg told us the man intentionally skipped portions in our letters that referred to the office prison's location; he skipped over complaints about our conditions and our case; he covered for portions describing the beatings being doled out to Afghan men. He translated the English and the German letters despite the fact that he did not speak German. What kind of commentary did he come up with to substitute for the pages and pages of German text? We all knew the cruelty Sonan was capable of inflicting. This translator had risked his life for us. We were awed.

By the time all of us finished with the phone, it was after two o'clock. Atif was anxious to leave. Najib handed Atif our pile of letters. Atif and Bismillah said goodbye and departed.

We never saw the two men again.

Shortly after Atif and Bismillah left the compound, Najib and Sonan showed up at our door with Georg and Peter. I was resting in the jailers' room when I heard the men's voices. The men were talking about our letters. I knew immediately what was wrong. My map describing our location never made it out of the compound with the lawyer.

Sonan called a meeting in our room. Georg, Diana, and I were the last to enter. I whispered to Georg: "That's my letter they are holding."

"Whatever you do, do not tell them you wrote it," Georg urged.

"We found this letter," Sonan said once we all were seated. "There is an address clearly telling the location of the other prison." He and Najib looked at Dayna and me.

"Which one of you wrote it?"

There was no way to get out of it. All the men had to do was ask each of us for a writing sample. "I wrote it," I confessed.

"You did a very bad thing," Najib said sternly. "It makes things very dangerous for you and very dangerous for us. Why did you do it?"

"My parents are very concerned about me with the bombs dropping," I explained. "I wanted to tell my parents where we were so they would not be afraid, so someone would know not to bomb our location."

I repented over and over. "I am so sorry if I have done something wrong. I will not do it again."

Georg interjected, enumerating all of the things SNI had done to help the Afghan people through relief and development. No one was trying to be deceptive, he insisted.

To our great relief the apology and explanation seemed to diffuse the men's anger, and they let us go.

Dayna: Once Atif and Bismillah left the country, we spent our days at the intelligence prison and random nights at the office prison. Najib would give us very little notice to get ready on the evenings we were being moved. We tried to salvage some routine and kept up with our worship meetings.

I enjoyed riding in the van to some extent: The Kabul bazaar areas were up and running; men were out riding their bicycles. You might never know the country was engaged in a war. Still, all of the shifting and moving between prisons exhausted us. Some grew concerned that passersby could see us through the van windows.

We caught wind of a rumor that our case had been passed to Mullah Omar for a ruling. Perhaps we might be pardoned. Someone told Georg that the chief justice was going to issue a decision. We heard another rumor that Atif was coming back to town. At any time, Kabul could fall and the Taliban flee. We needed to be prepared.

We began to think about contingency plans for our departure. At one point, we talked of going with Najib and his brother to their village should the Taliban retreat. Another prisoner whom Georg knew talked of letting us stay at a house in the city. Many ideas were discussed.

We talked about modes of exit—would we drive, would we fly? Driving, we figured, would prove extraordinarily dangerous. Silke believed strongly that we would be flown out. We talked about a helicopter rescue, but that scenario seemed too risky. We did not want any of the Afghan guards to be killed in a rescue attempt; nor could we imagine climbing up a rope into a helicopter—in such a position we would be open targets for marksmen. We women cast our lots for a rescue by handsome men.

However we left the country, we knew we would have to go out as inconspicuously as possible. At the end of October, we asked Najib to buy burqas for us, the women. He made a trip to the bazaar, then came to our room and helped us try on the burqas. He checked to see whether the length was right, whether they fit our heads properly. My burqa was too short, he concluded and offered to take them back to the bazaar to get me something longer.

The others wore their burqas once while we were riding in the van en route to our night prison. I was still waiting on Najib to buy me one that fit properly. Soon afterward Najib decided he wanted to hold on to the burqas for us. He seemed nervous that we might be planning an escape. "When you need them, I will give them to you," he said. That was the last we saw of the burqas.

One evening I wrote a joke song called "We Wanna Go Home." The song fit our mood and perfectly echoed our sentiments. We were tired of living in prison. We wanted out. I taught the song to the other women, and they immediately caught on. We got rowdy as we sang.

> *We wanna go home. We wanna go home;*
> *Lord, we're tired of this place, and we wanna go home.*
> *Lord, we thank you for all that you've done for us,*
> *For all of your faithfulness and love.*
> *Yes, we've enjoyed your presence and your companionship:*
> *But we wanna go home. We wanna go home.*

One of the lines, in tribute to Diana, went: "Lord, you've taken good, good care of us, and we don't mean to complain. But now we're ready to leave this blinking place. Yes, we wanna go home. We wanna go home."

Ursula always wanted to sing the song. For a while, we sang it every day. We sang it so obnoxiously loudly one night at the intelligence prison that when we heard a knock on the door we thought we had upset Najib and the men upstairs. We immediately quieted down.

To our surprise, a guard was bringing in an Afghan prisoner. When she took off her burqa we recognized her. Her name was Sila. We knew Sila from the reform school prison. We were not clear about her crime. The Taliban suspected Sila of working for the Northern Alliance, but she seemed less than lucid. Sila reported that most of the women at the reform school had been released. She told us that on the day we left the prison the women cried for hours.

My thirtieth birthday fell on November 4. My mother had told me during our last satellite phone call that my father's extended family was planning a big birthday party for me; they intended to raise money to buy blankets for the Afghan people. Our party was a less ambitious affair, but for us, we were living large. Heather suggested scrambled eggs for breakfast. We ordered ingredients for Ursula to make her special pasta and tomato cream sauce. Diana knew a recipe for no-bake black forest cheesecake. She figured we could cut our water bottles in half lengthwise for the cake tins. Heather spent some hours pitting canned cherries for a garnish.

The birthday consisted of breakfast and a morning worship time with the ladies; lunch and prayer with the men; and tea and cake with Sila, Sweeta-jan, and her eleven-year-old son. Silke made me a card depicting some of our little delights—playing cards, the heating coil, a teapot, a mouse, a burqa. She situated pictures of me in different exercise positions—doing my leg lifts, sit-ups, and push-ups—between the words "Happy Birthday" and "Dayna." The muscles in my legs appeared to be quavering during the exercises.

During our morning worship time, my friends prayed for me and spoke words of encouragement over my life. Kati, Silke, and Heather sang me a song they had written just for me. As we all sang one particular worship song, "Jesus, All for Jesus," I began to cry. Tears streamed down my face when I got to the line "All of my ambitions, hopes and plans, I surrender these into your hands." I sang the line with true feeling. I had no idea what was ahead for me. My plans to serve in Afghanistan for the next few years were now destroyed. I was turning thirty. I prayed God soon would answer the hope in my heart for companionship, but I was surrendering that hope to him. My life was in his hands.

In the evening, Heather organized game night. We played Two Truths and a Lie and a handmade version of Twenty-Five Words or Less. We laughed for hours. Everyone loosened up. Heather and the other women truly enjoyed one another.

All of us sensed we would be leaving soon. A few days after my birthday while I was writing in my jounal, I thought God told me, "You will be leaving *very* soon." Then I thought I heard him say we would get out before Thanksgiving. I did not know whether God truly was speaking to my heart, but I felt he wanted me to share these words with the group during our worship meeting. Diana confirmed that she was hearing something similar from God.

I read in Psalm 50: "He who sacrifices thank offerings honors me, and prepares the way of salvation." Inspired by this passage, we believed we were supposed to spend an entire worship meeting singing songs of thanksgiving, believing that God would prepare a way of salvation or escape for us as we did. We sang every "thank you" song we could remember. We wanted to go out of prison singing. "We'll go out singing your praises" was a line in a song I wrote.

Days later, we learned that the Northern Alliance had taken Mazar-e-Sharif.

"This may be the way we're going to get out," we said soberly.

The images given by the radio announcer were fantastical. Men on horseback entered Mazar-e-Sharif while Taliban fled in their trucks and tanks. We imagined that the Northern Alliance eventually would overtake Kabul and let us go free—we dreamed of dancing in the streets of Kabul with all of the freed citizens. But we were concerned that if the Northern Alliance came in, fighting might break out in the middle of the city. That scenario would be very dangerous—both for us and for the people of Kabul.

"Lord, let the Taliban flee without a fight," we prayed. "Let them flee without a fight."

part four

AAAZAAD!

eighteen

KABUL GEREFT

[T]here was lots of gunfire and shooting, several bombs dropped
very close by. One dropped and plastic in window almost exploded.
Very loud, building shook. Heard, beginning around 9:00, many men
in the hall, opening and closing . . .
—HEATHER'S LAST KABUL JOURNAL ENTRY,
   NOVEMBER 12, 2002

Heather & Dayna: In the days following the Northern Alliance's
capture of Mazar-e-Sharif, the demeanor of the Taliban running the
intelligence prison changed. Najib and the Taliban guards seemed distracted. Najib spoke curtly. He no longer asked us how we were or
what we were doing. He gave us less information about the war.

Georg brought us news from the radio. We heard reports that the
United States and Pakistan were urging the Northern Alliance not to
take Kabul. Many of us believed the troops would take Kabul anyway.
"They are not going to miss an opportunity to take the capital city," we
said.

On November 12, we learned that a video had been broadcast in which Osama bin Laden was said to have expressed foreknowledge of the September 11 attacks.

The same afternoon, Najib told us we would be spending the evening at the office prison. We had just stayed at the office prison the previous night. Though Najib did not move us according to a set schedule, we usually did not stay at the office prison on consecutive nights.

"We will be ready after dinner," we told Najib.

We sat down to an early dinner, anticipating our move. Ursula spent the day tending to a large pot of cauliflower vegetable soup; it was nearly five o'clock when she served us. Normally at mealtime, we would send portions of whatever we were having to Georg and Peter via a prison guard. On this evening, as we had only one pot for the soup, we decided to finish our meal and then send the entire pot over to the men.

Halfway through dinner, Najib entered the room. "You must leave immediately," he demanded.

We spoke in English among ourselves: "We are not going to let them push us around and make us rush. We will eat our meal in peace."

We told Najib we were not ready. "We are going to finish our food."

"You have to leave now," he insisted. "Take the food with you. The men can eat at the other prison."

Najib's tone was harsh and urgent. Fear flashed over his face. Realizing we had no other option, we consented.

Heather: We packed up the pot. I did not want to leave the dishes on the floor for the mice to pillage, so I picked up the metal bowls and spoons and set them outside by the water pump. I went back for the glasses.

Najib came in. "No," he snapped. "Leave it."

I folded the *destarkhaan* over the tops of the glasses and left everything in the middle of the floor.

Heather & Dayna: In those days we never knew when Najib would come and move us to the night prison. We kept a suitcase packed and ready at all times. The two of us shared a suitcase. That evening, we grabbed more things than usual—toiletries, coffee, cheese. We did not know whether we were leaving for good.

When we got to the van, Georg and Peter were there waiting. For the last couple of weeks on these trips, we women usually waited on the men. The routine went like this: We would go to the van. We would refuse, in accordance with Georg's instructions, to get into the van until Georg and Peter arrived. We did not want to give the Taliban a chance to drive off with us. Georg would always come some minutes later. Najib then would blame the delay on Peter, claiming he moved slowly. When Peter finally arrived, Najib would say to him, "You are old." Peter would agree. *"Bale, Peer astum."* Yes, I am old. This evening was different.

We got to the van, handed the men the pot of hot soup, and climbed in. As the van pulled into the office-building compound, Kati noticed that the bright spotlight at the entrance had been turned off.

We took the stairs to our hallway. Men congregated there; one, a prisoner and contact of Georg's, walked with a limp. Later we learned that the man had been trying to plot a dramatic escape from the prison for that evening in the event the Northern Alliance overtook Kabul. Georg told him quite plainly that we did not want anything to do with grisly schemes.

We entered our room. It was just before six o'clock. The atmosphere seemed tense. We could hear men moving around in the hallway. Then the bombing started. Explosions rocked the building. Gunfire erupted. One bomb dropped so close to the compound, the plastic over one of our windows blew up like a balloon. We wondered if the Northern Alliance was already in Kabul.

Heather: Due to the heavy bombing, I requested to go downstairs with Peter and Georg. The others insisted that they did not want to go.

"I will go to the basement by myself," I explained. Staying temporarily in the basement with Georg and Peter appealed more to me than sitting in an open room during the middle of a heavy raid and possible invasion by Northern Alliance troops. I called to one of the guards and requested he send for Georg.

Georg came up to the room. "If the bombing continues to get worse, I will request permission to have you brought down," he assured me.

Dayna: Georg told us that a guard he had befriended would come and take us underground if the bombing became any heavier. Spending the night in a dungeon with male criminals seemed a less-than-palatable arrangement, but we finally agreed it would be safer than staying above ground.

Heather & Dayna: Not much time had passed before Georg again came to our door. He came under the pretense of wanting to borrow medicine, but in fact he brought important news: Northern Alliance forces were ten kilometers outside of the city.

"Do not open the door unless you hear my voice," he firmly instructed.

At nine o'clock Kati and Silke went back to their room across the hall. We decided to lie down and try to sleep. "When we wake up, this city may not be in Taliban hands anymore," someone remarked.

Soon afterward a vehicle pulled up to the building. We began to hear movement in the hallway. By 9:30, the hall was abuzz with the activity of men. Pounding broke out on our door. "Come on. You must leave," we heard.

We went to the door and heard the voice of one of our guards, a youthful, almost tender-looking man who had treated us kindly during our nights at the office prison. He spoke through the door. We thought he was leaving and trying to tell us goodbye. Then we realized: "He is telling us that *we* have to leave."

The banging on the door grew more forceful. The men demanded we come out.

"We are not opening that door unless we hear our boss's voice," insisted Diana.

Finally we heard Georg: "Ladies, you must collect your things. These men have Kalashnikovs. They are nervous and upset."

We pulled on our clothes, gathered our belongings, and opened the door to Georg.

A group of armed men dressed for war, some with their faces wrapped in turbans, moved anxiously up and down the corridor. We recognized two of the men. One, the leader, was the large man from the intelligence ministry who came to our door with a video camera perhaps a week prior. Next to him stood the youthful guard who had treated us with favor. Najib was nowhere around.

"They are taking us back to the other prison," Georg said.

Heather: "That's a lie," I said to Georg. "They are telling us a lie. Najib would be here if we were returning to the other prison."

"Heather, we cannot do anything about it. We have to go with them."

"We will go," I said, "but I know we're not going back to that prison."

I was carrying my suitcase, pillow, and a burlap bag. A soldier turned to me: "Leave your things. You do not need them. You will be back in the morning."

"I have everything I own in this suitcase, and I am not leaving it behind." I knew we would not be returning in the morning.

He smiled. "Okay. For you, we can take your things." Everyone left carrying a small bag.

Heather & Dayna: As the men led us down the hall, some commotion broke out around Kati and Silke's room. The women were not opening the door. They said they could not hear Georg's voice. Once they heard him, they grabbed what they could and followed our column outside.

The men put us into what looked like an enormous sport utility vehicle. In the back, bench seats on either side of the truck bed faced inward. Diana was one of the first to climb in.

"What am I stepping on?" she asked.

"Rocket launchers," a Talib answered. The excitement never seemed to end.

We crammed into the truck. The quarters were tight and uncomfortable. On one bench, Diana, Silke, Kati, and Peter sat atop several rocket launchers. We sat with Ursula and Georg on an empty seat. More weaponry lay on the floor under our feet. Our bags were piled on top of us. From floor to ceiling the truck was packed; the atmosphere was suffocating.

Dayna: I was sitting on the end of the bench seat, and just before we drove off, a Talib got in beside me. He kept his Kalashnikov between his legs. There was little room even to twitch. The Talib and I sat cheek-to-cheek.

He asked me questions: "Where are you from? Are you from America?"

Heather and Diana urged me not to answer the man.

"What do I do?" I asked Georg.

Georg spoke firmly to the Talib: "Do not talk to the lady."

Heather & Dayna: We drove through the city while bombs continued to fall. As expected, we passed right by the intelligence prison.

"You have betrayed us!" Georg exclaimed in Pashtu. "You have lied to us. You told us you were taking us back to the prison. We are supposed to be your guests. You are treating us terribly."

Georg spent several minutes trying to get them to disclose where they were taking us. They laughed as if to mock us. We asked Georg to translate.

"Georg, is this the road to Kandahar?"

"I do not know yet," he replied. Kandahar, the Taliban seat of power, would be a very dangerous place for us to go.

It was difficult to breathe in the vehicle. We cracked the window and let in some cold air; then we closed the window against the cold. So went the ride: open the window, then close.

Dayna: Just beyond the city limits, we stopped on the side of the road so our driver could consult with some other men. We did not know whether men were being added to our caravan. Perhaps the men were discussing where they would take us.

I turned to the Talib next to me. "Where are we going?"

"Wardak." Wardak was the home village of several Taliban from the reform school prison. Mariam's family lived in Wardak.

Wardak was on the road to Kandahar.

The caravan started up again. Along the road, tanks and Taliban trucks fled the city. No bombs were dropping. A quarter of an hour down the road, the driver called something out to the guard crunched up next to me.

"*Kabul gereft. Kabul gereft,*" the driver said. Kabul has been taken.

Wow, I thought. *We missed it. We missed the Northern Alliance. We really missed our chance to go free in Kabul.*

"We missed it by thirty minutes," Georg said.

For some time, I had dared to hope our release would happen soon, that we would be home by Thanksgiving. I believed God had spoken to me. Now we were in the hands of men we did not know, men who were not interested in our safety, men who, in fact, had just been overthrown. We were hostages.

"Lord, mobilize more prayer for us," Diana cried out. "Wake up people to pray!"

It was a low moment.

Heather began singing, "There is a light in the darkness and his name is Jesus." Then she asked for a Bible. I gave her mine. She pulled out her flashlight and began to read to us. She spoke with strength. She took the lead. She who had been afraid now confidently comforted us in our distress.

Heather: I began to read our favorite passages of scripture aloud. We had woven many of the verses together into songs. I would read a passage. Then we would sing the accompanying song.

I read Psalm 121, and we sang, "The Lord Will Keep Me from All Harm," a song Dayna wrote.

Another of Dayna's songs, "Wait for the Lord, Be Strong and Take Heart," accompanied Psalm 27.

I read Psalm 55 and we sang a song of Kati's: "He Ransoms Me Unharmed."

Then Psalm 126 and Kati's "We Were Like People Who Dreamed." This song spoke of captives who returned to their homeland singing and dancing with joy over their dream come true. One line went, "Then it was said among the nations, 'The Lord has done great things for them.'"

We sang Kati's song from Psalm 86, "Hear and Answer Me," and Dayna's song from Psalm 31, "My Times Are in Your Hands." We sang the song Dayna and I wrote the day after our arrest, "Fear Not," from Isaiah 43.

We sang many of the songs we had written and some we had not written. Just as we had hoped, we went out of prison singing.

The driver turned on the radio to try to drown us out. We blasted the poor Talib soldier next to Dayna.

"These songs were written for this night," Diana said. "They were written for right now." We all started to laugh. In what should have been our most terrifying moment, we relaxed. I relaxed. We worshiped Jesus. The situation had gotten so beyond our control that we could not worry over it any longer. There were no props to lean on. Only Jesus would be our way of escape.

"God, what miracle are you going to perform to get us out of this one?" we said.

Heather & Dayna: Two hours later our caravan stopped again, this time for gas near Wardak, but we did not stop long. We got back on the road and drove farther south. At two o'clock in the morning, we pulled off the main road onto a small dirt road. We drove up a hill, passing some metal shipping containers, and eventually reached the front gate of a compound. The metal gate was green with decorative blue and yellow ironwork at the top. We assumed we were in front of a house.

"I guess we are going in there for the night," someone said. But the caravan of vehicles kept moving past the compound. We pulled up alongside a shipping container and stopped.

The heavyset intelligence official who had tried to video us back at the office prison came alongside the passenger's side of our vehicle. The youthful guard we knew accompanied him. We also noticed that Georg's prisoner contact, who walked with a limp, had come along as part of the caravan. The men engaged Georg. We understood that the men were talking about money. Could we get a large sum from our governments or families? We thought the men said that if we could come up with ransom money they would release us.

We had talked as a group about the money option before—would we give money if the Taliban wanted it? Some answered with a firm no.

Dayna: I did not feel right about money being given for our handover. The thought gave me a sick feeling. That way out would only encourage the whole hostage-ransom cycle. I did not want to be a part of perpetuating such activity. I wanted God to be glorified in our means of escape. I wanted it to be clear to the world that God got us out of Afghanistan through prayer, not through financial negotiations.

Heather: I admired the others' faith, but I did not mind pursuing the money route if that was the only option at hand. Time was of the essence. The situation on the ground in Afghanistan was deteriorating by the minute, and we had heard of no other surefire means to get away from our captors. We at least wanted to call our parents and diplomats and find out what would be best to do.

I asked the youthful guard from the night prison, "Is this why you have taken us—for money? Is this what you want?"

"Yes," he remarked casually. "You will be fine. They just want money. *Bandikhaana khalaas shud.*" Jail is finished.

Heather & Dayna: Georg complained that none of our governments knew of our whereabouts.

"We will take you to a satellite phone tomorrow so you can call them," the intelligence official said. "We will prepare a comfortable room for you for tonight."

Meanwhile, someone opened the back of our vehicle. The air was bitterly cold. The temperature had dropped well below freezing. We women were dressed in our long johns and dresses. We wore thin socks and plastic slip-on sandals. None of us had coats. Most of us were without blankets.

We got out of the truck. About two dozen armed Taliban in heavy camouflage jackets milled around the area.

One said, "You're sleeping in there." He gestured toward the shipping container.

We gasped. The container was about twelve feet deep, big enough to hold two large vans. Inside were a few dirty *toshaks* and a couple of blankets.

Georg argued with the men. "I cannot believe you would keep us in such conditions," he said, exasperated. "You are putting men and women together in the same place. This is absolutely unacceptable!"

"Do not worry," quipped the youthful guard from the night prison. "Tomorrow we will put you in a luxurious place. This is only for tonight." He smirked.

By this time the youthful, tender guard had metamorphosed into a warrior. He wore a thick camouflage jacket and an enormous turban. Rounds of ammunition encircled his torso. A scarf covered all of his face but his eyes. His manner was at once mellow and edged, casual and shrewd. He was no longer our friend. He was ready for war.

Dayna: Georg continued to argue with the men. Peter stayed with him. Heather refused to go inside the container out of concern that the Taliban would lock us inside. The rest of us were exhausted. We resigned ourselves to the arrangements.

"How can I help?" I said to the others. They were organizing the *toshaks* and blankets and determining who would sleep where. We all had our sheets with us, which helped for cleanliness. I felt very distressed but tried to make the best of the situation.

Kati and I went around behind the container, looking for someplace to use the bathroom. Armed men lurked everywhere. Kati and I stood in front of each other and held up our *chawdurs* as curtains. None of the men bothered us.

Back in the container, we huddled together for warmth. I balled into a fetal position, covered my head with my blanket, and tried to warm myself with my breath. It was no use. The night was miserable.

Heather: Several Taliban urged me to go into the shipping container with the other women.

"No," I told them. "I am fine out here." I was standing near the vehicle. Men hovered around me. I watched my back. I wondered if they would attempt to shoot me for refusing to go into the container.

"Look, all of your friends are in there," one Talib coaxed. "They are all warm and have blankets. You should be in there with your friends. You will be happy. Out here you will be cold."

"I am sorry. I am happy standing right here. I am not going in that container." I could not imagine going into the container. If I went inside, the men could close the doors and lock us in. They could blow up the container, which we understood was a common practice during the war between the Mujahideen. It was not safe for all of us to go inside the container. I was not going to be locked in anywhere.

"Heather, they are not playing games," Georg said firmly. "They mean business. They are angry. You need to come in here."

He tried to explain to the men that I believed they would attempt to lock the door if I went inside. But as he talked, the circle of men gradually closed in around me. In a minute or two I was standing at the door of the container. I did not want to get shot. I looked at Georg.

Finally, I went in and sat down right at the entrance. Georg and

Peter took spots near me. Just as I had suspected, one Talib moved to close the doors. I called on Georg to do something about it.

"You cannot shut the door," Georg insisted to the men. They conceded and posted an armed guard inside the doorway with us. Then they pulled a vehicle, in which other men were sleeping, right up to the door to protect against our possible escape.

Before the man with the limp whom Georg knew from our office prison left for the night, he took off his thick wool head scarf and handed it to me.

"You will freeze," I said. "I cannot take it."

"No, no. I insist that you take it."

I hesitated. "Take it," Georg said. "He wants to give it to you."

"Thank you so much for your kindness," I said, and wrapped the scarf around me. I took a sweatshirt out of my suitcase, and a Talib brought me a blanket. It was too cold to sleep, and I thought someone needed to stay awake and keep watch. I sat against the wall and prayed.

At about four-thirty, a man came to the door. He gave the guard a pot of tea and a bowl of burning cinders from a fire. The guard and I warmed our hands over the bowl. "Are you cold?" the guard asked.

He pushed the teapot over so I could put it between my feet. He offered me his blanket. "It's extremely cold," I urged. "You keep it."

At six o'clock the intelligence official came to the door. "We're leaving now. We will take you to a nice room. There you can call your families and your governments."

nineteen

A WORLD TURNED UPSIDE DOWN

Dayna: I got up with Silke the next morning to find a private spot where we could relieve ourselves. We walked some yards from the shipping container, and suddenly armed men seemed to come out of nowhere. They were like cats ready to spring in the event we tried to make a break and escape.

"Please leave us alone so we can use the bathroom," I exclaimed. "Please!"

The men did not back off. We had to use the bathroom right there. We covered each other with *chawdurs* while armed Taliban paced nearby keeping watch.

The heavyset intelligence official and the youthful guard stood with our group near the container. These men had traveled somewhere else to sleep for the night, likely to a warm place. They herded us into a different vehicle with the same bench-style seating but no rocket launchers. The intelligence official got into the driver's seat; a right-hand man climbed in on the passenger's side. We left the youthful guard and the other weapon-wielding Taliban at the shipping container and headed south on the road toward Kandahar.

We sang some songs and enjoyed the scenery along the bumpy, unpaved road. Our heads bobbed as we traveled. Open stretches of dusty terrain gave way to awesome, barren mountains. The area was much drier than Kabul's environs. A cloud of dust hovered over the land. We saw little vegetation and few passersby.

"Where are we going?" we asked Georg. He had been trying to get more information from the intelligence official.

"Ghazni," Georg answered.

Back in July, Heather desperately had wanted to go on a trip that Peter led to Ghazni. SNI was working on a water canal project in the area. Heather did not get to go.

"Well, Heather," I said, "at least now you get to see Ghazni."

Meanwhile, we all were looking forward to washing up. We felt nasty and wiped out. All I wanted to do was brush my teeth, wash my face, and get to a nice room in the city.

Heather: Down the road a bit, the intelligence official pulled over so a few of us could make a bathroom stop. I never dreamed the man would agree to let us out, but he obliged us and slowed down near a series of short walls. A few mud houses stood nearby. The gardens were dead from months of drought.

Diana, Ursula, and I ventured off, jumping wall after wall in search of something high enough to protect us from view. I had not walked out in open space since before our arrest in August. I felt both exhilarated and exposed. As we approached the truck on our way back, I noticed several Taliban vehicles parked in various spots along the road. I quickened my pace.

The day was beautiful. The sky was clear, the air refreshing. We passed through a few villages and finally reached Ghazni at close to ten o'clock. The city sprawled over the hills and rugged terrain. Many of the buildings were concrete. Traffic filled the streets. Taxis were out. Men rode bicycles and wheeled *karachis*. Dayna noticed that hardly any women were out walking.

Our vehicle turned right on a narrow street and approached a large dilapidated building on the left. Shards of glass hung from its windows. The concrete façade was cracked. A rusty barbed-wire fence encompassed the walls. The compound looked like a bombed-out military installation. We wondered how many times it had been targeted over the years of war.

I turned to Dayna: "Please, don't let this be where they are taking us."

"I hope that's not it," she agreed.

To our great relief, we drove past the compound.

Farther down the road, the intelligence official pulled up to a whitewashed building with a slant roof and a green gate. The windows were broken out, but this building looked better than the one we had just passed. The official got out of the truck and tried the gate. The gate was locked.

He got back into the van and turned the vehicle around. *We must be going to get the keys,* I thought hopefully. Instead we headed back in the direction of the military compound. This time we pulled over and stopped in front of the building.

"Get out," the intelligence official said. His tone was sharp and forceful.

Georg got out of the vehicle first and tried to get a sense of what was happening. We heard the boom of explosions. The vehicle shook with every blast. Clouds of dust rose toward the sky. People on the street fled in every direction.

The official looked skyward. "Oh, no," he said. "America."

Dayna: As soon as we heard the bombs, the heavyset intelligence man told us to stay in the vehicle. Heather refused. She did not want to be in a vehicle while bombs dropped on the city. We all got out.

The official pointed to the hull of a building. "We are going in there," he said.

We followed him to the entrance. On the ground by the door we saw a black machine gun sitting on a tripod. Nearby a young, mustachioed man bent over at what looked like a water tap and cleaned out a bowl. Unlike the Taliban, he wore no beard.

We entered the building and took a flight of stairs to the second floor. Heather lingered behind.

"Heather," Peter called. "Come upstairs. You have to come upstairs."

"I don't want to go upstairs during bombing," she replied. Then she followed us.

The stairs put us out on the second floor at the center of a corridor. The floors were cracked and covered in dust. Concrete crumbled from the walls. To the left we could see the street through busted windows that lined one side of the hallway. Opposite the windows were doors to rooms we assumed were prison cells.

"Is this a prison?" someone asked the heavyset intelligence man.

He nodded.

He took us down the hall in the other direction to a set of two connecting rooms situated in the corner of the building. Red carpets covered the floors. Some *toshaks* lined the walls in the first room, and a metal desk stood in front of the window. In the far room were more *toshaks* and a desk covered with radio equipment. I put my burlap bag down in this second room and tried to adjust my spirits. The youthful guard had promised us a luxurious place. I had expected at least a private room for the women. I wasn't sure how long we would be staying here. I did not feel good.

Georg talked with two or three Taliban guards who were now in charge of us. The intelligence official was gone. The guards wore sober expressions. They said nothing about our being their guests. They seemed irritated.

I asked for some water so that I could wash up. One guard reluctantly brought me a full bucket. I thanked him profusely and took the water to the bathroom. Diana went with me. Georg, who had already visited the facilities, warned us of the conditions.

The bathroom was all the way down at the other end of the corridor. We passed the prison cell doors and the row of windows looking out onto the street. At the end of the hall were two doors. One opened into a small room that contained a shower drain. I washed up in this room. In the second room was a hole in the ground filled up with feces. The room was dark.

Oh, Lord, I thought. *I don't want to be here.*

Our prison conditions had never been great, but at least we had been able to keep our space and ourselves clean. We had been able to maintain control of our lives in that way. Here we had no running water on our floor of the building, and we could not even take care of relieving ourselves in a sanitary way.

When Diana and I got back to the room, more Taliban had entered and were talking to Georg. One Talib wore a huge white turban. His teeth were rotten. He squinted as if he were looking at Georg with suspicion. The conversation was held in Pashtu, but we learned later what had transpired.

Georg explained to the man that SNI had worked in Pakistan and Afghanistan for eighteen years combined. "In your city, Ghazni, we worked on a water project, giving the citizens the ability to have clean drinking water and water to wash dishes. Men in the villages worked on the project and earned food. We love your country. We love your people."

"No," replied the squinting man. "You are very evil people." With that, he and the other guards walked out of the room.

I felt bad that Georg was the one having to deal with the officials and take the heat from them. He looked tired. I went into the far room, stood in a corner, and put lotion and powder on my face, trying to refresh myself.

Heather: The explosions continued. I looked around trying to figure out where on the upper floor of this building I could go and feel safe. I wanted to get away from the windows in our rooms. Broken windows also lined the hallway. Since our rooms were located in the corner of the building, I crouched against the wall outside of our door. Even so, nearby were a desk and some cleaning implements—loose items that would go flying across the hall if a bomb were to drop in the vicinity of the building. I sat in the hallway and cried. There was nowhere to go. I just wanted to feel safe.

The Taliban guards were going in and out of our rooms talking to Georg. One spoke to me in Pashtu and motioned for me to go inside with the others.

"No. I am not going in the room. I'm sorry."

"Heather, please come in the room," Georg pleaded. "It will be better if you come inside."

I did not mean to be disrespectful of my leader. I wasn't trying to be a thorn in the Taliban's side. I simply could not handle being in the room near the windows. I sat still and did not speak. Georg sighed.

Some time later, a guard brought in a metal tea tray and bread. The others began to prepare for breakfast and our morning worship meeting. I scooted over to the door and participated from the hallway.

Dayna: The guards brought in two big thermoses of tea, some bread, and some sugar. Ghazni bread was thinner than Kabul bread, and each piece was about the size of a pizza. I gave up trying to put on makeup and took out the cheese we had packed the previous evening when Najib told us we were moving to the night prison.

We ate, drank tea, and then began our worship meeting, the first meeting we ever had together with the men. "We sure are in a safe place," I noted sarcastically, eyeing the windows. We started to sing.

"We should pray for Heather," someone suggested. We prayed for her peace. Ursula felt ill, so we also prayed for her.

Suddenly, rounds of loud shooting broke out. I moved to the window. Taliban were running from our compound toward the center of the city. Heather came into the room and stood next to me.

Heather: "Have the Northern Alliance entered the city?" I wondered. "How did they get here from Kabul so fast?" I assumed the fleeing Taliban were moving to the front lines. I got underneath the metal desk in front of the window and prayed. A blanket draped the desk. At least it afforded some protection should glass shards start flying.

Dayna: Georg tried to keep us focused on prayer. Minutes later the shooting stopped. Complete silence followed. We continued to pray.

I noticed that Heather had gotten out from under the desk. She walked across the room to our bags and began to take things out of our suitcase. She was transferring papers and important items to her burlap bag. I needed to do the same. My letters and papers were in the suitcase's side pocket. *I need to get them,* I kept thinking. But I did not want to interrupt the meeting. I decided to wait.

Heather: I knew anything could happen at any minute. I secured my letters and journals in my burlap bag and got back underneath the desk. We all kept praying.

Several minutes later, a violent banging sound reverberated in the corridor. Someone was pounding with tremendous force on the front door of the prison. Our meeting stopped. No one said a word.

This is it, I thought. *The Taliban are angry, and they are coming back to kill us.* I swallowed hard, trying to gain my composure. I lay underneath the desk and prayed: "Jesus, help me to die gracefully. Help me to die honoring you. Let your name be the last word that crosses my lips."

Dayna: The pounding noise was overwhelming and unusual. Someone was obviously trying to get to us. We stood there in the room waiting to see what would happen next.

Footsteps sounded on the stairs. Seconds later, our door flung open. A scruffy, beardless man in ragtag clothing burst through the entrance. Rounds of ammunition were wrapped around his chest. In one hand he carried a rifle; in the other, what looked like a rocket launcher. His eyes were wide open; his hair was wild and coated in dust. He was panting and looked astonished to see us, a group of foreigners, there in the room at the Ghazni prison.

"Hello," he blurted out in English. That was the only English word he knew. Farsi came next.

"Aaazaad! Aaazaad!" You're free! You're free! *"Taliban raft."* The Taliban have left.

"Rasti?" Kati and I asked. Really?

He assured us it was true. *"Raft, raft,"* he said. They fled, they fled.

Only Kati, Heather, and I knew Dari well enough to understand him. We translated for the others. "He says the Taliban have left and that we are free!"

For a second no one moved. Then we hugged each other. Some other armed men entered the room. Georg spoke with them.

"Come with us. Come with us quickly," the men urged.

Heather: "Are we really free?" I cried aloud in English. I got up and went to the wild-looking man. "Is it true? Am I going to get to see my family today?" We had been lied to for so long, I was not sure whether I could believe this man's pronouncement. For more than a hundred days I had dreamed of hearing the words "You're free!" It seemed too good to be true. The man looked confused. He did not understand my English.

Unkempt men armed with rocket launchers moved in and out of our room. One man grabbed our suitcase. I thought he was trying to help me. Everyone moved out and flooded the stairwell. I picked up my burlap bag and pillow and ran. Men were coming up the stairs. No one was in charge. The whole place erupted in pandemonium.

"Come on! Come on!" Georg shouted. "Where's Dayna? Where's Silke? There's no time to mess around! We have to go!"

Most of us ran out of the prison with a group of men. We passed the heavy weaponry sitting by the front door.

"Come on, we are moving you somewhere!" hollered the men. "You're free! You're free!"

Gunfire broke out seconds later. "Turn back! Turn back!" shouted the men at the front of the pack. We turned around and made a bee-line for the door of the prison.

Inside, a young, blue-eyed, olive-skinned man stood shaking. He looked like a puppy that had just been beaten. His clothes were wrinkled and filthy; his eyes were alert with fear. We learned that he was the one other prisoner in the building when the men broke down the door. He came from Iran.

Dayna: Up in the room, I couldn't find one of my plastic sandals. Silke and an armed man were tearing up the room looking for it; the man also searched for things he could take. Georg shouted to us from the bottom of the stairwell. "Come on!"

"We have to go," Silke said.

I left the room frustrated but resigned, thinking I would run for my life wearing one shoe.

"There's no time to mess around," Georg yelled. "We have to go!" Silke later explained to him about the shoe.

A crowd that had started across the prison yard turned back. "There's still shooting in the city," someone said.

We were all shuffled into a room on the lower floor of the prison. Men came and went. Teenage boys and young men with pistols, automatic weapons, and rocket launchers packed the room. The men argued among themselves about what to do. Their eyes were dilated and they seemed wired. We wondered if many were high. No one was in charge.

One young guy paced the room, flipping his long, henna-streaked hair and drawing on a cigarette. At one point, a three-foot-tall bearded midget strapped with ammunition and carrying a gun walked by.

The Iranian prisoner sat down near us. He was the man I had seen at the water tap when we first arrived with the heavyset intelligence official. The Iranian was shaking now. Georg tried to calm him. One of the armed men said, "Don't worry. Don't worry. You're a brother."

If I could just get my hands on the suitcase, I thought, *I could grab my extra pair of sandals.* I turned to one of the fighters. "Have you seen a suitcase?"

The man left and came back with it. When I opened the suitcase, I saw that someone had rifled through our belongings. Our clothes were covered with dust; they had obviously been dumped out on the floor. As I searched through the contents, my heart sank. All of my papers were gone—my letters from family and friends, one of my journals, my wart picture and birthday card. Our large jar of Nestlé's coffee also was missing. I dug around, looking for my sandals.

Others seemed irritated that I was looking through the suitcase at such a tense moment. "Is she looking for socks?" someone muttered.

I took out my shoes and sat quietly, grieving over my letters. At least I still had one of my journals. I kept it in my burlap bag.

Heather: "You can leave now," a dust-covered man announced after forty-five minutes. "It is safe to go."

We got up and followed the train of fighters. The Iranian came with us. He carried our suitcase. I held on to my burlap bag and pillow. I did not want to lose them.

Several yards in front of the prison we heard more gunfire. We kept walking. The gunfire stopped. We turned onto a street, and a man with a weapon came out from behind a stone wall. To our relief, he greeted us. We waved. Someone mentioned a professional man in the city who spoke English. The men would try to take us to him.

We traversed the streets very quickly—all of us except for Peter. In his fashion, he took his time. Vacant buildings lined the streets. No one was out. We passed a six-foot-high sandbag wall. I scanned the scene. Everyone was nervous. We were open targets. A pack of kids charged across the street as momentary gunfire broke out.

"Jesus, protect us," I prayed.

Eventually, we wended our way into the bazaar area and saw people emerging from their houses. Women stood uncovered in the doorways. Children came out to the street. Men, still holding their weapons, shouted, "The Taliban just left! We're free! We're free!" Drivers in cars honked their horns. We began to hear music playing. People clapped, waved, and laughed. We waved back at the women showing their faces. We acknowledged the men—something we could never do under the Taliban.

As I walked down the road, I felt as if we were participants in a parade. The sky was perfectly blue, and a strong breeze swept through the city. I looked around with awe at the scene and wondered if I was seeing the first generation of children in a new Afghanistan to grow up free from the atrocities of war. My heart was moved. We were marching through history. Walking through Ghazni was like walking in a world turned upside down.

Dayna: One of the men next to me gestured toward the eight of us and proclaimed to the crowd: "They were held by the Taliban! We set them free!"

"*Tabreek!*" people shouted. Congratulations!

"Congratulations to you!" we cried.

Women smiled and greeted us from their doorways. Young teenage boys tried to practice their English. "Where are you from? What happened? We are so happy for you!" The atmosphere was light. The sense of restriction imposed by the Taliban had vanished. Fear had lessened. Though the city was still unstable, people were free—at least for a time—to rejoice and celebrate.

I turned to Heather: "I feel like we're in the middle of a movie."

"God is good," she said.

Yes, I thought. God was so good to let us participate in this moment. We were getting to be a part of what we longed to see—a new day for Afghanistan, a new day for the Afghan people. If we had been given our own way, we would have been released from prison much sooner, but we would have missed this incredible experience. We were living out the very thing for which we had prayed. We were in the middle of it all.

Heather: Somewhere on the journey the professional man we were supposed to meet connected with us. His name was Qasim. He spoke some English. "Come with me. I will take you to a place where you can rest."

We walked for more than half an hour. We passed through the bazaar, through a nice residential area with whitewashed houses and colored gates, and, finally, into another market area of the city. All of the shops were closed. Again we were reminded that the city was still very insecure. We walked through the streets believing we would not be harmed, but we did not know this city or its people.

Qasim led us into his office on the upper floor of a strip of shops. Within seconds the office was packed with people, mainly fighters. Teenage boys who wanted to practice their English entered. Qasim greeted his friends and, in Afghan fashion, kissed them on the cheeks. Qasim gave the man from Iran some money and dismissed him. We never learned where the Iranian went.

The office was posh. Against the wall in one room stood a cabinet containing cups and teapots. There were several tables and a sturdy wooden desk. Pictures hung on the walls. One poster depicting war in Afghanistan looked like an ad for a Rambo movie. We sat on plush red couches. I had not seen such a fine room during my entire tenure in the country. The teenage boys plopped down right next to us, skin to skin. Their behavior startled me. Under the Taliban, such behavior would have yielded serious consequences; but, apparently, we were among free spirits in our motley crew.

One commander proclaimed, "I love Massoud. I am with Massoud." Others echoed his enthusiasm. Eventually, we learned that these men were not officially Northern Alliance fighters. Many loved the Northern Alliance, but they had assembled as a local force to fight the Taliban in Ghazni. We entered the city less than an hour before the local uprising commenced and at roughly the same time two hundred Al-Qaeda fighters were leaving the city, Georg later learned.

"What about our sixteen Afghan brothers from your organization?" one man asked. The commander who loved Massoud informed us that the sixteen had been released. "The first thing the Northern Alliance did in Kabul was free all the prisoners," the commander explained. We hoped he was right. We had prayed daily that our Afghan coworkers would be released before us.

Our host served us a traditional meal of *Kabuli palau* and french fries. I could hardly eat because of the intensity of the events; adrenaline still raced through my veins. But the food tasted so good.

Meanwhile, Georg was working with Qasim and others trying to locate a phone to contact our embassies in Islamabad. In the end, no working phone could be found. Qasim said he would take us to a comfortable house where we could wait and rest.

Dayna: While the others were sitting in the office, some young boys led Ursula and me to a private house across the street to find a toilet. Crossing the street, I noticed two men walking by. They wore dark turbans and thick black eyeliner. I thought they were Taliban. I gasped. The street was full of people. No one seemed to think anything unusual about the two men. But their presence frightened me.

The young boys took Ursula and me up a flight of stairs to an elevated room with a diamond-shaped hole in the floor. Clods of dirt in the corner were the only available substitute for toilet paper, but Ursula handed me some pages she had torn from an old book. In the yard we encountered some children and two Hazara women. "How are you? Are you happy?" they asked. "Oh, yes," we replied. "We are very happy."

When we returned to Qasim's office, we freshened up and got our things together. I pulled out my makeup bag, sat on the floor, and turned my back to all the men in the room. Then I set a little mirror on the red couch where I was sitting and applied face powder, eyeliner, mascara, and lipstick—the works. Ursula and Heather followed my lead. I felt much better.

Before we left, I approached the commander and asked whether he could try to locate my missing letters. Surely, one of his men must have them. He laughed. "Oh, the papers are not important."

I told him the papers were important to me, and he said he would ask around and look for them. I doubted my letters would turn up, but at least I could ask.

Qasim brought a van around to the front of the building, and we got in. There were curtains on the windows. "Close the curtains," Qasim insisted. "We do not want anyone to see you."

The curtains did us no good. A mob of more than a hundred people surrounded the van as we prepared to drive away. People beat on the hood and banged at the windows. We felt like rock stars making a getaway after a concert.

twenty

MILES TO GO BEFORE I SLEEP

Heather & Dayna: Qasim drove us out of the city to a compound of houses belonging to one of his friends. Up until that afternoon, we understood, the friend had been a Talib of rank. Once the uprising started, the friend quickly decided to become an ex-Talib.

Driving into the ex-Talib's home compound was, by Afghan standards, like entering a palace gate. We drove through two large blue steel doors into a large courtyard, which opened onto a second, even more spacious courtyard area. Two homes abutted the first courtyard; three homes adjoined the second. The homes were two-story mud houses; white iron guardrails protected the balcony areas. Each courtyard had its own well and trees. Children, chickens, and cats roamed freely.

Our host welcomed us into the first house in the first courtyard. Everything looked brand new—furniture, pillows, carpets. The walls were freshly painted lime green and sky blue. As soon as we set our things down in the hospitality room, a horde of Afghan men trooped in behind us. We women were exhausted and asked to be moved to the women's quarters.

In the women's room we met two of the three ex-Talib's wives. One woman held an infant. The women served us tea and sweets. A Hazara woman, a servant in the compound, joined us. The women told us that they had only just returned to the house after spending the night at a safe house in the mountains to escape heavy bombing around the city. Many of their female relatives were still hiding out and planned to return that afternoon. Taliban fighters had turned against one another, the women explained, and could not hold a united front against the local uprising.

While we rested, Georg continued to meet for hours with various Afghan men of note who came and went during the afternoon. The men turned on a radio, trying to discover whether news sources had reported our removal from Kabul. We hoped our parents knew. Georg planned to go to the ICRC office in town to communicate with the Red Cross in Pakistan early the following morning. There was talk we might get out of the country in two or three days.

Dayna: I asked the Afghan ladies if I could take a bath. They told me to gather my things and then brought me to the mother of the ex-Talib; she oversaw the work of the household. The mother led me to a closet-size concrete room that adjoined a simple but colorful living room. She set up a pitcher and brought me a bucket of hot water from the courtyard with a cup to use for pouring water over my head. She had heated the water in a large metal canister using hot coals from the fire.

After my bath, I asked the mother if I could borrow soap to wash some clothes. She wouldn't think of it. "I will wash your clothes," she insisted. "No, I will do it," I said. "No, I will do it," the mother pressed, and I relented. Later, I saw a young Hazara girl washing my clothes. I was brokenhearted. "Let me help you," I offered. But she wouldn't let me.

Heather & Dayna: Late in the afternoon our host, the ex-Talib, moved everyone into another one of the mud houses. He ordered a room to be set up for us so that we could rest. Lace curtains draped the bay windows. The walls were painted lime green. A thick Persian rug covered the floor. In the corner of the room were *toshaks,* pillows, and fleece blankets stacked nearly to the ceiling. The room was set up for all of us—men and women. Though we were uneasy with the coed arrangements, we tried to take our rest.

An Afghan man in his twenties came into the room frequently to talk with Peter. He wore a Western-style sports jacket.

Dayna: I helped Peter with translation. The other women encouraged me not to engage the Afghan. "Do not talk to him," they advised.

Later the Afghan asked me for my address in America.

"I'm sorry," I said. "I don't give my information to men." In the end, he turned out to be a very nice man.

Heather & Dayna: At dinner, the ex-Talib sent Peter and Georg to eat with the men. He—the ex-Talib—and Qasim ate with us. We had never eaten a meal alone with Afghan men and felt very uncomfortable with the setup.

"Georg, please do not leave us here," Silke said. Georg insisted that he had to go with the men. He had to build relationships to help us get out of the country. His face looked strained.

One of the ex-Talib's young sons did most of the serving while we stayed at the compound. The proud father told us that his son had attended the Kabul *madrassa* adjoining our reform school prison.

"My son often misbehaved and did not have enough responsibility here at home," the ex-Talib explained. "At school he learned discipline and hard work." His son lived at the *madrassa* during the time we were imprisoned in the reform school compound with Mariam and the Afghan women.

Heather: "Were you beaten?" I asked the boy. "Yes, every day," he said. "I am sorry you were treated badly," I replied. It broke my heart that he had been abused.

Heather & Dayna: At the end of the evening, we stressed to the Afghans that we did not want to sleep in the same room with Georg and Peter.

They seemed surprised. "You do not want to sleep with the others?" they asked.

"Oh, no," we said strongly. "We prefer to sleep alone." We gathered that the family was trying to let us live by what they assumed were Western standards.

Dayna: Before bed, the six of us spent time thanking God for the amazing way he had freed us from prison. I cried over the loss of my letters and papers and other belongings. I did feel silly crying over the loss of material things when there was so much for which to be joyful. We had our lives. But I needed to express my sadness so that I could move on and rejoice over our freedom.

Heather: God had worked an incredible miracle. I was overjoyed. Nevertheless, I did not feel totally free yet. Though I celebrated and thanked God for the marvel of our release from prison, I also knew that much needed to happen in order for us to get out of the country safely. We were out of prison, but we were still behind enemy lines. I would feel completely free when I landed on Pakistani soil.

Heather & Dayna: We slept comfortably and deeply in luxurious bed linens, a marked contrast from our previous night in the ice-cold shipping container. A few bombs exploded in the distance, but otherwise the night at the compound was peaceful. When we awoke, Georg had already gone to the ICRC office. The ex-Talib's son came to the door early to serve us breakfast. He and his father joined us for fried bread and black tea.

Dayna: Georg returned briefly in the morning with a local commander and other men of rank. He asked me to put together on the spot a speech in Dari thanking the men for helping us, and expressing our deep gratitude and sincere appreciation for their support.

Heather: For the moment, Dayna became our ambassador.

Dayna: Later, we asked if we could borrow a radio. We wanted to continue listening for any reports about our plight. A man brought a radio to us, and when we turned it on the first thing I heard was an interview with my mother. Information had gotten out that we had been taken from Kabul

"Are you frightened?" an interviewer asked my mom. She sounded casual. "I'm confident the Taliban will take good care of the detainees. The Taliban took good care of them before all of this."

I thought, *Oh, Mom, you should have been worried this time!* Later, I found out that she thought we were with Najib. One of Georg's contacts, the man who risked his life translating our letters, had gotten out of the intelligence prison before we were taken from Kabul and had sent word to Islamabad of Najib's contingency plan to take us to his village.

Heather: We each took some alone time before our morning worship meeting. I went outside to pray and became distracted watching the women. Sitting in the yard, I was afforded a rare glimpse of daily life in an Afghan household. The women were carrying heavy loads between the courtyard and the house. Some were pumping water from the well, while others washed clothes. When else might I have an opportunity to observe Afghan women in such an intimate way?

"Can I help?" I asked.

"Oh, no, no," one of the women said. They would not hear of it. We were their guests.

I decided to write down some of my observations. I wanted to remember what I saw:

"Walking through the *awlee* [courtyard] are 30 chickens (black, white, red) of various sizes and a handful of grey tabby cats. . . . The young children run around the *awlee* playing with stones, broken glass, and anything else they can find. The women run back and forth carrying water buckets, chopping wood, hitting [*toshaks*] w/wood [and] w/a rubber rope and pulley gathering water from the 30 foot well."

The mother of the ex-Talib approached me and asked me what I was writing. I explained, and she confided that she wanted to learn how to write English. I wrote out the English alphabet for her, but she was hesitant about taking the piece of paper.

"This must be secret," she said. She did not want the Afghan men to know. I passed it to her discreetly.

Dayna: "What are you doing?" asked a teenage girl and two Hazara women. I was sitting on the steps listening to the CD player.

"I am listening to music to God. It gives me peace. Would you like to listen?"

The teenage girl listened for a while.

I saw the women pulling buckets of water out of the well. I went to them and asked, "Can I try?" It was easy at first, but as the bucket got nearer the top, I could barely pull the rope. The women laughed at me. Then Heather joined us.

"Ooh, she's strong," they said. "She can do it really well."

The women then asked me if our aid agency could give them a pump for their well. They explained that drawing the water was very hard work and took a toll on their hands. I told them I would talk to our boss about it.

Heather & Dayna: As we started our morning worship meeting, Qasim came into the house.

"We are moving you," he said. "Georg wants you to come to a different location. You need to leave with me."

We refused. Qasim did not have a note or any proof that Georg wanted us to move. Qasim was offended that we did not trust him. We were wasting time, he said. Nevertheless, we did not want to risk being separated from Georg. We continued with our meeting.

An hour later, Georg returned and told us that, in fact, we did need to leave. He did not feel safe in the ex-Talib's house. We learned that the family of the heavyset intelligence official lived nearby. The intelligence official had brought us to Ghazni so that he could visit his family, Georg explained; then the man planned to take us to Kandahar. While we had been sleeping the previous night, armed Afghan men stood watch in our compound, pacing the roofs and guarding against a potential raid. Georg thought we needed to move into town closer to the ICRC office.

We packed up our things, and Qasim took all of us to the home of one of the ex-Talib's wives. By now it was lunchtime.

The wife's house was a nice, modest home with carpets and *toshaks* and decoration on the walls. Here, too, we noticed a poster depicting the war in Afghanistan. We were taken to a cozy room, and the men stayed with us awhile. Friends of the ex-Talib came to the house and wanted to take photographs with us. Then the men went off to eat in a separate room.

Some teenage boys served us pickled eggplant, rice, Afghan meatballs, french fries, and fruit for lunch. Then Georg came in to say goodbye and left with Qasim for the ICRC office. We stayed in our room, and some of us played cards.

Not much time passed before Qasim returned. This time he brought us a note: "Dayna and Heather, you need to come right now to the ICRC office. Georg." The two of us got up and went with Qasim. Peter joined us.

When we arrived at the office, Georg was talking on a satellite phone with David Donahue in Islamabad. Donahue wanted to speak with each of us personally to make sure we were safe. He wanted to hear our voices for himself. It was wonderful to hear his. We told him we were well and shared with him briefly what had happened since our departure from Kabul. Then Donahue relayed several important pieces of information:

Helicopters were coming tonight. We were to be at the pickup spot at 11:30 P.M. We could not bring anything with us.

Tonight helicopters were coming. We tried to stay calm. We asked if our parents were informed. They were not. Donahue wanted to make sure that the rescue went as planned before getting our parents' hopes up. Further, with our lives and the lives of U.S. soldiers at stake, the mission needed to be kept under wraps.

"Much has to go right for the rescue to take place," Georg told us after we finished the phone call.

He explained that several local commanders would have to be in agreement over our pickup spot. The city was incredibly tense. Shooting was breaking out among people of different ethnic groups. Taliban surrounded Ghazni. If the commanders did not agree on the details of the pickup, the rescue would be too dangerous to attempt.

Before he sent us on our way, he said: "You and the other ladies must pray." We couldn't wait to get home and deliver the exciting news.

"We will be rescued tonight," we announced to the others back at the room. Everyone was shocked. Things were happening very fast. We explained that Georg had urged us to pray for agreement among the commanders.

"And there is one other thing," we said. "We can't take anything with us—no purses, bags, or luggage."

Mayhem ensued. We spent the next couple of hours dressing, undressing, and stuffing everything we could inside of our clothes.

Dayna: The Germans decided that they were taking their purses; and in the end, everyone who took a purse got away with it. Kati wanted my little pocket Bible as a memento; she used it all the time in prison. I let her take it. She secured it in her tiny purse.

I figured out a way to strap the CD player on my back with an elastic strap from my pants. I planned to cover up the hump with my *chawdur.* I stuffed my socks with lipstick and my inhaler. I stuck a container of face powder down the leg of my long johns. My prescription eyeglasses and sunglasses went down my pants, too. I stuffed my whole makeup bag into the front of my long-john bottoms and my journals down my back.

In the end, I was wearing both pairs of NBC long johns, a black long-sleeve shirt, and a blue jean dress my mom had sent me from Pakistan through Atif. Everyone convinced me to pull on a black dress from Pakistan, too. I could barely breathe by the time it was all over.

Heather: I put on several items of underclothing, including both pairs of NBC long johns. On top of those I wore two dress-pants sets, called *shalwar kamiz,* and a black Kuchi dress I had ordered from the bazaar when we were staying at the intelligence prison. I ordered the dress specifically for our rescue. I had never worn it until this evening.

I stuck the roll of film from Georg's camera, courtesy of Najib's brother, in my underclothes. A tube of liquid eyeliner went in my socks; I was wearing three pairs. I put a set of disposable contact lenses in my embroidered pencil case—this was the pencil case the large-nosed senior Talib left in my cloth backpack the day of our arrest. Necklaces made by the Afghan girls at the reform school prison also went inside the pencil case, which I stuffed down the front of my shirt. My journals and letters went down the front of my pants; the tight long johns held the mass in place. I put my hefty reference Bible that the Taliban let me take out of our house in Wazir down the back of my pants. I saved three head scarves; one was the thick wool scarf that Georg's prisoner contact had given to me at the shipping container.

Heather & Dayna: All the while, the Afghan women could not make out what we were doing. Clothes and items were strewn across the room. We were laughing hysterically. It felt wonderful to laugh again.

One woman popped her head in. "We are having a fashion show," we told her, and smiled. Obviously, we were not allowed to explain what was really going on.

As it started to get dark, the woman told us we needed to move into another room where she had set a gas lamp.

We took some of the items out of our clothes so we could move freely and carried our things into the side room. Some people played cards.

Dayna: I pulled out the book I was reading, *Men Are from Mars, Women Are from Venus.*

Heather: I took a turn listening to the CD player to spend time with God, but two young, rowdy boys soon interrupted me by pushing all of the buttons. I let them listen to the music awhile, hoping to quench their curiosity, but they continued to pester me.

Heather & Dayna: Inspired by the CD player, we began to sing celebratory worship songs. One was called "You Have Turned My Mourning into Dancing," the same song we sang and danced to in our room at the reform school prison when we were praying for the Afghan women's freedom. We got up now and began to dance and celebrate our release. Six o'clock came and went. We decided to pray. Soon it was 7:30. "Where is Georg?" we began to wonder. We hoped the delay was a sign of progress.

"We are concerned our boss is not back yet," we said to the Afghan woman tending to us. "Why might he not be back?" We knew she did not have the answer.

We continued to pray: Jesus, help Georg wherever he is, empower him to negotiate, give him favor with the right people, protect him, and make it all work out.

Heather: *Let it happen tonight,* I prayed. *Please let it happen tonight.*

Heather & Dayna: At nine o'clock, Georg still had not returned. Curfew fell at eight o'clock. Was Georg safe?

We had not eaten in nearly ten hours and were hungry. The Afghans served us seasoned potatoes in oil for dinner. Afterward, some of the women wanted us to dance for them.

Dayna: The mood was still positive and we were goofy. I performed some American-style dance moves—in the vein of *Saturday Night Fever*—for the ladies. It was fun to make these ladies laugh. They had been working so hard serving us.

Heather & Dayna: At some point we all restuffed our clothing. We knew that the minute Georg walked in we would have to leave to make it to the pickup point by 11:30.

Georg entered the house after ten o'clock holding a satellite phone. Several men, including the local commander, Qasim, and the ex-Talib, accompanied him.

"Everything is falling apart," Georg said. "There is no agreement among the commanders."

It turned out that the local commander had decided not to raise the issue of the rescue with the other commanders in the area. Any agreement on the location and circumstances of our rescue would take days to achieve, the local commander said. Meanwhile, if the pickup went forward tonight as planned, the other commanders would suspect that whoever facilitated the ordeal had received a great deal of money. The other commanders would want to share the money, the local commander told Georg.

Furthermore, the local commander explained that everyone in Ghazni was expecting a Taliban counterattack. Men all over the city were armed. In the end, the commander refused to take us to the pickup spot. U.S. officials in Islamabad had spoken to him earlier by satellite phone and tried to convince him to help us, but with no effect. The rescue could not happen tonight. Soon after he came in with Georg and the other men, the local commander left the house.

While we stayed in our room, Georg was on and off the phone with U.S. officials. Georg talked on the phone in the courtyard where some of the men were standing and then reported the developments to us at intervals.

The U.S. officials told Georg that the rescue had to happen that night. The next day was not an option.

"Can you do it in the morning?" Georg asked a U.S. official.

The rescuers would have to come very early in the morning, before curfew lifted.

That would not work on our end. No one would take us anywhere before curfew lifted.

In the commander's absence, the ex-Talib claimed that he could not help us. "I cannot change the decision of the commander. I cannot act without the commander's permission."

The ex-Talib said he would not take us to the pickup point for anything, not for any amount of money. He came to our room to explain his position to us. "Do you want me to die?" he asked. "I am a father and a husband. If I do this, I could be killed. The commander will think I have taken a bribe."

"Can you go back and get the commander so we can talk to him?" we asked.

"It is after curfew," he answered. "I could be shot."

At one point Georg said, "I have talked for hours and no one will move. It is not happening."

Diana began to pull out her *toshak* and blanket and prepare for bed. "It's not happening tonight," she said as if to resign herself. Some of us joined her and started preparing the room for bed.

The U.S. official pressed Georg again: You have to make it happen tonight. It must happen tonight. It will not happen tomorrow. Do whatever you have to do to get out of there, but make it happen.

The helicopters were on their way, the official said.

Meanwhile, the ex-Talib stayed on top of Georg, pressuring him to give it up.

"Look," Georg said fiercely. "The helicopters are already in the air. They are going to land in this courtyard if they have to, but they are coming to get us tonight."

"Pray," Georg told us.

We began praying loudly, fervently. "God, do something!"

At about eleven-thirty we heard a loud banging on the courtyard door. The Afghan women were terrified. Some were shaking and having difficulty breathing. It was hours past curfew. Only enemies would be coming to the house at this time of night, one woman said. We grabbed the lantern and hid in the hallway.

We could hear men's voices outside. The local commander had arrived. We learned what transpired after the fact.

"We have to move you," the commander told Georg. "It is not safe for you. We have heard of some Taliban intelligence people who may try to come here and take you."

Sensing that the commander had another agenda, Georg looked at the man and spoke firmly. "We are not moving."

"You must come with me now. You will be harmed if you stay here. Get ready. You have to come."

Inside the house, the ex-Talib and Qasim pressured us. "Come on, get your things. We are moving you somewhere else."

Outside, Georg turned to the commander: "You can kill us, but we are not moving."

Moments later, something extraordinary happened. The commander came into the house. We do not know what caused him to alter his position, but for whatever reason he completely changed his mind. He looked at us. "Okay," he said. "Let's go."

"Where are we going?" we asked.

"We're taking you to the helicopter." We froze.

"Come on! Now!" Georg shouted.

Heather: I had taken my Bible, journals, and letters out of my clothes. Our *toshaks* and blankets were spread out in the room. I grabbed my journals and letters and stuffed those in the front of my pants. I could not pull my pants out fast enough to get my Bible in place. I ran to an Afghan woman: "Help me, help me." She stuffed the Bible into my pants and I flew out the door.

Dayna: Everyone ran out of the house and took the lantern. The side room was pitch black. I had unstuffed most of my things. I groped for the journal but couldn't find it. I couldn't find the CD player. I tried to get my sandals on but could not manage the Velcro straps. An Afghan man called out, "Just go barefoot."

"I can't go barefoot."

As I was trying to get the strap to hold, a woman came to the door.

"*Bakshish?*" she asked. Alms?

twenty-one

ARISE

Heather & Dayna: Out on the road, we followed the commander and a few of his men. We were not going to the prearranged meeting place after all. The U.S. official told Georg about an open area nearby. We did not need a vehicle. We could walk.

"Do not speak English," the Afghans warned us.

Ghazni lay in complete darkness. Potholes pocked the road. Some of us stumbled.

"I can't see a thing," someone whispered.

"Be quiet," others instructed. "Do not say a word."

Qasim and the ex-Talib saw us off and returned to the house. The

Afghan wearing the Western sports jacket continued on with the commander and two other armed men. To ensure the safety of the rescuers, the U.S. official told Georg that no Afghans were to be in the vicinity of the pickup spot. Otherwise, someone might get shot.

Our destination was a disused airfield about the size of four football fields. We approached a concrete slab, the remains of an airstrip. Mud houses surrounded the slab. Two shipping containers provided our only cover.

Georg talked on the phone with the U.S. official. We set the lantern down in front of us and waited. Ursula opened her purse to look for matches. We needed matches in case the lantern went out. She did not find any.

Dayna: In the darkness I took a wrong step and fell down a four-foot drop off the tarmac. The others helped me up. Thankfully, I was not hurt.

Heather & Dayna: The Afghan men handed us their blankets. "You are cold," they said.

"Please leave," we urged them. "It is dangerous for you."

The men stayed.

After some minutes, we still did not hear any helicopters approaching. We thought we heard airplanes overhead. It was hard to tell.

"Is that it?" someone would whisper every few moments. Even our whispers carried in the eerie silence.

The U.S. official talking to Georg said the rescuers would get to us in fifteen minutes. Then the phone battery died and we lost our connection.

Sometime in the next half hour, we saw the helicopters. We cheered as quietly as we could. "This is it! This is it! They're coming!"

Two enormous machines circled above the field searching for us. They would come in close, skirt the mud houses, and recede. Come in and then recede. The circling went on for some time.

"Don't they see us?" someone asked. Twice the machines came so close that we were certain the rescuers had spotted us—we felt we could almost touch the helicopters. But each time, they pulled back and flew into the distance. Minutes kept passing.

Heather: Please, Jesus. Please, Jesus. Please, Jesus. Do something. Do something.

Heather & Dayna: Across the concrete strip, we saw a light come on near one of the mud houses. Someone was searching the area with a flashlight. Dogs barked in the distance. People were hearing the commotion and waking up. A man approached us from behind. "Who are you? What are you doing?" he asked.

"Nothing is going on," the commander replied forcefully. "Go back to your house."

Then the commander turned to Georg: "This is too dangerous. We must leave. The whole city knows you are out here. Everyone is armed. You could be ambushed. The Taliban know where you are. We must go."

We waited. The choppers continued to pass overhead. "There must be something we can do!" we exclaimed.

"It is not safe," the commander said again. "We must go."

We watched the helicopters approach and recede. We picked up the lantern and waved it in the air, but with no result.

"They are not going to see us," Georg said. "He is right. It is not safe."

Dayna: I was willing to follow Georg if we needed to leave. I felt vulnerable. I knew we could be shot like the commander said. We were out in the open. *I guess God will get us out another way,* I thought.

Heather & Dayna: "Georg," someone pleaded, "just five more minutes."

Heather: I was not going to leave. We were in danger standing out in the field, but I knew the helicopters were not going to come back the next day. If we returned to the house, we would be open targets. The Taliban knew where we were. This was our one chance. We had to make it. We would leave tonight or we would not leave at all.

Dayna: Heather grabbed Ursula's purse.

"I am looking for matches," Heather said. "There have to be some in here."

"Heather," Ursula insisted, "there are no matches in my purse."

Heather: I did not care. I would see for myself. I continued digging for matches, and I found some.

"Georg," I said, "we can start a fire. We can burn my head scarf. They will be able to see a fire."

We knew the helicopters were not looking for a fire—the flames might throw the rescuers off. But what choice did we have?

"Go ahead," Georg answered.

We spread out the wool head scarf given to me by the prisoner at the shipping container and poured oil from the lantern on it. I was sad to lose the keepsake, but nothing mattered outside of building the fire. The scarf burned quickly. I added another of my head scarves. Dayna added hers.

Heather & Dayna: The local commander and his men found pieces of wood and laid them on the fire. One man picked up some planks and broke them. The cracking sound hung in the air. We cringed. Surely everyone in the area was awake by now.

The Afghan in the sports jacket gave us a blanket to burn.

Dayna: I felt badly burning his blanket.

Heather: I did not mind burning anything at that point, not when the fire could mean the difference between life and death, freedom and captivity.

Heather & Dayna: We lifted up the burning blanket, trying to catch the attention of the helicopters. The pilots brought the huge machines in close. They swooped overhead, creating an overpowering gust of wind. Dust blew up our noses and into our mouths. The flames of the fire washed back on top of us, catching one of our dresses on fire. We crouched in each other's arms.

"They've seen us! They've seen us!"

But the machines drew back. One circled overhead. Surely, they had seen us. We did not understand what was taking the rescuers so long to land. Twenty minutes passed before anything happened.

Dayna: I saw the shapes of people coming toward us.

"Do you speak English?" a man said.

"Yes," I replied without thinking.

The others gasped and got onto me for answering. "We don't know who those people are!" someone whispered.

Heather: I leaned forward so I could see. Several huge shapes emerged from the shadows. These men were not Taliban. Covered in gear, they looked like Martians. I could see their guns.

Dayna jumped behind me and cried, "Don't shoot! Don't shoot!"

Heather & Dayna: Over the noise of the choppers, we heard: "Are you the detainees?"

"Yes!" we exclaimed.

Behind us the Afghan men looked on with dazed expressions. "These are our friends," Georg explained. "Please do not shoot." The soldiers acknowledged Georg's request.

"Listen and do exactly what we say!" one rescuer commanded.

"Count 'em off," another voice said.

Someone counted. "They're only seven," he yelled.

"No," we answered. "There are eight of us!"

He counted again. "They are all here. Let's go!"

The rescuers led us across the field, placing their hands on our shoulders to guide us.

"Watch your step. Look out for holes," one soldier warned.

"Let's run! Come on, let's run!" one of our group called out.

"Keep your pace," a rescuer responded calmly. "This is a good pace." Along the way Diana collapsed into a ditch.

As we moved ahead, we looked up. Towering over a little mud house in the distance was the chopper.

Heather: I thought: *We are in the middle of a movie!*

Everything seemed to be happening in slow motion. I had never seen such a spectacular sight. In the complete darkness, a ring of light circled above the propellers of the monstrous machine. *What must the poor Afghan in the house below be thinking?* I wondered.

Georg and I were the first ones to board the chopper. As we climbed into the dark hull, Georg fell down and I tumbled over him. We moved to the front, tripping as we went, and took seats on the floor. Diana boarded and sat next to me, and I leaned against her. The whole operation had been so sensational. But I would not feel completely safe until we reached Pakistani airspace.

"How high does this chopper fly?" I asked one of the men.

"Don't worry, ma'am. You're going to be just fine."

Another soldier bent down and said, "I want you to know that since your first day in captivity on August 3, my family and I have never stopped praying for you."

No words could have been sweeter.

I sat close to Diana and let my gaze drift upward. Tacked to the ceiling of the chopper was an American flag. It was a beautiful flag. I finally rested and worshiped Jesus.

Dayna: I sat with Kati on top of some boxes. "Is it okay if we sit here?" I asked one of the soldiers.

"You're good," he said.

Another soldier approached and yelled into my ear over the noise of the engine: "I just want you to know that my family and I have been praying for you since the first day you were taken captive, and most of these guys in here have been praying, too. It's an honor for me to be on this operation and to be used by God to help get you guys out."

I was touched by his words. God heard the prayers of many and used these great guys to save us. No one had been hurt. We were so grateful.

The men handed out water. Then they held up a laminated sheet of photographs and asked us to identify ourselves.

I thought back to the night Kabul fell. I had grieved that night sitting among the rocket launchers in the Taliban vehicle. *I guess I didn't hear from God,* I had told myself. *It doesn't look like we will get out very soon at all. How will we ever make it out before Christmas, much less Thanksgiving?*

But I did hear. We did get out "very soon." God did speak to me. And God was faithful.

After the aid workers made contact with Islamabad from Ghazni, the U.S. military quickly assembled a team of Special Operations Forces rescue personnel. A rescue team had planned to pick up the aid workers as Kabul was falling, but Taliban forces took the aid workers out of the city.

The new rescue team included a U.S. Navy "SEAL platoon plus" (a SEAL platoon normally consists of sixteen men) and a small number of Air Force Special Tactics airmen. The team was divided into a "recovery force" and a separate "quick reaction force" (QRF). The QRF would stand by to intervene should something in the rescue process go awry.

The team flew three or four MH-47 Chinook helicopters off of ships in the Arabian Sea. The total round-trip for the rescue operation was eighteen hours. The force refueled several times in the air and in Pakistan twice—once before entering Afghanistan, then on their trip out. Six other U.S. special operations were in progress simultaneously elsewhere.

At the Ghazni airfield, the rescue team touched down two times before they actually located the aid workers. In both cases, rescue personnel encountered groups of what appeared to be Taliban fighters. Neither group seemed inclined to fight. The fighters cheered for America, and both times the rescue team got off the ground safely.

Only after the aid workers started a fire with their head scarves were rescue team personnel able to spot the group through night-vision goggles. The team touched down, verified the group's identity, and loaded them on one of the choppers.

Heather & Dayna: Three hours later, we landed in Pakistan and boarded a C-130 Hercules. Dozens of people were on board. We ate our first meal, an MRE—Meals Ready to Eat—and took off some of our layers of clothing. We shook hands with the soldiers who rescued us and talked with them awhile. We badly wanted to know something about them—even their first names—so we could better express our appreciation; but they could tell us nothing.

We landed in Islamabad at 8 A.M. Once we came to a stop, one of the crew members opened the door of the plane and told us to wait. We could see our parents standing on the tarmac.

Heather: The first person who came into view was my father; he wore a red, white, and blue windbreaker. When they allowed us to walk off the plane, I ran as fast as I could into his arms to receive the hug on free soil for which I had waited one hundred and five days.

Dayna: I went to my mother. I was so relieved all of this was over for her. She wept with joy and hugged me tightly. Then she hugged the other women as they got off the plane, since none of their mothers could be there to greet them.

Heather: The embassy staff cheered and welcomed us. We were so happy to see them. Donahue bent down and picked up the plastic bags of extra clothing we had stripped off in the plane.

My dad turned to him: "Donahue, your job is finished. Now it is your time to rest."

Heather & Dayna: There are many more stories we could tell. We could tell about our welcome in Islamabad, about the utter dedication of our military and the government officials who worked night and day for months trying to get us out of Afghanistan. We could tell about the celebration that erupted at our church in Waco once news of our release was made public. The international news media were set up near President Bush's ranch in Crawford, Texas—just over twenty miles from our church—to cover a visit by Russian president Vladimir Putin. When word of our rescue got out, the press descended on our church parking lot and reported the passionate worship of the hundreds of local people who had prayed fervently for our safe release.

We could tell of media interviews and hair salon appointments in Islamabad, and the love shared with us by Pakistanis on the streets. We could tell of the welcome dinner hosted by the German ambassador and of the special phone call that came for us that evening at his home.

"This phone will ring in a moment," a U.S. official told us gently. "The President will be on the line."

We could tell of our reunions with loved ones, our return to America, and the countless letters we received from people who prayed for us. We could tell of our meeting with President Bush at the White House and the media marathon that followed. "We believe that God is using America to bring restoration and hope to this nation we love so much," Diana wrote to the President, thanking him on behalf of the eight of us. We could tell many more stories, but other books would have to contain them.

A NOTE TO THE READER

We are so thankful for all that God did for us throughout our ordeal in Afghanistan. God truly is a God of miracles and a God who answers prayer. No matter how desperate our situation looked at different points along the way, God always came near to comfort us.

Still, we believe this story of God's love has a purpose that reaches beyond our lives. By demonstrating his love and rescuing us while we were in peril, we believe God desired to express his heart for all people. Through his son Jesus, God is setting people free from prisons even today—the prisons in our hearts. No prison is too dark for the unconditional love of God to overcome.

Our wish is that some aspect of this story has touched your heart and brought you hope in the midst of your own personal experience. God says in Hebrews 13:5, "Never will I leave you; never will I forsake you." He promises always to be with you, no matter what obstacles come your way. He will guide you and give you peace. He promises that all who put their trust in Jesus will receive the gift of eternal life.

If you have never met Jesus in a personal way, and you would like to follow him, we want to give you an opportunity to respond. If the suggested prayer below reflects your desire, then as you pray it, Jesus will come into your heart as he promised. God is not as concerned with your words as he is with the attitude of your heart.

> *Lord Jesus, I want to know you personally. I need you. Thank you for dying on the cross for my sins. I open my heart to you and ask you to come in and be my Lord and savior. Thank you for forgiving me and healing my heart. Thank you for giving me eternal life. Please take control of my life and be my leader. Make me the kind of person you want me to be. Amen.*

If you prayed to know Jesus personally, he now lives inside your heart. He has given you a new life and a fresh start. To deepen this relationship with Jesus:

1. Read your Bible every day.
2. Talk to God every day in prayer.
3. Worship, fellowship, and serve with other followers of Jesus in a church where Christ is preached.
4. Share with others how God's love has changed your life.
5. As Christ's representative in a needy world, live out your new life by demonstrating love and concern for others.

We would love to hear from you. If you decided to follow Jesus or would like to learn more about walking with him in relationship, then please let us know. Visit our website at *www.prisonersofhope.com*.

ACKNOWLEDGMENTS

After returning to the United States in late November, we were awed by the overwhelming support and love we received from countless people. In fact, as we traveled and shared our story, we came to realize that the reach of others' support extended farther than we ever imagined. From a bathroom in the Geneva, Switzerland, airport to a church in New York City to our local grocery store in Waco, Texas, people graciously have expressed their love for us and shared in the joy of our release.

If we spent a lifetime saying "thank you" to everyone who labored to bring us home, we would not be able to convey our gratitude fully.

We will never know all of the people who prayed, worked endless hours, and risked their lives on our behalf. Kindly allow us to attempt to share our deep appreciation for all that you have done.

We offer sincere thanks to the numerous people around the world who remembered us in prayer. Your prayers paved the way for us to return home alive. God heard and answered you. You are heroes in this story. To the churches and followers of Jesus who gave their time and energy to praying for our well-being, we commend, thank, and encourage you. May we continue to be a people of prayer, service, and sacrifice.

To our own church, Antioch Community Church—your dedication and commitment to us remains almost unparalleled in our eyes. We honor you for your unwavering support throughout the years. You have given us more than we will ever be able to repay. Thank you for praying literally twenty-four hours a day for our release. You gave heart and soul, hour after hour—even staying up through the night—pouring out prayer on our behalf. You made enormous financial sacrifices for us. We are humbled by and so thankful for your devotion. When the going gets tough, there is no team we would rather be on. We love you!

In particular, we would like to offer thanks to Dawn Manoleas of ACC for her steadfastness and servant's heart. We are also deeply grateful to our associate pastor, Danny Mulkey, who spent ten weeks in Islamabad so that someone from our church would be available to us when we were released. We love and appreciate you.

To our friends from Waco with whom we served in Afghanistan: Thank you for daring to live for something bigger than yourselves, even when it costs you everything. You model for us what it means to lose our lives so that we might find them. We are proud to call you our friends.

We extend our deepest love and gratitude to our pastor and friend, Jimmy Seibert. Once again you have shown yourself to be a man of humility, grace, and courage. Your leadership and your commitment to serve Jesus no matter the price have changed our lives.

You have risen to this most recent challenge and handled it with such grace and honor. Well done! We know you were always there for us. Thank you for believing in us and for selflessly spending yourself to help us chart our way through this latest piece of the journey. We dearly love you and pray that you see all your dreams fulfilled.

We would like to thank the U.S. military personnel and government officials who worked tirelessly behind the scenes for three and a half months to help us. We recognize and are so grateful for the sacrifices you made.

We will always remember the commitment of the U.S. Special Forces who bravely put themselves in harm's way in order to get us out of Afghanistan. Thank you for your unflagging determination to rescue us on that memorable night. We are utterly indebted to you.

We are still awed by the dedication of the staff at the U.S. Embassy in Islamabad, Pakistan. We would like to thank especially U.S. Ambassador Wendy Chamberlin, U.S. Consul General David Donahue, Deputy Chief of Mission Michele Sison, and Deputy Consul General Abdelnour Zaiback. Thank you for persevering on our behalf and for supporting our loved ones during an uncertain time. You all did an amazing job, and we will never forget you.

We would like to express sincere gratitude to our president, George W. Bush, and his administration for demonstrating strength and leadership during a crisis of enormous magnitude. While in prison we prayed almost daily that you would be given the wisdom and grace to navigate unpredictable events and lead a changing world. We graciously thank you for your resolve to commit American resources and lives in order to rescue us and bring us home.

We are grateful to the people of Shelter Now International for allowing us to serve with them. May you receive double for all you lost through this crisis, and may your coming years of service to the Afghan people be even more fruitful than previous years.

We also appreciate the media for faithfully covering our story and spotlighting our circumstances. And we want to thank Waco, Texas, and Baylor University for rallying around us during our ordeal. Thank you, Waco, for your tremendous encouragement. You always will be our home away from home.

Warmest appreciation to the staff at Doubleday and WaterBrook Press for all of their hard work on this book project. We especially thank our editor, Trace Murphy, who believed in the book and went the extra mile to accommodate us, and his assistant, Siobhan Dunn, for her diligence. Special thanks to Don Pape, Steve Cobb, Laura Barker, and Ginia Hairston at WaterBrook Press; Eric Major, Director of Doubleday Religious Publishing; and Steve Rubin, president and publisher of Doubleday.

Thank you also to Dell Computer Corporation for giving us the laptops that we used to work on this book.

We appreciate Bettye Miller, our reporter and researcher; Christian Lowe, our researcher on military matters; and Bob Cornuke, Amanda Spitzer DeRocher, Juan Medina, and Patrick Byers for contributing their photographs. Special thanks to David Aikman, our editorial and foreign policy consultant, for his wisdom, constant accessibility, and commitment to the project.

We would like to express our gratitude to Stacy Mattingly, our book writer. You did it! What a miracle! Thank you for giving your life for the last three months to write this manuscript. Thank you for putting in all the long days and near-sleepless nights to complete the work. You have done a phenomenal job, and we are proud of you!

To the Ambassador Agency: Not only have you represented us with excellence during a whirlwind season, but you also have become our friends. Special thanks to Charles Robinson for your hard work and commitment. We especially appreciate and warmly thank our agent and Ambassador Agency president, Wes Yoder, who has given countless hours serving us. You have been the man for the job. Thank you so much for your heartfelt dedication.

I, Heather, want to thank the people of my hometown of Vienna, Virginia, and Lewistown, New York, for all of their support during our imprisonment. Special thanks to Vienna Presbyterian Church for holding a prayer vigil during our ordeal and a celebration service upon our release.

I would like to honor the abiding love and support of my entire extended family. Thank you for the energy you gave doing media interviews and so much more to keep our story alive. I am forever grateful and love you all dearly.

To my sister, Haley Mercer: I am so proud of you. I believe in you. Thank you for your letters while I was in prison. They were such a source of strength in times of weakness. I lovingly remember my sister, Hannah A. Mercer, whom I will love always and always. You are never far from my heart.

I extend boundless thanks to my mother and her husband—Deborah and Del Oddy. Thank you for taking a risk and coming to support me in Afghanistan. Your presence there, and in Pakistan, meant the world to me. Thank you for doing everything you knew to do to get us released. I know it was not easy. I love you both dearly.

To my father, John Mercer: I never once doubted you would be the first one on the doorstep of Afghanistan to bring us home. You handled yourself and the situation with grace and courage. Thank you for never giving up. Thank you for always being my greatest fan and supporter. May you and Elaine have many wonderful years together. I love you with all my heart.

I, Dayna, want to extend a big thank-you to my hometown of Nashville, Tennessee, with special thanks to First Presbyterian Church and Belmont Church in Nashville, and to Christ Fellowship in Franklin, Tennessee. Thank you for your prayers and support.

I am grateful to my relatives in Louisiana, particularly my aunts Jackie and Claudia, and the community of Denham Springs, for my Blanket Blast birthday party, which encouraged me and helped the Afghan people. And special love to my grandmother, Edna Curry ("MawMaw"), who went to be with the Lord five days after our rescue.

Particular thanks to the Cassell family for their incredible help increasing awareness of our plight and raising prayer support—especially to Leanne, who volunteered to take innumerable media calls.

I am utterly grateful to my mother, Nancy, and my stepdad, Jim. Mom, thank you so much for coming to Afghanistan to see me and for waiting for me for three months in Pakistan. I can never repay you for all the love you have shown me. Jim, thanks for allowing Mom to go to Afghanistan and for trusting God to take care of her. I am grateful for all the time you spent making the public aware of our situation. You sacrificed a lot and endured some lonely months. I appreciate you.

I also want to thank my dad, Tilden, and my stepmom, Sue. Thanks for all you did here at home talking with government officials, giving interviews to the media, taking hundreds of phone calls, and answering letters. Thanks also for all the encouraging notes you sent to me while I was in prison and for your prayers. It meant a great deal to me that you offered to come to Afghanistan on a moment's notice if you were needed. You all are awesome.

Thanks to my brothers Clay and Daniel and my stepsister, Evyn. The cards you sent me in prison touched my heart and made me smile. Thanks, too, for praying for me and asking your friends to pray. I love you guys.

To the numerous other people who supported us in any way— we thank you. Finally, we honor Jesus for his faithfulness in keeping us throughout our imprisonment. No matter how difficult our days became, he never abandoned us. All of his promises are true. Thank you, Lord, for the privilege of partnering with you on earth. We love your presence. Your friendship is steadfast, and your love cannot fail.

NOTE: Many of the names in this book have been changed to protect the identity of people with whom we had contact.